THE TYPE 2 DIABETES SOURCEBOOK

THIRD EDITION

David Drum and Terry Zierenberg, R.N., CDE

New York   Chicago   San Francisco   Lisbon   London   Madrid   Mexico City
Milan   New Delhi   San Juan   Seoul   Singapore   Sydney   Toronto

The *McGraw·Hill* Companies

Library of Congress Cataloging-in-Publication Data

Drum, David E.
    The type 2 diabetes sourcebook / David Drum and Terry Zierenberg.—3rd ed.
       p.   cm.
    Includes bibliographical references and index.
    ISBN 0-07-146231-7 (book : alk. paper)
      1. Non-insulin-dependent diabetes—Popular works.   I. Title : Type two diabetes
sourcebook.   II. Zierenberg, Terry.   III. Title.

    RC662.18.D78   2006
    616.4'62—dc22   2005016579

14 15 16 17 18 19 QVS/QVS 21 20 19 18 17

ISBN 0-07-146231-7

Interior design by Rattray Design

McGraw-Hill books are available at special quantity discounts to use as premiums and sales
promotions, or for use in corporate training programs. For more information, please write to the
Director of Special Sales, Professional Publishing, McGraw-Hill, Two Penn Plaza, New York, NY
10121-2298. Or contact your local bookstore.

This book is printed on acid-free paper.

To my grandmother, Mrs. L. A. McKinnell.
—D. D.

In memory of Robert P. Rood, M.D., whose passion
for teaching has been my inspiration.
And in memory of Roxanne Godden, R.N.
—T. Z.

Contents

12 PREGNANCY

13 CHILDREN WITH TYPE 2 DIABETES

14 MENTAL HEALTH

Foreword

READERS OF THIS newly revised edition of *The Type 2 Diabetes Sourcebook* will learn that it is possible to successfully treat Type 2 diabetes. It is possible to delay the further advance of the physical damage caused by diabetes and, in some cases, even to reverse it. Good control of diabetes depends so much on a knowledgeable and motivated patient, and the new *Type 2 Diabetes Sourcebook* provides you with a powerful educational tool.

There is a growing worldwide epidemic of Type 2 diabetes, and the most important new development is that it is occurring with increasing frequency in young people. Type 2 diabetes is usually associated with obesity, and because of this relationship, efforts should be directed to preventing and controlling it in both children and adults through appropriate lifestyle changes. *The Type 2 Diabetes Sourcebook* contains necessary advice to halt the progression of this potentially preventable disease, no matter what the patient's age.

This revised edition also discusses the increasing number of medications for diabetes that may be incorporated into a treatment plan prescribed by your physician. These supplementary medications work best when used in conjunction with a program of beneficial diet and exercise, though when sensible and nonthreatening recommendations for lifestyle changes are diligently applied, there is less of a need for drugs to control diabetes. This book admirably covers the many practical aspects that a person with Type 2 diabetes must address in order to live a long and happy life.

To produce this useful book, Terry Zierenberg, an outstanding diabetes educator, has collaborated with the staff of the Diabetes Care Center at Encino-Tarzana Regional Medical Center and David Drum, a skillful medical writer. They have set out the important facts you need to know, arranged in simplified language for ready understanding. This new edition is a valuable ally for patients and their doctors to combat the major threat to the successful management of this most common and costly form of diabetes—a lack of knowledge.

The Type 2 Diabetes Sourcebook provides a wealth of information to help strengthen the necessary partnership between you and your doctor. A knowledgeable patient is the best medicine in the treatment of this disease.

—CALVIN EZRIN, M.D., R.C.P., F.A.C.P.
Clinical Professor of Medicine, UCLA

Acknowledgments

THE AUTHORS THANK the following individuals in the health-care community who provided generous support and useful advice during the preparation of this manuscript: Calvin Ezrin, M.D.; Linda B. Gledhill, Area Executive Director, Western Region, American Diabetes Association, Los Angeles; Helenbeth Reynolds, R.D., University of Minnesota, for the American Dietetic Association; Steve Degelsmith, Ph.D., M.F.C.C., Conflict Solutions and Consultations, Granada Hills, California; Therese Farrell, M.S., R.D., C.D.E., Encino-Tarzana Hospital, Tarzana, California; Josie Curran, R.N., Encino-Tarzana Hospital; Diane Woods, M.S., R.D., C.D.E., Encino-Tarzana Hospital; Debbie Solomin, M.P.H., R.D., Encino-Tarzana Hospital; Terri Hansen, R.N., C.D.E., Glendale Adventist Medical Center, Glendale, California; Roger Curtis, Sitcur Analysis, Los Angeles; Los Angeles insurance brokers Elaine Fried and Howard Fried, The Howard Fried Agency, Alhambra, California; pharmacist Allen Silverman, Tarzana Pharmacy; Jean Partamian, M.D.; Richard

David, M.D.; David Kayne, M.D.; Debbie Rehman-Lux, M.F.C.C.; Diane Gilman, D.P.M.; David Aizuss, M.D.; Robert P. Rood, M.D.; Yehuda Handelsman, M.D.; Julius Griffin, M.D.; Norman Lavin, M.D.; Paul Sogol, M.D.; and the Diabetes Care Center staff at Encino-Tarzana Regional Medical Center, Tarzana, California.

Introduction

DON'T THINK OF yourself as a victim of diabetes. Rather, think of yourself as a person with diabetes who has choices to make. As you will see, making good choices may literally change your life.

This newly revised third edition of *The Type 2 Diabetes Sourcebook* provides you with updated information in several crucial areas, including strategies for nutritional and lifestyle changes, new standards for lab tests, and recently approved new medications for blood sugar and blood pressure control. While it is not intended to replace the medical advice of the doctor who treats your diabetes, or the recommendations of other specialists whom you consult, this book will complement your treatment in one crucial way: you will be armed with the most up-to-date information you need to live well with Type 2 diabetes.

In addition to some basic facts about Type 2 diabetes, a condition that may seem bewildering and foreign to you, especially at first, this book explains which medical treatments and referrals you should expect from your health-care team, based on important treatment recommendations by the American Diabetes Association. We suggest ways in which you may work as a partner with your doctor and your medical team to apply the best available strategies of diet, exercise, and medication to achieve optimum health.

As you will learn, even small changes in lifestyle can help you better manage the effects of diabetes. Included are case histories of people who are now living successfully with diabetes. *The Type 2 Diabetes Sourcebook* also provides many useful suggestions for coping with the physical and mental ramifications of the disease.

Chapter 1 provides an introduction to Type 2 diabetes, along with an explanation of risk factors and an overview of the incidence of diabetes in North America. Chapter 2 introduces the concept of empowerment, explaining how men and women with diabetes may choose to take some control over the management of this disease.

In Chapter 3 you will be guided through your interactions with the medical system, including tips on building a partnership with your doctor and selecting a good health-care team. Chapter 3 also contains what has been called the American Diabetes Association's "Bill of Rights," which recommends crucial standards for clinical care, that you should expect from your doctor.

Chapter 4 explains the basic pathophysiology of Type 2 diabetes, a disease that alters the way in which the human body metabolizes food. This includes a look at blood glucose and its effects on the body, insulin, and insulin resistance, which is a defining characteristic of Type 2 diabetes.

The vitally important principle of self-management is introduced in Chapter 5. It is an essential concept because the day-to-day monitoring and management of diabetes is in your power.

Chapter 5 also contains techniques for dealing with the greater levels of physical and emotional stress that you may encounter when living with this disease.

Chapter 6 explains your most important self-management tool, blood glucose testing. This chapter takes you through a step-by-step explanation of the simple equipment you may use to track your blood glucose levels and suggests ways to use testing to achieve better health.

Chapter 7, the most in-depth chapter in this book, addresses nutrition, an aspect of self-management that is necessary for all people. You will learn a number of strategies for changing your eating style and better understanding your unique nutritional needs.

Chapter 8 suggests ways to help you develop a more physically active lifestyle, another change that has been proved to help control both blood sugar and blood pressure. Strategies for incorporating more physical activity and exercise into your life are offered, as are some simple precautions to be taken with any program of exercise.

Chapter 9 deals with the drugs prescribed by doctors to help patients manage their diabetes, including the newest diabetes drugs, such as exenatide, pramlintide, and acarbose, as well as more established medications such as metformin and insulin.

Chapter 10 looks at the latest standards for laboratory tests you may take at your doctor's office and explains what the results may mean to you.

Chapter 11 discusses the day-to-day management of diabetes, including many simple forms of daily hygiene and preventive maintenance that you can take to avoid medical problems before they occur. This chapter also discusses how to care for yourself on sick days, when your blood sugar is high.

Chapter 12 looks at diabetes that develops during pregnancy and includes some tips for keeping yourself healthy for and during pregnancy.

Chapter 13, a new chapter written especially for this revised edition, focuses on children and young people with Type 2 diabetes. While Type 2 diabetes was once considered a disease of middle-aged people, children entering adolescence—and those even as young as four years of age—are now being diagnosed with this disease.

Chapter 14 discusses the often-neglected emotional and social effects of diabetes, which involve you, your family, and friends. This chapter includes suggestions for improving communication between you and your friends and loved ones, as well as guidelines for working with a mental health professional or a diabetes support group.

Chapter 15 discusses the financial aspects of diabetes, including an estimate of the costs you may incur. Also included are tips on working with health insurance companies and Medicare, and suggestions for saving money on medications and supplies.

Chapter 16 looks at the long-term complications of diabetes such as heart and blood circulation problems, and problems involving the eyes, the kidneys, and the feet, as well as information on new strategies for treating particular complications and how to exercise and engage in physical activity despite them.

Chapter 17 examines some promising developments in diabetes research and discusses the importance of long-term self-management.

Additional useful information is presented at the back of the book, including a completely updated "Resources" section that lists toll-free telephone numbers and website addresses for educational, professional, and volunteer organizations. We've also included a glossary of diabetes terms that will demystify some of the medical jargon you may encounter along the way.

Achieving good health involves more than receiving medical treatment for a particular disease. For this reason, the best treatment these days utilizes a multidisciplinary approach, which focuses treatment on the whole person rather than on the physical body alone. This "whole person" approach is the philosophy behind this book.

Although the topic of this book is Type 2 diabetes, ultimately this book aims to teach you how to maintain and maximize your good health in the fullest sense of the word. Good health involves the entire person and includes all aspects of physical and mental health.

1

About Diabetes

Diabetes Is a Chronic Disease That Can Be Controlled

DIABETES IS INVISIBLE, a chronic disease that does not go away. Diabetes is not like a broken arm—it can't be seen and will never completely heal. Diabetes is a disease that can only be managed. Although you can enjoy a long, full life with diabetes, the disease will affect the way you and your family live. But take comfort in knowing that diabetes is one disease over which you, the patient, can exercise an enormous amount of control.

In this thoroughly revised third edition, which includes useful information on several new drugs and treatment strategies, the emphasis remains on the control of diabetes through self-management. With good self-management, control of diabetes may be achieved for many years. Self-management means that you choose to participate in your own medical care and in the management of your disease. The first steps you take will probably involve simple changes in your lifestyle, rather than exotic medical treatments. If you have just been diagnosed with diabetes, be assured that you have plenty of time to learn how to take good care of yourself, because diabetes progresses very slowly. Diabetes will not kill you today or tomorrow. In fact,

1

although it is a serious disease, the pace at which diabetes progresses is quite slow.

Even if you have just been diagnosed with Type 2 diabetes, you have probably been living with it for several years. Frequently, diabetes is not even diagnosed until it is detected by a routine blood test or by the onset of symptoms, such as a slowly healing infection, which can lead a knowledgeable medical doctor or a dentist to suspect the presence of diabetes. Unfortunately, the symptoms of diabetes are so subtle that they can slip past the radar, practically unnoticed, for many years in an otherwise healthy person.

The first thing you have done to help yourself has been to visit a medical doctor and be diagnosed with diabetes. This knowledge allows you to take action, to focus on learning more about the disease and how to control its effects. Your primary source of information about the treatment of your diabetes or any other medical condition should be your medical doctor and your medical-treatment team. Unfortunately, given the seismic shifts currently under way in our health-care delivery system, your doctor may not have the time to explain the rationale for each aspect of your treatment right away.

The management of diabetes may seem overwhelmingly complicated at first. It is not. There are many things *you* can do to take control of diabetes. Treatment typically involves changes in diet, the adoption of a more physically active lifestyle, and often medication. Stress reduction is an acknowledged component of diabetes care, and one dealt with at length in this book. Unfortunately, many physicians have little time to provide guidance in this area, since stress management is unique to every individual and is beyond the primary area of expertise of many doctors. Regular visits to medical specialists and a program of daily hygiene are also important in your care.

Diabetes is a time-intensive disease for both doctors and patients. It is widely acknowledged that good diabetes care rests on a foundation of patient knowledge. When the American Diabetes Association, or ADA, updated its important clinical practice guidelines in 2005, as explained in Chapter 3, it set higher standards for good medical care, standards grounded in the best current science. Knowing what care you should receive is vital, since not even all doctors are aware of these guidelines. A survey published in *Annals of Internal Medicine* in 2002, for instance, estimated that only 30 percent of the people with diabetes had a hemoglobin A1c, or HbA1c, test in the previous year—this is a crucial test that should be given to all people with diabetes at least twice a year. In the same survey, 37 percent of respondents said they did not have an annual dilated eye examination, and 45 percent said their medical team did not give them annual foot examinations, which are also recommended. For good reason, the American Diabetes Association recommends a referral to a diabetes educator as part of a good comprehensive medical evaluation. It is imperative for people with diabetes to understand the parameters of good health care and also to receive it as a matter of course. However, some health insurance plans are curtailing rather than increasing their payments for vital educational services. In the current cost-cutting environment, which includes a shift toward managed care, the responsibility for at least a portion of your education about diabetes is frequently handed back to you.

Since Type 2 diabetes appears and is treated differently from Type 1 diabetes, books attempting to cover both types can be confusing. Each reader is, after all, dealing with one type of diabetes. For this reason, this book addresses only the treatment of Type 2 diabetes, which is simply referred to as "diabetes" in much of the text. Although the information is thorough and up-to-date, some medical and scientific terms have been simplified. Every attempt has been made to make this information as accurate and current as possible.

Fortunately, information about diabetes is more available to the average person than ever before. Major advances in the management of diabetes have been made in the past century. Some of the greatest advances have occurred within the past twenty years. After 1980, for instance, advances in technology have allowed patients to monitor the levels of the important blood sugar, glucose, in the privacy of their homes. Although the first glucose-testing devices were large and cumbersome, digital and computer technology, miniaturization, and other improvements have produced an extremely simple, accurate, and lightweight tool that instantly checks the status of the patient's health. Simply knowing the level of glucose in your blood gives you the basis to control your disease. Other innovations in diabetes care include new medical treatment techniques and improved medications.

The Impact of Diabetes

The American Diabetes Association estimates that nearly one of every five Americans will contract diabetes. In the United States, another person is diagnosed with diabetes every sixty seconds. More than 625,000 new cases of diabetes are diagnosed in the United States each year. According to the World Health Organization, an estimated 177 million people in the world have diabetes, and this number is expected to nearly double to 300 million by 2025. The current incidence of diabetes in the United States includes more than 18 million Americans already diagnosed and about half again as many who remain undiagnosed. All of these undiagnosed cases are people with Type 2 diabetes.

The American Diabetes Association estimates the financial impact of diabetes at $132 billion per year in the United States alone. This estimate includes direct medical costs totaling $92 billion, along with $40 billion in indirect costs such as lost time at work, disability, and premature death. In the future, with more and more young people being diagnosed with diabetes, these costs are expected to double every five years. Complications that can arise from diabetes make it the leading cause of blindness, kidney disease, amputations, and heart disease. Because of this enormous and growing impact on American health, the United States spends about $12 billion on diabetes research each year, and this research continues to pay off.

Your own diagnosis of diabetes may have unsettled, shocked, or upset you. You will soon move past this period of grieving, which is quite natural. But first, you must accept that you have a serious disease. You must learn something about diabetes. Then you must manage it intelligently, with as much self-discipline as you can muster each day. It is possible to live a normal, satisfying life with diabetes.

As later chapters will explain, self-management will take a bit of time and effort each day. Take comfort in knowing that scientific research shows that the time you invest in yourself will improve your health and your quality of life now and in the future. Good self-management can not only make your life better right now but also slow—or even stop—the progress of complications such as heart disease, which may develop later on.

A diagnosis of diabetes is not a death sentence, but it may be an intimation of your own mortality. It is a fact of life that every living thing is mortal. If you're having trouble dealing with the idea that you have diabetes, try to accept your own mortality, and work backward from there. Look at it this way: with or without diabetes, you may live eighty, ninety, even a hundred years, but you cannot expect to live forever. That you have diabetes is merely a fact of your life. You may learn how to manage the disease in a way that improves the length and the quality of your life. Therefore, it makes a lot of sense to simply accept the fact that you have a disease, and then manage its effects as wisely as you can.

Accepting diabetes is a process. You may experience emotions such as anger, fear, or depression. But those powerful emotions will pass. Understanding diabetes and how to manage it is the next step, one you will make with the help of your doctor and medical team. Good self-management requires education, and then the application of effort, patience, and tenacity. Ultimately, your own continuing efforts will empower you.

Who Gets Diabetes?

A number of risk factors are known to exist for diabetes. Type 2 diabetes most frequently strikes men and women with a family history of diabetes, people who are over forty years of age, and people who are overweight. Women who have a baby that weighs more than 9 pounds are frequently at risk for developing Type 2 diabetes. Sedentary lifestyles, physical stress, emotional stress, and high-fat diets also are recognized risk factors. A medical condition called impaired glucose tolerance, impaired fasting glucose, or prediabetes, which is present in approximately 20 million Americans, is another identified risk factor for Type 2 diabetes.

Although people from all ethnic groups are diagnosed with diabetes, Native Americans, African Americans, Latinos, and Americans of Asian or Pacific island descent are statistically much more likely to have it. In a few Native American communities, more than half of the adults have Type 2 diabetes; on average, these Native American groups are twice as likely to have diabetes as non-Hispanic whites. Pregnant women in some Native American communities have an extraordinarily high incidence of gestational diabetes of 14 percent. Statistically, African Americans are 1.6 times more likely to have diabetes, and Hispanics are 1.5 times more likely to have diabetes than non-Hispanic whites. The typical person diagnosed with Type 2 diabetes is between fifty-five and sixty years old. More frequently, people under the age of twenty-five are also diagnosed with Type 2 diabetes, which is one reason that the disease is no longer called maturity-onset diabetes, the more descriptive name it bore for years. Groups with a higher incidence of diabetes are beginning to produce more children with Type 2 diabetes as well.

Diabetes is a disease that may be rooted in industrial progress. Even today, it is rare in so-called developing countries. However, statistical studies show that as countries develop an industrial base, the incidence of diabetes skyrockets. This upsurge in the incidence of diabetes occurred first in Japan after World War II and has more recently appeared in Korea, Taiwan, and other industrializing Asian countries. That greater numbers of people in these countries suddenly began to be diagnosed with diabetes indicates that something associated with industrialization brought their latent diabetes into full bloom. Industrial progress is often accompanied by massive shifts in eating patterns; whole populations stop eating simple foods such as black bread, rice, and tortillas and begin consuming larger quantities of more complex food products, such as meat and milk from domesticated animals, and more processed and conveniently packaged food products. In addition, the most privileged citizens of newly affluent lands quickly assume the sedentary, exercise-free lifestyle that passes for luxury in our time—a lifestyle that may help set them up for a diagnosis of diabetes.

Medical doctors have been able to diagnose diabetes for centuries. However, most of the advances in the treatment of diabetes have occurred in the twentieth century. Insulin, for instance, was not discovered until 1921. Many advances in diabetes care have come about because of the sophistication of our measuring devices, which allow medical doctors to measure small quantities of chemicals such as glucose, cholesterol, and damaged proteins in the blood. It was only in 1979 that the National Diabetes Data Group concluded that there were actually two basic classifications for diabetes—Type 1, in which absolutely no insulin is produced in the body, and Type 2, in which insulin is produced but not properly utilized by the body.

Who Gets Diabetes?

Some racial, ethnic, and age groups have higher rates of diabetes than others. The lifetime chance of getting diabetes is approximately one in five. According to the American Diabetes Association, the most recent statistics are as follows:

Group	Age	Incidence
U.S. population	All	6.3%
U.S.	60+	18.3%
U.S.	Under 20	<1.0%
U.S. men	20+	8.7%
U.S. women	20+	8.7%
African Americans	20+	11.4%
Latinos	20+	8.2%
Native Americans	20+	14.5%

Good Health

Good health can be defined in a number of ways. The World Health Organization has defined health as "the complete state of physical, mental, and social well-being, not merely the absence of disease." With this definition in mind, we turn first to the cornerstone of good diabetes care—empowerment. In the next chapter, you'll learn how the empowering spotlight of good self-management can shine its bright, healing beam on you.

2

Empowerment

How You Can Help Yourself

A GREAT MANY people live quite successfully with diabetes. One aspect of this achievement is empowerment. Empowerment involves your choice to take a measure of control over your own life. This chapter introduces the concept of empowerment, an attitude that can embrace every aspect of your diabetes treatment. Empowerment may involve working with your health-care team and with family and friends. But most of all, empowerment involves a continuing process of educating yourself and putting what you learn into action.

Don't think for one moment that a diagnosis of diabetes means that you can't live a rich, full, productive, fun-loving, even extraordinary life. Tennis star Billy Talbert, baseball champions Jackie Robinson and Catfish Hunter, and hockey star Bobby Clarke didn't let the fact that they had diabetes stop them from excelling in brutally competitive professional sports. Diabetes did not compromise the brilliant show business careers of comedians Jack Benny and Mary Tyler Moore, guitarist B. B. King, or vocalist Ella Fitzgerald. Businessman Ray Kroc didn't let diabetes stop him from parlaying one little hamburger stand into the world's largest and most successful fast-food chain—McDonald's. And although U.S. Supreme Court Chief Justice Oliver Wendell Holmes had diabetes, he wrote many brilliant and well-researched legal opinions before he died at the age of ninety-four.

It is possible to see diabetes as a challenge, one that may become a turning point in your life. Weight lifter Ron Gillembardo began lifting weights after he was diagnosed with Type 2 diabetes at the age of thirty-eight. The diagnosis inspired him to lose 100 pounds in two years. Gillembardo's exercise of choice, weight lifting, sparked a continuing passion that led him, at the age of forty-five, to become the oldest man in history ever to compete in the Olympics powerlifting event, which he did in 1992 in Barcelona—an accomplishment he attributes to his diagnosis of diabetes.

The old joke about psychologists also relates directly to the concept of empowerment:

Question: How many psychologists does it take to change a lightbulb?
Answer: Only one, but the lightbulb has to want to be changed.

Empowerment means learning about and managing at least some aspects of your diabetes. Unfortunately, some people believe that health care is solely their doctors' responsibility. The problem with this attitude is that diabetes cannot be cured with a prescription for medicine, an elaborate machine, or even a surgical operation. Diabetes is not a death sentence, but it is a long-haul, long-term disease. Living with diabetes is a lot more like running a marathon than running a 100-yard dash.

The good news is that you begin to empower yourself the moment you begin to participate in your own health care. Your efforts may make a huge difference both day-to-day and over the long term.

The best news about diabetes is that you can make a big impact on the course of the disease. To make a difference, you will need to practice good self-management. You have a choice about whether you will become involved in your own health. Although it may not be easy, self-management can be integrated into your life, and even become routine, as the following story illustrates.

Ruth's Story

Twelve years ago, when she reached the age of thirty-eight, a woman we shall call Ruth was diagnosed with Type 2 diabetes. The news frightened and shocked this mother of two children. She was in the midst of a bustling, busy, productive life.

"I was scared," Ruth remembers. "I asked, 'Why me?' I wondered if it was a death sentence for me."

In retrospect, Ruth had suspected something was amiss. When she was sixteen, a doctor told her she had "a touch of sugar" in her blood, gave her diabetes pills for a year and a half, and then pronounced her "cured." When she was twenty, a physician mentioned in passing that she was "borderline diabetic." When she was pregnant at twenty-four, another doctor told her she was "slightly diabetic" but assured her the diabetes would go away after her pregnancy.

But subsequently, blood tests confirmed that Ruth had Type 2 diabetes, a disease that ran in her family—a disease about which she knew little.

At her doctor's suggestion, Ruth attended educational classes in which the importance of blood sugar testing, nutrition, and proper diet were explained, as were the possible complications of diabetes.

"I was scared when I went in, and the educational classes were even scarier," Ruth concedes. "They talked about the neuropathy, the blindness, and other complications. I thought it was all going to happen right then and there. About that time, my gynecologist learned that I had diabetes; he said I would have to remove my IUD and suggested I get my tubes tied. All of a sudden, I felt like this high-risk person. It was overwhelming."

Then Ruth's mother, who had never talked much about her own diabetes, died. Ruth's life "got all mixed up," and she endured great emotional stress.

Ruth heard about a diabetes support group that met in a nearby town. One evening, she attended a meeting. Although she was frightened, she liked the people in the group and was encouraged to come back. Over the years, the group has become an important part of Ruth's personal support system. When she began attending the meetings, she was taking diabetes pills and working to change her diet, but she was afraid to begin glucose testing at home.

"At the time, I was afraid to stick my finger," Ruth recalls. "One thing that the support group helped with was explaining to me that the finger would hurt for only a second but that I could hurt myself for life by not pricking my finger. I had a hard time with this at first. I used to meditate before pricking my finger. It took a few years before I came to a total acceptance of it."

Another part of Ruth's support system has been a knowledgeable and supportive physician. The doctor who treats her is an endocrinologist and doctor of internal medicine who specializes in the care of diabetes. She says his caring attitude reminds her of an old-time family doctor who made house calls. Ruth has learned how important it is to be honest with her doctor, particularly about the results of blood sugar tests.

She admits it took her some time to adjust to the ups and downs of blood sugar testing results.

"I used to wonder why I couldn't get the numbers right," she says. "I used to feel so frustrated that I was doing things right, but the numbers would come out wrong. For instance, I'd eat the same thing one day as I did the day before, and the numbers would come out different. Finally, I realized it's not a right-or-wrong kind of thing. I know now that you can do everything right and things can still go haywire. It's a constant roller-coaster ride and constantly changing."

As she became more accomplished at self-management, Ruth swept like a tornado through her personal life, a supermom who worked full-time as an accountant, held a second job, raised two children as a single parent, attended college classes, sat on a hospital board, and maintained an active dating life.

But five years after being diagnosed with diabetes, about the time her doctor wanted her to begin taking insulin, Ruth suffered a major heart attack. This knocked her down into a depression.

"To be stopped in my tracks with a heart attack was devastating . . . to be forty-three years old and to have a major heart attack. I felt I couldn't do anything," she recalls.

A mental health professional helped her move through this crisis in her life.

During Ruth's recovery from the heart attack, she received help and encouragement from her diabetes support group. For instance, she was having to kick her newspaper from her front porch into the house, since she was not allowed to bend over to pick it up. A friend from the support group gave her a "grabber" device to help her pick up the newspaper and reach other things around the house.

Her doctor started her on a newly approved diabetes medication, Glucophage, which allowed her to lower the amount of insulin she took each day. Ruth asked for help from her support group when she began insulin, and she got it. Taking insulin has now become as routine for her as blood testing.

"I sure wish I didn't have diabetes, but it's become a part of my life," Ruth says. "I have finally reached a point where I feel that my life has some form of balance. I reached a point where I could accept it. Now I take insulin and test my blood sugar just like I go to the bathroom and brush my teeth. Today, it would almost be strange not to do those things. By learning how to take care of situations like high or low blood sugar, I get a sense of being safe and secure. The more I know, the better off I am. It's very important to keep learning and to keep growing."

Responsibility

Diabetes puts responsibility on you. This responsibility may be frightening at first, particularly if you're still grappling with the idea of having a chronic disease. Fortunately, the progress of diabetes is slow. If you choose to educate yourself, you have adequate time to learn. When you understand how to manage and control the effects of diabetes, your knowledge will empower you, and perhaps your family. Good self-management of diabetes may actually become routine.

Whenever you choose to do so, you can educate yourself. You can assess where you are, what you have gone through, and what may lie ahead.

With the help of medical professionals, you can learn to take control of the day-to-day management of your disease. Work with your health-care team to set goals for yourself that are reasonable in the context of your life. Your participation helps develop a treatment plan that is appropriate to you and to your life as you live it right now. You can work at your own pace to

Benefits of Social Support

Social support makes people more likely to participate in their own health care, according to a recent study of the influence of family and friends on a group of people with Type 2 diabetes.

The difference between mean compliance scores among people with various types of social support and those without support is listed in the following table.

Compliance in General Health Care

Type of Support	vs. No Support
Support of family plus friend	22% higher
Support of family plus support group	17% higher
Support of family	17% higher
Support of friend plus support group	8% higher
Support of friend	4% higher

Compliance in Diabetes Self-Management

Type of Support	vs. No Support
Support of family plus support group	35% higher
Support of family plus friend	27% higher
Support of family	22% higher
Support of friend plus support group	10% higher
Support of friend only	1% higher

Source: *The Diabetes Educator*, September/October 1996.

adopt a healthy, affirming lifestyle that may greatly improve the quality of your life.

Although Western culture worships individualism, when it comes to diabetes, it's not always best to try to tough it out alone. In fact, most people do a better job of maintaining their overall health (and dealing with diabetes) if they have emotional support from friends, family, or a diabetes support group. Recent research conducted at the University of Hawaii by Chen-Yen Wang and Mildred Fenske has verified the important role of social support in overall health. Within a group of men and women with Type 2 diabetes, those who had a supportive family member, a diabetes support group, or even a sympathetic friend did significantly better both in caring for their own overall health and in managing their diabetes. As shown in the sidebar "Benefits of Social Support," those who took the best care of themselves had both a supportive family and a diabetes support group. People with no social or emotional support took the poorest care of themselves. The moral of this research, and many other studies that reach similar conclusions, is that it may actually benefit your health if you discuss what you're doing with a sympathetic family member or friend, or find a good diabetes support group to help you along your way.

A Belief System

A therapist experienced in working with people who have diabetes defines empowerment as "a belief system that involves having the tools and feeling competent and effective in what you're doing and how you do it." The emotional and physical benefits that accompany empowerment are immense.

Certainly, thinking of yourself as a victim without any choices to make in your life doesn't work. Yes, you have diabetes, probably because you had a genetic predisposition to the disease. Diabetes is merely a fact of your life, not your life itself. No matter what the future holds, you will continue to have choices to make in your life, including fundamental choices about how much you wish to participate in your own care. By simply educating yourself about diabetes and then practicing good self-management, you can improve your health, save money, and lead a higher-quality life.

Some of the benefits of good self-management may result in better health in the future. The United Kingdom Prospective Diabetes Study, or UKPDS, a large twenty-year trial completed in 1997, involved more than five thousand Britons who began the trial newly diagnosed with Type 2 diabetes. The study showed that the members of the group who maintained tight glucose control—that is, kept their blood sugar levels as near as possible to normal—significantly reduced their risk of complications. Keeping blood pressure under control was equally important. In one part of the trial, two groups were asked to follow a low-fat, high-fiber diet, with half of all calories ingested in carbohydrate form. One group was treated with both diet and medications and given instructions on how to achieve good control. Compared with the group receiving only dietary treatment, the group members with tight control achieved an 11 percent reduction in important HbA1c test levels. In addition, they achieved a 12 percent reduction in complications, including a 25 percent reduction in risk of small-blood-vessel complications, especially eye problems. They also reduced their risk of heart attacks by 16 percent.

In another part of the trial, people with Type 2 diabetes who had high blood pressure were instructed to check their blood pressure regularly and to use drugs to reduce blood pressure. After nine years, the group whose blood pressure was more tightly controlled had a significantly lower incidence of complications including heart attack, stroke, and eye problems. This 24 percent reduction in diabetes-related complications, 37 percent reduction in small-blood-vessel complications, and 32 percent reduction in diabetes-related deaths led the authors to state that "the management of blood pressure should have a high priority in the treatment of Type 2 diabetes."

Robert Turner, M.D., head of the British study, said, "We know now that if we aim for lower-to-normal blood glucose concentration, and near-to-normal blood pressure, then it is possible to reduce the risk of complications and maintain the health of the patient. It's not that we need a new treatment. We can use the present treatments that are available more intensively."

A Fork in the Road

At this moment, think of yourself as at a crossroads in your life. Visualize yourself as a little boy or girl walking along a road, carrying a bag of groceries home from the store. You come to a fork in the road. To the left is a shadowy road marked by a beat-up sign reading Poor Self-Management. Down the crooked, winding road of Poor Self-Management lives a gang of unruly kids called the Complications—Heart Disease, Blindness, Amputations, Kidney Problems, and Neuropathy. To the right is another road and an illuminated sign reading Good Self-Management, where the bright lights usually keep the Complications away. You may be at that fork in the road right now. It's your choice as to which way you will turn.

Successful self-management involves listening to your body. You'll need to develop an ability to listen to the messages your body sends you, indirectly in the form of feelings and symptoms that may be subtle, and directly in the form of blood sugar readings and test results. As a general rule, the more you and your health-care team can tailor your self-management to fit your life, the more successful your self-management of diabetes—and your own empowerment—will be.

Overcoming Obstacles

Take a moment to reflect on the events of your life. If you've lived a few decades, you have already overcome some obstacles and setbacks. You have won victories. You have gathered the strength you needed at important times. To begin empowering yourself, pause to recall your personal victories and recount some of the things you have already accomplished, already achieved, or already won.

Diabetes is simply one area of your life in which you can choose to help yourself. Yes, it may well take some willpower. Perhaps it will require a continuing display of personal courage. Self-management involves you, your doctors, your medical team, your social circle, and the greater world. Self-management involves learning a little bit of science and applying this knowledge adroitly to yourself. Yes, this process will take education, time, and energy. It may require self-discipline, manual dexterity, and some emotional strength. Diabetes will affect the way you live your life. But you can make the necessary changes.

It is even possible that you will become a better and stronger person, because your efforts may become one of the turning points of your life.

Beyond Grieving

Accepting that you have diabetes, and that you are not quite as healthy as you thought you were, involves a process of grieving. It is normal to ache with grief when you experience or anticipate the loss of something precious to you. Many persons diagnosed with a chronic disease experience a profound grief, an intimation of their own mortality that is better seen as an emotional process than as a single, isolated event. According to author and research psychiatrist Elisabeth Kübler-Ross, who has long studied the emotional aspects of serious illness, the process of grieving often involves a series of emotional changes or plateaus. The attendant emotional turmoil may include an initial shock or denial, followed by anger, guilt or bargaining, depression, and eventually acceptance. But hope is a constant in this process because it allows us to look past the present moment toward something better. The way each person handles and moves through grieving varies, but weathering this emotional process can be the first step to accepting and then to managing your disease.

With diabetes, you may worry about your health on a practical, everyday level—fretting that you aren't getting the details right, that you're not being "a good diabetic" every day in every way. You may become upset when you discover a gap in your knowledge that takes time or effort to fill. You may simply have to allow yourself some time to adjust to the big changes that have muscled their way into your life. Accept that some aspects of self-management may be emotionally or physically stressful, particularly at first, during the most emotionally vulnerable times.

Putting attitudes about diabetes to rest among family or friends is not always a picnic, either, particularly if they seem to be overly worried about you or, on the contrary, don't seem to share your level of concern. Something as simple as beginning an exercise program or changing the recipe for a dish your family eats at holiday meals may spark heated arguments and stir up emotional stress. These aspects of diabetes may seem overwhelming. Diabetes may add greater stress to your life.

The best news here is that you can learn to manage negative stress. This should be a priority because stress directly affects your body in a harmful way—by jacking up your blood sugar. Relieving stress can benefit your health almost immediately by helping bring your blood sugar levels down. As explained in

Steps to Empower Yourself

Here are a few general ways in which you can empower yourself:

- Identify your own attitudes toward learning more about the management of diabetes, particularly your own feelings about accepting a measure of responsibility for it. If you resent having diabetes, for instance, admit that you resent it and then move on.
- Learn more about Type 2 diabetes, including how you and your health-care team can better manage its effects.
- Put something you have learned into practice today.
- Periodically record your efforts in a record book or on a chart.
- Share your successes with other people who have diabetes—family members, friends, or members of a support group. Keeping a written diary or seeing a therapist may be helpful in some cases.
- Realize that your life has other aspects such as work, children, or family that are more important to you than the management of your diabetes.

Chapter 5, you may learn ways to relieve the stress associated with diabetes, one aspect of giving yourself a more pleasant and more manageable life.

At first, the medical issues may seem very complex. Rest assured that you can understand everything you really need to know if you begin to educate yourself and then make an effort to continue learning. Working with your doctor and a good diabetes educator will help you understand how your body works, what symptoms you must watch for, and how to handle the various questions and problems that arise. Before you know it, you may well become the family expert on diabetes.

A Process of Mastery

Another way to define empowerment is "a process by which people gain mastery over their affairs." In the case of diabetes, this empowering process involves self-management, which is discussed at greater length in Chapter 5. At its best, the self-management process will energize and inspire you because you will gain a measure of control over your destiny. This will help and empower you.

It's more difficult to deal with a chronic disease than with a simple medical problem such as a case of strep throat. You take the antibiotics your doctor prescribes to clear up the strep throat, and your payoff is immediate. Your sore throat feels better in a few days because the infection has healed. With diabetes, the reward for taking good care of yourself day after day is that you feel only about the same. The physical "payoff" isn't as immediate or as visible as the disappearance of a sore throat. In an age of instant gratification, diabetes is one of the great frustrations. Self-management is something you must patiently work into the fabric of your life without a lot of payback. Ideally, any intervention strategy must work within the physical, mental, and social framework of your life, and it must be a good "fit" for you. You must set goals for yourself in cooperation with your medical team, choose between therapeutic options, and practice good self-care behaviors to empower yourself. You must accept, through a combination of knowledge and faith, that your efforts are worthwhile, because self-management lacks immediate, tangible rewards.

In the beginning especially, accepting some responsibility for your health can be frustrating, fraught with emotion, and hampered by the grieving process that is normal after any bad medical news. True, you will never have to live like Nathaniel Hawthorne's Puritan-era heroine Hester Prynne, wearing a big red *D* around your neck that marks you as a person with diabetes. But the going is still tough sometimes. For the moment, accept the idea that empowerment might liberate you because it gives you the knowledge to help yourself.

Educating Yourself

When they choose to participate in the process, many people succeed in following many or all of the recommendations given to them by health-care professionals. This educational give-and-take is best seen as a partnership between you and your health-care team, not like the trips the ancient Greeks made to the Oracle of Delphi, where they knelt in the darkness to receive words of wisdom and prophecy from the gods. Keeping yourself healthy is a time-consuming process with many rewards, but it can be frustrating. It is also an educational process that should continue for your entire life.

Excellent diabetes educational programs exist all over the world, offering group or individual instruction. These programs work. The U.S. Centers for Disease Control and Prevention, in Atlanta, estimates that for every dollar spent on outpatient education, between two and three dollars are saved in hospitalization costs alone. Some of the best diabetes educational programs are for inpatients in the hospital; other good programs, designed for outpatients, are open to the public for a reasonable fee. Most major diabetes centers in the United States offer these programs, as do many clinics, hospitals, and health maintenance organizations. To continue learning, you may also join the local affiliate of the American Diabetes Association. This can be quite useful, since most affiliates have periodic educational meetings, workshops, or panel discussions that feature guest speakers and experts who can answer your questions. The American Diabetes Association is always looking for volunteers. Support groups for people with diabetes are another way to educate and empower yourself.

Outside these formal settings, you can read books, go to the library, subscribe to magazines specializing in diabetes, or even take it upon yourself to search the burgeoning informational databases on the Internet and the World Wide Web, some of which are listed in the back of this book.

Empowerment is both an art and a science. The science involves such necessary skills as checking your own glucose levels and understanding your test results. The art involves integrating what you learn as gracefully as possible into your life. You take the first measure of control over your destiny when you choose to help and empower yourself.

Empowerment is an important concept that begins with your education and ultimately involves a choice to help yourself. Some support from family and friends will likely help you maintain a good program of self-management. A central factor in developing a program of good self-management is your medical team, and particularly your doctor. Ideally in partnership with you, your doctor leads the group of people who constitute your medical team, the subject of the next chapter.

3

Treatment

*You, Your Health-Care Team, and
the Patient's Bill of Rights*

THESE DAYS, THE best diabetes care involves a multidisciplinary approach. Specialists from several disciplines deal with the whole person who is you. This chapter offers a brief explanation of some of the people you might find on your medical team, their roles, and what you might expect from them. Tips for selecting a good doctor and a good health-care team are included. Also presented is a checklist of the things that the doctor who treats your diabetes should do on your first visit—the American Diabetes Association's clinical practice recommendations, known as the Patient's Bill of Rights.

Ideally, a team of specialists will be ready and willing to help you learn the fundamentals of self-management. Headed by your medical doctor, in partnership with you, this team should include a physician who specializes in the care of diabetes—either a diabetologist, an internist with advanced training in diabetes, or an endocrinologist, a specialist in the endocrine system.

Another member of your health-care team may educate you in the day-to-day self-management of diabetes, which encompasses the basics of blood glucose testing. This person may be called a certified diabetes educator, nurse educator, or physician-trained assistant. A medical nutritionist or registered dietitian may help you modify your eating style by planning nutritious meals or developing a plan to help you lose weight if that is recommended. Some doctors or diabetes programs also enlist the expertise of an exercise physiologist, a specialist in the effects of exercise on the body, who will help you develop a program of physical activity tailored to your abilities and needs. Nurses, dietitians, and exercise specialists may also be certified diabetes educators, which means that they have certified in-depth knowledge of diabetes in addition to their professional training. Mental health professionals such as a psychiatrist, psychologist, or social worker may join your team if you have trouble handling the emotional turmoil that sometimes accompanies diabetes.

Rather than maintaining all of these specialists on staff, some doctors refer their patients to good, established diabetes educational programs. Offered through hospitals or clinics, these programs provide classes in basic coping skills and sometimes host diabetes support groups and ongoing educational programs. Other doctors prefer to handle most of the recommendations for lifestyle changes themselves.

Research has shown that a team approach usually works best, because each specialist handles a key aspect of your treatment. However it is composed, your medical team should work with you to help empower you and give you the confidence you need to take a hand in your own care.

Any successful program of lifestyle changes, of course, should be built around your needs and involve your participation from the beginning. If you are willing to participate even a little, the treatment plan should incorporate that amount of participation. Some involvement is preferable to none. Your medical team should give you the sense that what you do makes a difference, because it does.

A feeling of "buying in" to a partnership with your health-care team should develop quickly. Your desire to follow through with the program that you help design will be important in the long run.

Selecting a Doctor

You choose your doctor, if not your entire health-care team. If you're enrolled in some form of managed care such as a health maintenance organization, or HMO, your choice of a doctor to treat your diabetes may be limited, although you probably will have some options even within the HMO. Most doctors are caring and competent. However, if you absolutely don't like a particular doctor, you can always find a way to visit a different doctor. Changing doctors will not cure diabetes, but it may improve how you feel about your treatment.

Here are some questions you might want to ask any doctor who treats diabetes:

- How much specialized medical training have you received in the treatment of diabetes?
- Are you now treating many patients with diabetes?
- How much input do you expect from me during my treatment?
- What is your treatment philosophy regarding lifestyle changes and the use of prescription medications?

Ideally, the doctor who treats your diabetes will have received special training in treating diabetes and will be experienced in treating people who have it. The treatment of Type 2 diabetes involves both lifestyle changes and medicines, but lifestyle changes are almost always the preferred first approach. You might want to think twice about a doctor who relies only on medical interventions, such as pills and insulin, and never even considers a more holistic approach to diabetes, incorporating changes in diet and increased exercise. The best treatment always involves the whole person.

While it's true that some doctors seem to think that *M.D.* stands for Medical Deity, many physicians are in fact sympathetic people, confident in their ability to help you but also aware of their limitations. Given adequate time and accurate information, a good doctor should be able to clearly analyze the state of your health and give you the tools you need to help yourself, including referrals or suggestions for dietary and lifestyle changes, and medications when necessary. More and more, the ideal relationship between a patient and a physician is being seen as a collaboration, more like a business partnership than the relationship between a vassal and a king.

After you have been diagnosed with diabetes, your doctor will recommend a treatment plan, explaining the risks and benefits of the recommendations. Your doctor only recommends a plan to treat your diabetes. You must choose to accept the recommendations. Participating in the creation of your treatment plan will help you integrate the plan into your life.

Remember that you are a consumer of health-care services, and you should expect to get everything you pay for. Utilizing the combined educational skills of all the people on your medical team broadens the scope of your treatment and can make it more effective. Look for a team that pays attention to you, people who treat you like a person and not just another number. The ability of your medical team to tailor your treatment plan to you is a leading indicator of that plan's success.

The Joslin Diabetes Center in Boston, one of the oldest and best diabetes treatment and research facilities in the United States, has prepared the following checklist to help guide people in the selection of a health-care team. This checklist is excerpted from *The Joslin Guide to Diabetes*.

A Good Health-Care Team
- They are knowledgeable about diabetes and its care.
- They listen to your concerns and help you identify solutions to problems.
- They are sensitive to the challenges of life with diabetes.
- They return phone calls within an appropriate time.
- They consult you and consider your lifestyle, likes, dislikes, and abilities when developing your diabetes-care program.
- They work with you to help maintain the best diabetes control possible.
- They help you learn as much as possible about diabetes and how to prevent complications.
- They routinely perform necessary tests and evaluations.
- In accordance with the findings of the Diabetes Control and Complications Trial, they believe it is important to keep your blood sugar (and blood pressure) as close to normal as possible.
- They participate in activities of the American Diabetes Association.

All Joslin Diabetes Centers and their affiliates meet these guidelines, as do other good diabetes programs, medical clinics, and health maintenance organizations in the United States.

When you find a doctor's office or clinic in which you feel comfortable, you may well feel at home before you leave the office. Give these professionals a chance to know you, and give yourself a chance to know them. Your confidence in your medical team is a primary element in designing a program with which you can live for some time. Your program should eventually come to fit your lifestyle like a comfortable pair of shoes, because you will need to practice good self-management for a long time.

Take immediate steps to follow the plan you helped create, and communicate any problems you have to your doctor or medical team. Your responsibility includes letting the appropriate person know about any problems you have in following the recommendations you've been given and asking for suggestions.

The doctor who treats your diabetes will probably spend a lot of time with you on your first visit. After that, make sure to return for follow-up visits as you are asked to do, or for emergencies. Of course, report all medical emergencies at once. Set and keep return appointments with other members of your health-care team. When you don't understand something, assert yourself and get answers you can understand.

Good Listening

Doctors are taught in medical school to listen to what their patients say, but some tend to forget this lesson under the pressures of their work—which often involves seeing a great number of patients over the course of a day. The doctor treating your diabetes should listen to you, especially on the first visit, because a person who's been living with a disease for years may be expected to have more insight into it than anyone else.

Within reasonable limits, your doctor should be able to answer a few questions during each visit. It's your job to ask the questions and get them answered. For instance, if your doctor says your HbA1c test is "OK" or "a bit high, but acceptable," you might ask for the test results and write them down, or even request a photocopy of those results. If you're curious, ask your doctor what an ideal result on this test might be for you. You may have to specifically request certain information, because most doctors have some patients who don't wish to know any of the details of their medical treatment, or who get angry or confused when presented with information they don't understand.

As soon as possible, let your doctor know that you want to be educated to the maximum extent about your treatment. Many doctors will respond positively to this approach.

Since you may not remember medical information for long, it's a good idea to start a personal medical file containing information about your treatment. Your medical file can document the dates and times you saw particular doctors or specialists, their instructions or recommendations to you, test results, and other pertinent data. Some people chart or graph their test results, and computer software programs are available to help you do this. Keeping good records gives some individuals a sense of comfort, since it's easy to feel that your life has spun out of control in a brisk, somewhat impersonal medical system. Printed materials, tape recordings, written instructions from your medical team, drug prescriptions, and other medical information may be kept in this file. The main advantage of keeping such a file is that you can easily retrieve any information you've collected because it's all in one place.

Remember, you do not have to adore your doctor, but you should trust his or her ability to treat diabetes. Doctors are human; the best ones will listen and talk honestly to you. However, some aspects of your medical condition may not have clear or easily explained answers, and they may take more time to explain than the doctor has available. Nevertheless, if you ever lose faith in your doctor's ability to treat you, you have the option of consulting another doctor.

Your First Visit

On your first visit to the doctor who will treat your diabetes, you'll be asked to provide your medical history. The process should include questions about any relatives who have had diabetes, any symptoms of complications, and medical treatments you've had. Be completely honest and frank in answering these questions, even those you may find somewhat embarrassing. Accurate information will help your doctor understand your problems and treat you. After your doctor has reviewed your medical history, you should receive a complete physical examination and certain laboratory tests and referrals.

Since the treatment of diabetes is time intensive, your first visit will probably be your longest one with the doctor. Expect to spend some time in the office. If you are anxious about your health, or if you want a little comfort or support, take your spouse, a family member, or a friend along. This individual can be your personal advocate. With permission from your doctor, you can let your personal advocate sit in on your visits, since two heads are better than one when it comes to remembering information. You may also tape-record any conversation with your doctor, although you should ask permission in advance. Most doctors have no problem with tape recording, since they know it helps their patients to remember.

Although you may leave the doctor's office with a lot of information, including brochures and written materials, don't expect to learn everything you will need to know on your first visit. You should be able to schedule follow-up visits to members of your health-care team as needed. If you have questions early on, certified diabetes educators are often a good source of information to tap first.

The Patient's Bill of Rights

On your first visit, you'll be given a complete physical examination. This examination should comply with clinical practice recommendations for a comprehensive diabetes evaluation set by the American Diabetes Association—sometimes called the Patient's Bill of Rights. These recommendations were updated in 2005. Based in Alexandria, Virginia, the American Diabetes Association has a membership that includes medical professionals and volunteers as well as committees of expert physicians that recommend and set standards like these for good diabetes care.

According to the Patient's Bill of Rights, a complete medical examination begins with a medical history and standard measurements of your height, weight, blood pressure, and pulse. You should be asked about your diagnosis of diabetes, related test results, and any complications you've had. In conjunction with this visit, you should be given tests to check your blood glucose level, your HbA1c level, and your cholesterol and fat levels, as well as a test for microalbuminuria and a urinalysis to check the level of protein in your urine. Depending on your age and symptoms, you may also be given other medical tests at this time. For instance, a test of the feet, using a plastic bristle called a monofilament, should be administered every one to three years to locate any developing nerve problems early. The late Robert P. Rood, M.D., noted that the rate of amputations in the United States could be reduced by half if every doctor included this test along with an examination of the feet in every physical exam of every person with diabetes. However, he observed that only about 8 percent of doctors actually take the shoes off their patients—a percentage that should be much higher.

The American Diabetes Association recommends that the doctor who treats your diabetes examine your eyes, mouth, hands, fingers, and feet, checking for sensation and pulses. Your doctor should also check your skin, especially any places where you have injected insulin. Further, your doctor should feel your neck to palpate your thyroid gland, feel your abdomen to check your liver and other organs, listen to your heart through a stethoscope, and generally test your reflexes.

You should be asked about any medications you are taking. You should be asked about your eating habits, your weight history, and the amount and frequency of your exercise. You should be asked whether you smoke tobacco (it's been estimated that one in six people with Type 2 diabetes smokes). According to Irl B. Hirsch, M.D., an associate professor of medicine at the University of Washington School of Medicine, in Seattle, if you do smoke, then your doctor should urge you at every visit to quit and should discuss methods of quitting and drugs that can help the process. If you're a pregnant woman, you should be asked about problems you might have experienced during pregnancy, as well as previous pregnancies.

A comprehensive evaluation includes a referral to a diabetes educator, if the doctor's office or HMO does not have one on staff. Adults and children who are overweight, as well as pregnant women, should be referred to medical nutrition therapy. Usually provided by a dietitian familiar with diabetes, medical nutrition therapy can help develop an eating plan to control weight, blood sugar, blood pressure, and other metabolic outcomes. The American Diabetes Association (ADA) recommends the development of a program of regular physical activity, sometimes called an "exercise prescription," appropriate to the patient and any complications or problems he or she has. As needed, the ADA also recommends referrals to a psychologist, psychiatrist, or social worker, particularly at key points such as after a diagnosis or after major changes in medical status. Shortly after being diagnosed with diabetes, you should also be given a referral to an ophthalmologist or optometrist for a dilated eye examination.

If your doctor skips any of these steps, do something about it. Taking off your shoes and socks before the doctor comes into the room may remind him or her to check your feet. One well-informed woman shyly wiggles her toes if her doctor seems to be forgetting this important step. You can even take a checklist into the office with you if you think your doctor might miss something, although this will probably not be appreciated.

Medical doctors are busy, so please don't waste your doctor's time on irrelevant chatter. But when it's necessary, assert yourself on your own behalf.

Your Treatment Plan

By the end of the first visit or series of visits, you should have worked out a diabetes-care plan with your health-care team. Your treatment plan should consider you and your lifestyle—your physical condition, your work or travel schedule, your eating preferences, your cultural background, and any other medical problems you might have. Although some similarities exist, you are not exactly like every other person who has diabetes. Therefore, your treatment plan should feature lifestyle changes, but it should not be the exact same one given to all patients who see your doctor. If necessary, you may have to adapt the plan to yourself. Doing so gives it a much higher chance of success and gives you more control and participation in the process.

Every good diabetes-care plan should include the following, some of which come in the form of referrals:

- Educational sessions on how to measure blood glucose levels, how to keep records, and how to treat low blood sugar
- Advice on eating, prepared by a registered dietitian or nutritional specialist, now called medical nutrition therapy

- Recommendations on lifestyle changes that you should make, such as regular exercise and stopping smoking
- A written list of any prescribed medicines that you will use for control
- Instructions on when to return to the doctor and when you should call if you have a question or an emergency

In addition, your plan should include a referral to visit an eye doctor, a foot doctor, a dentist, and other specialists as needed. Heed the recommendations your doctor gives you for referrals and follow-up appointments. If you happen to miss an appointment, call and set another one.

If you are a woman who may wish to have children, a good diabetes-care plan will include some form of birth control and family planning. It's certainly possible to have healthy children if you have diabetes, but planning for pregnancy in advance will give you the best chance for a successful pregnancy. Gestational diabetes, or diabetes that occurs during pregnancy, is addressed in Chapter 12.

Frequency of Visits

As a rule of thumb, the better your health, the less frequently you will need to see your doctor. Two or three doctor visits per year are sufficient if you have no complications and have good glucose control.

Your doctor may want you to come back or call in more frequently in certain situations, such as when you are making major changes in your diabetes-care plan. If you are having trouble controlling your glucose levels, or just beginning insulin or other medications, you should see your doctor at least four times per year.

Follow-up visits to the doctor who is managing your diabetes should include the following:

- Measuring your weight and blood pressure
- Examining your eyes and feet
- Asking to see your blood glucose records
- Taking blood for an HbA1c test, and urine for a urine test
- Asking about any problems you've had since the last visit, such as other illnesses or other life problems
- Asking what adjustments you've made to your plan
- Asking about any problems you're having in following your plan
- Asking about incidences of high or low blood sugar
- Asking about symptoms of possible complications
- A review of your treatment plan to measure progress and identify problem areas

In addition to the doctor who treats your diabetes, you may have a primary care physician, typically a doctor of internal medicine or a family practitioner, who oversees your basic health care. These general practitioners were once called family doctors. Ideally, your primary care physician should understand diabetes and know when to refer you to a specialist. In some cases, the primary care physician can be the primary medical manager of your diabetes, using diabetologists or endocrinologists only as consultants in your care. It is estimated that 80 percent of the people with diabetes in the United States are under the care of a primary care physician, while only about 20 percent are under the care of an endocrinologist. The doctor who treats your diabetes is important. In 1999, a survey printed in *Diabetes Care* stated that the number one cause of poor diabetes care was the doctor.

Frequency of Visits

Here are some generally accepted guidelines regarding frequency of visits to doctors and other specialists. These recommendations may vary from person to person, depending on the individual's physical condition and the recommendations of the personal physician.

More than once a year
- The medical doctor who is treating your diabetes should be seen at least twice a year, and at least four times per year if you are using insulin.
- A dentist or periodontist should be seen every six months.

At least once a year
- Primary care physician
- Ophthalmologist or eye doctor
- Nurse educator or certified diabetes educator
- Registered dietitian or nutritionist
- Exercise physiologist

As needed
- Foot specialists (podiatrists)
- Mental health professionals
- Family planning service providers
- Other medical specialists
- Support groups

Communication

You must communicate with your doctor and your health-care team. It's your responsibility to alert them to your problems, since they cannot read your mind or anticipate every situation that could come up. These people are often in a hurry, so some planning will help assure that your most serious questions are answered. Polite assertiveness is often effective. Ask the doctor to repeat any answers that you don't understand the first time. If you have a lot of questions, notify your doctor's office beforehand so that the receptionist can try to schedule extra time for you.

To make sure that you get your most compelling questions answered, it can help to approach a visit to your doctor as something like a business meeting. Experts on doctor-patient communication suggest the following steps to make the most of a meeting with your doctor, steps that could easily apply to meetings with any health-care professional:

- Write down a few questions in advance.
- Mail, fax, or deliver a copy of your questions before going in to see the doctor.
- After your doctor has examined you, present the questions on your list, one at a time, until all of them are answered.
- Write down or tape-record the doctor's answers so that you will remember them.
- Repeat back to the doctor what he or she said to you before you leave the office, so that you can get any misunderstandings corrected right away.

Diabetes treatment takes time, particularly at first, when you are educating yourself about your care. Some health-care organizations, hospitals, and clinics have very good educational programs, and you should avail yourself of these whenever possible.

If you are having a lot of trouble in the early stages of your diabetes, it may be possible for you to visit one of the major diabetes clinics and stay for a few days while you are examined and given various tests. Some of these clinics have excellent educational programs and classes that will teach you the basics of good self-care in a comfortable setting.

Your health-care team includes specialists who all have roles to play in your treatment. As you learn their roles, you will learn whom to ask about what. For instance, the registered dietitian or nutritionist is probably the best person to consult if you are having trouble changing your eating patterns or are reacting to a particular food. A mental health professional is probably the best person to see if your diagnosis or prognosis is causing you to have serious problems overcoming emotions such as anger or fear, or if you are experiencing a depression.

In this partnership approach, it's your job to notify your doctor or nurse if you have symptoms you don't understand, if a particular medication is not working as expected, if your blood sugar is unusually high, or any other time you experience significant problems. Given the current state of the medical system, you may have to speak up for yourself to get the services you are entitled to receive.

Many problems may be solved with a phone call rather than a doctor's visit. Before you have medical problems at home, ask your doctor or nurse when the best time is to call with questions. When you do call, ask when you may expect to receive a response. Some doctors set aside a certain time of day to return calls, and asking about a doctor's schedule may save you some time sitting by the telephone, waiting for a return call.

When you see a new doctor, take along a list of your current medications—including each drug's name, the quantity you take, the number of times you take it, and how you are taking it if it's different from the manner prescribed. Your new doctor will probably want to see your previous doctor's charts, test results, lab reports, and imaging studies such as x-rays. You can contact your previous doctor and request copies of these items, allowing adequate time for the office staff to assemble them, and then pick them up in person and deliver them to your new doctor, either in person or by mail with a cover letter.

Remember that nobody has a greater stake in your good health than you. Consider yourself an integral member of your health-care team. You're not the medical expert or the exercise expert or the diet expert, but you're the world expert on you. Know your rights, as recommended by the American Diabetes Association, and insist on good medical care from your doctors. Don't be obnoxious or abusive to people who are trying to help you, but assert yourself when necessary. If you need to blow a trumpet in the examining room to get a nagging question answered, blow that trumpet, because sometimes asserting yourself is the only way to catch the attention of a busy medical professional.

It can be empowering to educate yourself about diabetes and to develop a treatment plan with your doctor and the other specialists on your medical team. Know your medical treatment rights, as outlined by the American Diabetes Association. If you know what good diabetes care is, you'll be more likely to receive it. As the next chapter explains, diabetes involves a set of known biological facts that can be understood. You can put this information to good use in the management of your diabetes.

4

Biology

*How Diabetes Develops and
Affects the Human Body*

THIS CHAPTER EXPLAINS how diabetes can affect the human body. When you have diabetes, your normal metabolism is slightly thrown off. The most crucial relationship in diabetes is the one between a digested sugar, called glucose, and the essential hormone insulin. There are several ways in which high levels of glucose can affect the normal actions of the human body. If you understand these effects, your treatment will make more sense.

A diagnosis of diabetes is a call to action. A fasting plasma glucose (FPG) reading of greater than 126 milligrams per deciliter (mg/dl) or 7.0 millimoles per liter (mmol/L) taken after eating nothing and drinking only water for eight hours prior to the test is the current standard for diagnosing diabetes. The fasting plasma glucose test is the easiest of the tests to administer, and it is also the recommended test to screen for prediabetes, a condition in which blood glucose levels are high and the person is at greater risk for diabetes. Prediabetes, or borderline diabetes, is also called impaired glucose tolerance (IGT) or impaired fasting glucose (IFG).

Fasting Plasma Glucose Levels

Normal	< 100 mg/dl (5.5 mmol/L)
Prediabetes	100–126 mg/dl (5.5–7.0 mmol/L)
Diabetes	126 mg/dl (7.0 mmol/L)

A random glucose reading of greater than 160 mg/dl (or 8.9 mmol/L) at any time is also considered a positive screening result, but a diagnosis of diabetes should be confirmed by further testing. An oral glucose tolerance test is often used to confirm the diagnosis. Glucose above 200 mg/dl (11.1 mmol/L) with symptoms of diabetes, after two hours of an oral glucose tolerance test, also confirms a diagnosis of diabetes. The hemoglobin A1c test is also used to diagnose diabetes. Still another test, the C-peptide test, measures approximately how much insulin your body produces.

Diabetes is a disease that creates a continual problem with the way in which the body utilizes food. The breakdown of food is a part of the constant ebb and flow of food and energy within your body, a process called metabolism. Diabetes is increasingly being seen as a metabolic problem. In people with diabetes, the body digests food normally, but the nutrients that pass into the bloodstream cannot be properly utilized by the body's cells.

Genesis of Man

Diabetes has been around for a long time. About 1500 B.C., medical scribes in both Egypt and India mentioned a disease characterized by great thirst and the passing of large amounts of sugary urine. The relationship between diabetes and sugar in the human diet was recognized early on, and many early treatment attempts involved limiting the dietary intake of sugar and sweets.

One treatment recommended in India three thousand years ago involved strenuous exercise.

Although physicians have diagnosed diabetes for thousands of years, they have only recently begun to understand how to treat it. For many years, people with diabetes could expect to live foreshortened lives. A standard estimate for people with diabetes was that, all things being equal, diabetes could shorten life by as much as one-third.

Why do human beings get diabetes? For almost 2 million years, anthropologists tell us, our primitive ancestors roamed the earth trying to keep themselves alive in a hostile world by hunting and gathering food. Huge amounts of physical energy were burned away just by staying alive in a world without fast food, TV sets, automobiles, or central heating and air-conditioning.

The meat consumed by our ancestors came from free-roaming wild animals, whose bodies contained a much lower percentage of fat than domesticated animals, whose activities are restricted. Fish had to be caught, antelope hunted, eggs found and gathered, and edible plants located and harvested, all with a constant expenditure of physical energy. For tens of thousands of generations, our ancestors exhausted the food sources in one area and then abruptly moved on. In this harsh, primitive lifestyle, the humans who lived long enough to reproduce were those whose bodies could hoard enough nutrients to keep them alive between meals, sometimes for long periods.

Civilization as we know it has lasted less than 1 percent as long as the hunter-gatherer phase of human existence, which became defunct only with the invention of agriculture just a few hundred generations ago. Considering the full period in which human beings have roamed the earth, all human history since the Renaissance is merely a wink in time. Evolution is slow; human anatomy hasn't changed much over the past few centuries. We no longer need periodic bursts of great physical strength or to retain nutrients in our bodies for long periods. Consequently, great numbers of people get fat and flabby. And many of us get Type 2 diabetes, a disease strongly associated with obesity and a lack of physical exercise.

The Biology of Diabetes

To understand the biology of diabetes, think of the human body as a series of interlocking systems that work together to keep us alive. The circulatory, respiratory, and digestive systems all must function cooperatively for the body to be able to utilize food. The circulatory system, consisting of the heart and many miles of blood vessels, continually moves blood past the digestive tract and the lungs, back and forth to every part of your body, making a complete circuit approximately every twenty seconds. Your respiratory system, which includes your lungs, continually huffs and puffs in oxygen from the air and pumps it into the bloodstream. When you eat, food goes through the gastrointestinal, or digestive, system, where your stomach breaks it down into tiny digestible bits. These molecules of food move through your intestines into your bloodstream, where they accompany the oxygen in your red blood cells to the farthest reaches of your body, to provide energy and fuel for your cells.

Much of the food we eat is broken down into a simple sugar called glucose, the most important carbohydrate in our metabolism. Since glucose is oxidized and used directly by the brain and nervous system, we must always have some glucose in our bloodstream. Normally comprising approximately one-tenth of 1 percent of our blood (roughly equivalent to a spoonful of sugar), glucose is a vital substance, but problems occur when too much or too little of it is held in the blood.

After we eat, the amount of glucose in our bloodstream temporarily rises until it is absorbed by our cells to provide energy and nourishment. When diabetes is present, glucose cannot be properly absorbed by the cells. Consequently, glucose levels rise. This backup of glucose in the blood damages the body. Excessive glucose levels, called high blood sugar, are a continuing health risk for every person with diabetes and must be controlled.

Glucose and Insulin

In the bodies of most people, glucose is absorbed into the cells with the aid of an essential hormone, insulin, which lowers blood sugar. Insulin is produced in a gland called the pancreas, one of several glands in the endocrine system. Located just behind and below the stomach, the pancreas is about the size of a tennis ball and weighs about 1 pound. Insulin is secreted from small clusters of cells on the pancreas, the islets of Langerhans. Insulin is normally secreted as we need it, in perfectly timed and perfectly measured amounts. In most people, the first-phase insulin response begins almost immediately, within ten minutes of eating. Insulin's presence helps the tiny particles of glucose move from the blood into the cells of our body, a process that nourishes us and sustains life.

Insulin is a crucial hormone for people with diabetes, whether they are Type 1 or Type 2. Insulin is most necessary for people with Type 1 diabetes. Type 1 diabetes, once known as juvenile-onset diabetes, is sometimes called insulin-dependent diabetes mellitus, or IDDM. People with Type 1 diabetes don't produce any insulin in their bodies; because they can't metabolize glucose, it backs up in their blood in life-threatening amounts. People with Type 1 diabetes must have insulin injections in order for their bodies to utilize glucose, and they often

Damage by Excessive Glucose

With the exception of the brain, the organs of the body most likely to be damaged by diabetes are those that do not require the presence of insulin to metabolize blood glucose.

Can be damaged
- Eyes
- Kidneys
- Nerves
- Blood vessels

Generally not damaged
- Brain
- Liver
- Muscles

must fight simply to retain a healthy weight. In people with Type 2 diabetes, the cells are resistant to insulin's normal action, and the story is more complex.

Lack of insulin is not the only problem in Type 2 diabetes. Type 2 diabetes, the most common form of diabetes, was once known as maturity-onset diabetes because it most frequently appears in older people. Since supplemental insulin is usually not necessary to sustain life, Type 2 diabetes is also known as non-insulin-dependent diabetes mellitus, or NIDDM. In Type 2 diabetes, the body produces insulin, often in greatly excessive amounts. However, this insulin produced is inadequate to normalize blood sugar. This occurs because the person with Type 2 diabetes has become resistant to insulin's effects, a condition called *insulin resistance*. People with Type 2 diabetes have insulin resistance, and they are frequently overweight.

Metabolic Syndrome

Diabetes is increasingly being viewed as an aspect of what is called metabolic syndrome, a fairly common condition characterized by insulin resistance and its many related effects, including high blood sugar, high blood pressure, high levels of certain fats in the blood, and obesity. Rates of Type 2 diabetes and obesity are increasing in lockstep with incidences of metabolic syndrome. Obesity, particularly the type characterized by abdominal fat, the "apple-shaped" figure, is one of the criteria for metabolic syndrome, and most people with Type 2 diabetes are also overweight in this way. High levels of stress are associated with this configuration as well. Men with a waist of 40 inches or more and women with a 35-inch or greater waist meet that diagnostic criterion for metabolic syndrome. Working to normalize weight by good eating habits and exercise helps control not only diabetes and obesity but also metabolic syndrome.

For people with Type 2 diabetes, the metabolic effects of the disease are not sudden and can be difficult to spot. Compared with Type 1 diabetes, Type 2 diabetes is a much less dramatic disease, a tortoise versus a hare. The glacial pace with which Type 2 diabetes appears is part of the problem, since treatment cannot begin until diabetes is actually diagnosed.

Type 2 diabetes is generally defined as an impairment of metabolism associated with insulin resistance and an insufficiency of insulin production to compensate for the resistance. All people with Type 2 diabetes produce some insulin, and many produce two to three times the normal amount. People producing adequate insulin can often control their diabetes with disciplined lifestyle changes. However, about one in every six people with Type 2 diabetes has a pancreas that does not produce enough insulin to metabolize even a normal amount of glucose. Members of this small group benefit from lifestyle changes, but they must also take medications to stimulate insulin production or take supplemental insulin.

Approximately 88 percent of people with Type 2 diabetes are overweight, and excessive insulin production is a factor. The appetites of these individuals are in fact stimulated by the excess insulin, causing them to eat more. Overeating and excessive weight gain may actually be caused by a condition called *hyperinsulinemia*, a result of too much insulin in the blood. In addition to its important role in metabolism, insulin helps the body hold fats by inhibiting the hormones that break them down. Insulin also increases sodium retention by the kidneys, contributing to high blood pressure.

The Importance of Insulin

In Victorian times, research scientists seeking the cause of diabetes honed in on the pancreas, a comma-shaped gland located behind and beneath the stomach. In 1921, insulin was discovered. Before long, commercial insulin was given to human beings, allowing a measure of control over diabetes. In the 1950s, medical researchers discovered the resistance to insulin at the cellular level that is characteristic of Type 2 diabetes. This allowed Type 2 diabetes to be precisely identified as a related but distinct form of diabetes, which could be approached and treated in a different way.

Insulin is secreted by the pancreas of the average person at a rate of approximately 20 to 30 units per day in rhythmic pulses perfectly timed with the absorption of food. Insulin chemically ushers glucose into the cells of the body, where the glucose combines with oxygen to produce energy; it then breaks down into carbon dioxide and water. Insulin helps convert glucose into fats called triglycerides. Insulin also helps convert glucose into another form of sugar, called *glycogen*, which is stored in the body for emergency use.

A lack of insulin (or insulin ineffectively used) throws off the natural balance of the body, known as homeostasis. Trying to maintain homeostasis without proper insulin is a bit like trying to win a football game without a quarterback. The absorption of glucose into the body is continually blocked in people with Type 2 diabetes, even though the two key elements—glucose and insulin—are present, usually in excessive amounts.

For many years, researchers believed that fat cells somehow impeded the ability of this insulin to "open the door" to each cell's absorption of glucose. The current thinking is that a chemical substance produced in fat tissue, called the *tumor necrosis factor alpha*, is somehow transferred from fat cells to muscle cells, thereby impairing the normally ravenous consumption of glucose by the muscles. Another hormone produced in the pancreas, *glucagon*, normally has a counterbalancing effect to that of insulin and plays a role in Type 2 diabetes.

Whatever the cause, people with Type 2 diabetes don't utilize all of the glucose created from food. This is a simplified explanation, by necessity, because glucose goes through several chemical processes before it is converted to energy. The human body is a complex but well-orchestrated place in which an estimated 6 trillion chemical reactions take place every second.

High Blood Sugar

Most people don't even notice the gradual rise in their blood sugar levels because the backup of glucose in the blood occurs slowly, over many years. Consequently, at the time that Type 2 diabetes is diagnosed, most people have very high blood glucose levels, and steps must be taken immediately to bring those levels down.

In addition to the glucose produced directly from food, more glucose is added to the bloodstream by the liver and other organs that are biologically programmed to release sugar in times of deprivation; this release assures that the brain always has enough glucose to function. The liver typically cranks out extra glucose after you sleep for six or eight hours or when you don't eat, because it gets biochemical signals from your body that glucose isn't getting into your cells. Supplemental glucose production kicks into high gear when you get sick. High blood sugar sometimes occurs during pregnancy and during times of extreme physical and emotional stress, since adrenalin is one of the five hormones in the body known to counter the effects of insulin.

High and low levels of blood sugar do not normally remain in the bloodstream for long, because the swift insulin response keeps blood sugar at about 0.1 percent of our blood. Our bodies deal with normal fluctuations of glucose and insulin as a matter of course, but the human body has difficulty with greater fluctuations, particularly with levels that remain high. High blood sugar levels are dangerous because they damage the body over time.

The very high blood sugar levels associated with Type 2 diabetes are not healthy for many reasons. Since your cells can't absorb all of the glucose backed up in the bloodstream, the cells can actually be starved for nutrients, even with high levels of glucose nearby. The extra weight carried by many men and women with Type 2 diabetes strains the body in several ways, as high levels of fats clog the blood vessels and help elevate blood pressure. High levels of glucose can nourish the bacteria that cause infections inside the body and can inhibit the normal infection-fighting abilities of white blood cells; both of these factors slow the rate of healing and compromise the immune system. Two other harmful effects of high blood sugar levels are protein glycosylation and oxidation, which occur at the cellular and molecular levels, too small to ever be seen by the naked eye.

Glycosylation

When blood sugar levels are high, small simple blood sugar molecules attach themselves to the larger and more complicated protein molecules in the blood, a process called *glycosylation*. A bit of glycosylation occurs in every person, but high blood sugar causes much more of it. Glycosylation creates protein molecules that are damaged; they in turn disable other proteins, called enzymes, that are needed in many processes within the body. Glycosylation causes the protein-rich membranes of the red blood cells to stiffen, resulting in cells something like partially frozen water balloons. Stiff cell membranes make it more difficult for nutrient-carrying red blood cells to squeeze through the body's smallest blood vessels, which can cause these vessels to rupture. Stiffened red blood cells scrape against and slightly scar the walls of larger blood vessels, making the blood vessel walls stiffer than normal and forming shallow pockets that trap fatty substances such as cholesterol. These factors can raise the blood pressure and increase the risk of heart attack and other complications.

Besides the cell membranes, the eyes, skin, cartilage, and blood vessel walls also need high levels of protein to function properly. These areas are especially compromised by high concentrations of glycosylated proteins. In addition to this damage, glycosylated proteins may link together, forming harmful cross-linked biochemical products known as *advanced glycosylation end-products*, or AGEs. Among other things, these AGEs may contribute to the aging process. Fortunately, excess glycosylation may be slowed or halted with good blood sugar control.

Diabetes impairs the normal process of oxidation. Within the cells, oxygen is used to convert glucose into energy. Unfortunately, about 2 percent of the body's available oxygen causes trouble by converting into free radicals. These chemically unstable molecules set off small but ultimately harmful molecular chain reactions that damage the molecular structure of other cells. Free radicals are believed to contribute to cancer, brain damage, and, possibly, severe insulin reactions, according to health writer John Walsh. Free radicals are believed to initiate the process that ends with the creation of AGEs. As these damaging chemical processes occur, beneficial chemical substances called antioxidants can disable free radicals and restore chemical stability to wild, unstable cells. Unfortunately, levels of antioxidant vitamins, such as vitamin C and vitamin E, are often lower than normal in the bloodstreams of people with diabetes.

Taking positive steps to lower your blood sugar level will improve your health, even within the molecular depths of your body, because lower blood sugar will help you properly utilize food and inhibit potential damage from glycosylation and oxidation.

A disciplined combination of healthy eating and a vigorous, active lifestyle helps you control diabetes. One physician estimates that most people with Type 2 diabetes should be able to control their disease for twenty to thirty years using lifestyle changes alone, if their blood sugars have not been out of whack for too long.

Diabetes is a disease of the metabolism: something goes wrong with the way in which the body utilizes food. Its roots are deep in human history. The hormone insulin plays a key role in helping the body to metabolize glucose, but when this process is impaired, the high blood glucose levels that result can damage the body in many ways over time. The upside is that you have the power to lower and control your blood sugar level in a number of ways, including the use of self-management and stress-management techniques, both of which are explained in the next chapter.

5

Self-Management

Managing Negative Stress Helps You Manage Diabetes

SELF-MANAGEMENT IS a process of learning and applying new knowledge. A few basic tools are what you will need to achieve good self-management. These include changes in lifestyle, medications, and regular self-testing. Since having diabetes can be extremely stressful, one of the first aspects of self-management that you may choose to integrate into your life is stress management, an aspect highlighted in this chapter.

"It is by the presence of mind in untried emergencies that the native mettle of a man is tested," wrote American poet and essayist James Russell Lowell. Joseph Califano, former secretary of Health, Education, and Welfare, observed, "You, the individual, can do more for your health and well-being than any doctor, any hospital, any drug, and any exotic medical device." And, both of these remarks apply to diabetes.

The self-management of diabetes depends on learning to act on your own behalf. A program of good self-management will help you feel physically and emotionally better in the short run, improve the overall quality of your life, and keep you as healthy as possible in the years ahead. How far you take this concept is up to you.

Self-management primarily consists of educating yourself, monitoring your medical condition, and working with your health-care team to adopt lifestyle changes. Self-management may also involve an effort to combat negative or excessive stress, something you can influence and control.

Sisyphus spent his life trying to push a huge boulder up a hill, only to have it roll down again. Self-management doesn't have to feel like that kind of impossible, unending task. For the first few weeks, however, as you educate yourself, self-management will consume time and energy. It may frustrate you. It may seem endless. You may well feel like Sisyphus at times, as familiar routines are broken and new responsibilities are assumed. In the beginning, you may feel that you'll never get a break from diabetes. Keep in mind that the basis of self-management is exercising some discipline over our indulgences, those urges and impulses to which we have so often abandoned ourselves.

Believe it or not, you can successfully integrate the basic tools of self-management into your life. Many of the things you'll do may become as routine as finding a few minutes each day to comb your hair or brush or floss your teeth. After all, you don't feel resentful about having to brush your teeth every time you pick up your toothbrush—you just do it. As the following story demonstrates, making self-management work for you is a matter of learning what to do and then applying that knowledge to your life.

Steve's Story

A successful executive, whom we shall call Steve, took quick, effective steps to bring his diabetes under control within a year, a goal he achieved with the help of a supportive wife and a good medical doctor.

A former college quarterback, fifty-three-year-old Steve had risen through the ranks of a large company to become a regional sales manager, supervising people in several states and traveling frequently. His job challenged him, but he enjoyed it.

A few weeks after he got married for the second time, Steve began having troubling physical symptoms. He inexplicably gained weight and experienced bouts of dry mouth and blurry vision. He went to his doctor for tests. Although he felt fine at the time, his blood glucose level tested extremely high, above 600 mg/dl. He was told that he was "borderline diabetic."

The first thing Steve did was to sit down with his doctor and his new wife and ask what he could do about his high blood sugar. Then, he says, he began "attacking it aggressively."

His doctor, an internist with many patients who have diabetes, prescribed Glucotrol. He also told Steve about an educational program offered through a hospital in a nearby town. Steve and his wife attended the classes and read books about diabetes. Steve joined the American Diabetes Association and searched the Internet for medical information. He bought a glucose meter, began blood testing, and started a daily exercise program. Although he didn't smoke and only occasionally drank, he worked to change his diet, too.

"We just did what the books suggested, such as eating smaller portions of certain foods," he says. "Right now, we eat very little red meat. We eat a lot of fish, chicken, turkey, fruits and vegetables, and grains and cereals."

Steve has already lost 30 pounds. His exercise program features a daily one-hour walk, which he takes before dinner, sometimes accompanied by his wife and sometimes walking his dog. He takes a brisk stroll of three to four miles around the suburban neighborhood where he lives. He wears a good pair of Reebok walking shoes and checks his feet every day to make sure that they are fine before he exercises.

"Walking before dinner is a good time for me because it helps me shake off the minor stresses of the day," Steve says. "It also helps me because I'm less hungry after I exercise. My wife is buffing up too. This has helped bring us together as newlyweds."

After less than three months of aggressively combating his high blood sugar, Steve reports that his blood glucose level has fallen to between 75 and 100 mg/dl. He has another 10 pounds to go in achieving his weight-loss goal, but his blurry vision has gone away. His cholesterol level has fallen from a high of about 400 to 239 at his last test. Steve's doctor recently took him off the diabetes medication, which was no longer necessary because his blood sugar level was under control. Steve is almost a textbook case of what people with Type 2 diabetes can do to educate and help themselves.

"My wife and I got into a positive frame of mind on this thing and decided that we could take control of it," Steve says. "If you want to be successful in life, you've got to set goals. I encourage people I work with to do that, and it carries all through my life. I'm a positive thinker. I don't dwell on the negative, and I don't have friends who dwell on negative things. If you know you have a situation, you just go out and take control of it. You've only got one life. You might as well go for it, if you want to live that life well."

Five Concepts of Self-Management

Good self-management of diabetes embraces these five general concepts:

1. Blood sugar testing
2. Nutrition

3. Physical activity
4. Medication
5. Stress management

Each of these concepts may be foreign to you now, but your medical team can help educate you. You can then build on this basic information to learn a few things on your own.

The five aspects of self-management may be bewildering, especially at first, when it seems that as soon as one question is answered, two more questions pop up in its place. You will soon realize why all five concepts are important, but you may not know which one to put first, which you may let slide, or exactly how much time to devote to one or another. This effort may be confusing. You may feel like a person who has never juggled suddenly being pushed onto a stage and told to keep four or five balls in the air. Don't think that you have to learn it all right away; just apply some of what you know every day. Good self-management involves a judicious use of these five tools, which you will learn about and then handle in your own way.

Give yourself a period of time, perhaps a month, to begin the process. Learn at your own pace. Integrate what you learn into your life one piece at a time if that suits you, or in one grand swoop if that's more your style. Do not force yourself to try to move faster than you are able. Apply what you learn at a comfortable pace, but continue moving forward a little bit each day. What matters is that you learn eventually and that you use what you know on your own behalf.

One aspect of self-management that is linked to all the others is blood sugar testing. Your medical team will instruct you in simple home-testing techniques that you can use to check your blood sugar levels, and they'll also help you set reasonable blood sugar goals. As will be explained in Chapter 6, the blood sugar levels that people with Type 2 diabetes strive to achieve may be a bit above normal, but they are adequate to prevent damage to your health.

Nutrition, covered in depth in Chapter 7, involves creating a new style of eating that centers on healthy foods in reasonable quantities. A good eating style includes regular meals that are spaced out, with regular small snacks in between. The adjustments you make, perhaps with the help of a registered dietitian or a nutritional consultant, should be suited to the lifestyle you already have and your need to control your weight. Any changes in eating style should be reasonable and attainable within the framework of your life.

Adopting a more physically active lifestyle, as outlined in Chapter 8, is something else that will benefit you both immediately and over the long term. Established in conjunction with your doctor, an exercise physiologist, or a personal trainer, or perhaps on your own, the changes you make in this area of your life should also mesh well with your lifestyle.

The medications prescribed by the doctor who treats your diabetes, as explained in Chapter 9, are a fourth aspect of your self-management strategy. Although medications are not always used to treat Type 2 diabetes, they should be employed as needed, to bring immediate benefits that outweigh the risks.

Stress management, discussed in the pages that follow, is the final aspect of self-management and is perhaps the most easily undertaken because it is entirely within your control. Managing negative stress incorporates methods or techniques that you select to benefit yourself. Stress relief is useful to all people, and particularly those with diabetes, because stress raises blood glucose levels, which harm the body over time.

Taken together, these five principles form your tool set for self-management. By educating yourself, by practicing what you learn, and by seeking appropriate medical advice from your medical team when you need it, you can manage diabetes, one day at a time.

"A Long Sorrow"

Physicians have known for years that physical trauma, such as surgery or illness, can affect people with diabetes, markedly elevating their blood sugar levels. Emotional stress also has an obvious relationship with diabetes. As early as 1684, a doctor around Shakespeare's time observed that diabetes was due to "a long sorrow."

The emotional and psychological trauma of negative stress, sometimes called distress, may be treated by several methods, including education and psychological counseling. However, the medical community's longtime awareness of the ill effects of stress hasn't led most doctors to recommend particular methods of stress relief, perhaps because this subject is out of the realm of their expertise. The selection of techniques to relieve stress is also somewhat personal.

Incidents of acute stress affect your body rapidly and in measurable ways. Four hormones, including adrenaline, jump into your bloodstream in a fraction of a second. The release of stress hormones speeds up your metabolism, makes your heart beat faster and pump more blood, and slightly raises your blood pressure. Stored glucose is released from the liver and muscles, and blood sugar shoots up. Stress hormones in the bloodstream increase the rate of breathing, begin shutting down the digestive system to divert blood to the muscles, dilate the eyes, heighten hearing, slightly shrink the sex organs, and constrict the arteries in your arms and legs. Some people with diabetes say this stress-induced adrenaline rush first resembles the symptoms of out-of-control blood sugar—immediate weakness, shakiness, or an escalated fast-beating pulse. This so-called fight-or-flight reflex, caused by acute stress, prepares the body for strenuous physical action—struggling with a tiger, perhaps, or running for one's life.

Diabetes Is Stressful

Having diabetes is stressful too. There is a built-in high level of stress in the demands of coping with an invisible, chronic, ever-present disease. Diabetes takes time and energy to understand, and it can be difficult to manage. Diabetes can strain a family's finances or knock retirement plans askew. In addition to that, the threat of complications hangs over the heads of many people with diabetes, creating more worry and distress. In the 1950s, researchers first noticed a rise in both blood glucose levels and ketone levels in men and women with diabetes who were merely exposed to conversations about areas of stress in their lives.

The stress associated with diabetes may become acute or temporarily intense at certain times, such as immediately after your diagnosis of diabetes or when you experience complications. But most of the time, diabetes is a constant chronic stress that lingers in the mind. Chronic stress is chemically and emotionally different from acute stress, which can be more rapidly resolved.

In chronically stressful situations, a steroid hormone called cortisol is released over a period ranging from several minutes to a few hours. Similar to adrenaline, cortisol causes the blood pressure to rise and the pulse rate to slow. Among cortisol's measurable physical effects, the number of white blood cells in your body drops a bit, slightly depressing your immune system. Some amino acids (a form of digested protein) actually change into sugar, or glucose. Other hormones that can be released by stress include growth hormones, thyroid-stimulating hormones, and glucagon. All of these hormones elevate blood glucose.

Chronic stress is constant and primarily emotional, like many of the stresses of modern life. Without regular exercise, most of us have no physical release for this pent-up stress. When you live with an excessive level of chronic stress, you must either seek ways to reduce it or face the perils of physical or mental exhaustion. When you add diabetes to this mix, negative stress can further elevate your blood glucose and wreak havoc on your body.

The emotional stresses unique to people with diabetes include the "invisible" and chronic nature of the disease, the frustrations often experienced in trying to control the many variables that can affect blood sugar, and even the very unpredictability of the disease. Diabetes puts physical stress on your body, as does a lack of exercise or excess weight. Stress alone may throw off your normal routine of self-management, creating more stress when something as simple as missing a meal or not exercising throws your metabolism for a loop.

Although you probably had diabetes for quite a while before you were diagnosed, the idea of having a chronic disease may have hit you hard. For some, a diagnosis of diabetes is up there with life's most stressful and emotionally upsetting events, such as the death of a spouse, divorce, a jail term, or being fired from a job.

The stress of having diabetes may be compounded by what at first seems to be a huge amount of information that you are asked to absorb and retain to keep your diabetes in control. Even small variations between your goals and your first efforts at control may set you off, frustrate you, or vex you.

How Stress Works

The "general adaptation syndrome" reflects the way in which physical stress affects the body, according to the late Hans Selye, M.D., a pioneering researcher in this field. For purposes of simplification, we use a beast in the jungle as the stressor, although the stressor can actually be something as small as a virus or bacteria entering your body, in which case this drama would be played out in miniature through an immune response. If the general adaptation syndrome could be metaphorically extended to the national scale, it would look something like war and peace.

- **Alarm phase:** You see the beast in the jungle. Biochemical alarms prepare your body. Your brain perceives the danger, sending electrical messages down the nerves, while hormones such as adrenaline shoot out into the bloodstream. Your breath quickens, your muscles tense, and your body prepares for "fight or flight" with a quick burst of temporary strength.
- **Resistance phase:** You respond to the beast in the jungle by resisting its apparent intention to harm you. You may turn tail and rapidly take flight, or pick up a club and defend yourself. Both alternatives utilize the new supply of stress-induced physical and mental energy.
- **Exhaustion phase:** You may have run as far away as you could, or fought the beast to the point of exhaustion. Your body has given everything it can to adapt to the stress of meeting the beast; it can give no more.

"For me, the anxiety of being new to diabetes seemed to affect my intelligence," one well-spoken woman in her forties confessed. "For instance, once when I was trying to write a note, I couldn't even write the word *sure*. I had to cross out that word three or four times before I got it right. Then, I saw a headline in the newspaper that read 'Panacea Cure,' but I read it first as 'Pancreas Cure,' which was where my mind was. I got to the point where my own anxiety was scaring me."

The first few weeks can be a very stressful time not only for the person diagnosed but also for loved ones. Life goals and future expectations may have to be revised. Accepting changes can be a painful process for any family, as Chapter 14 explains.

It's certainly an adjustment to move into the maintenance phase of self-management, with all the required learning and changes to lifestyle. But it is an adjustment that millions of people all over the world have made.

"I've had to learn to control the outside factors in my life to manage stress," a woman told her support group. "The other day, I had two major events to attend; I knew both would be very stressful. I chose to attend only one event because I knew I couldn't attend them both. I've had to learn to make these choices since I was diagnosed with diabetes, to keep my blood sugar in control."

Stress may contribute to either excessive weight loss or weight gain. Hans Selye observed some years ago in *The Stress of Life* that excessive obesity may also be a manifestation of stress, especially in people with certain types of frustrating mental experiences. A person who does not get enough satisfaction from work or from relations with other people may be driven to find consolation in almost anything that may provide comfort. "Even though the predisposition toward diabetes is inherited," Selye stated, "it depends largely upon the way the body reacts to stress whether or not a latent diabetic tendency will develop into a manifest disease." In some cases, he noted, diabetes does not spring from an insufficient production of insulin, but from an overproduction of stress-related hormones that raise the blood sugar.

Night eating syndrome (NES) is a condition in which more than half a person's food intake is consumed after 8 P.M., and some experts on stress estimate it may occur in one-fourth of all people who are obese. NES is characterized by low appetite during the day and an increased appetite at night, as well as a tendency to eat sweet or starchy foods, feeling tense, feelings of anxiety or guilt while eating, and eating if one wakes up at night. Recent research has shown that people with NES have abnormal responses to certain hormones, indicating that this condition may be due as much to stress as to hunger. Stress contributes to high blood pressure and insulin resistance. People under stress may be more prone to put on the deep abdominal fat that contributes to metabolic syndrome and heart problems, too.

Stress contributes to fatigue, as does high blood sugar, poor nutrition, dehydration, lack of exercise, and smoking. Stress is known to deplete the body of stores of certain necessary vitamins, such as vitamin C and the B vitamins. Among its other ill effects, stress depletes the body of a necessary chemical called serotonin, most of which is manufactured in the body during deep sleep. Serotonin depletion leads to carbohydrate cravings, making it more difficult to maintain a program of healthy eating and to lose weight, according to Los Angeles endocrinologist Calvin Ezrin, M.D. Whether or not you have diabetes, you should make it a priority to recognize and control stress.

If worrying about diabetes has affected your sleeping patterns or your normal weight, or has resulted in great changes in your moods, you are exhibiting signs of depression or anxiety that should be treated by a psychiatrist, psychologist, or other mental health professional.

Stress-Management Techniques

Fortunately, you can learn to avoid or manage stress by using any number of safe, sensible techniques. All of these may be enjoyable, and many are quite inexpensive. One or more may already be part of your program of self-management. Some may be practiced a few minutes at a time, at work or at home, while others are best learned from expert instructors in formal classes or in groups. Some may enhance your social life. The bottom line is to find stress-relieving techniques that suit and benefit you.

Remember that reducing stress will help you control diabetes because lowering stress can help reduce dangerously high glucose levels. Beginning a program of stress management will give you more control over your life. Fortunately, it's quite safe to experiment with any of the stress-relieving techniques described in the following sections of this chapter. If you need a further inducement to control excessive stress, consider that research has begun to show that relieving stress can beef up your immune system and decrease the likelihood of contracting other health problems such as heart disease, mental illness, and cancer.

Positive means of coping with stress include behavior modification, exercise, good eating habits, meditation, biofeedback, distraction, relaxation techniques, counseling, support groups, and even prayer. Negative ways of dealing with stress include drinking, smoking, overeating, skipping meals, isolation, internalizing feelings, abuse of family or friends, and skipping doctors' appointments. Avoid all negative ways of dealing with stress because they actually add to your stress levels by depleting you physically and mentally.

Even if you are lucky enough to have a doctor who is knowledgeable about the latest breakthroughs in diabetes care, education is one of the most powerful tools you have to help alleviate stress and make your life more comfortable and satisfying. Educating yourself is the first step toward improving the quality of your life.

Changing Your Behavior

You have two ways of changing your behavior to deal with stress that you can anticipate. The first is to avoid the stressful person or situation, and the second is to take steps to minimize the effects of stress on you. Many times, you can reduce stress by planning ahead and making an effort to avoid situations or people that you know will be stressful. For example, if Uncle Jerry always ropes you into a heated political argument during family dinners, ask your hostess not to seat you next to him. Or if Uncle Jerry tries to bait you into an argument from across the room, simply don't participate. If driving in rush hour traffic is particularly stressful for you, perhaps you can arrange to travel at a time of day when traffic isn't so bad, keep a cellular telephone with you to call ahead if you're going to be late, or just hop into a taxi or bus. Make it a goal to not let petty annoyances get blown up into major frustrations. When you invest a big part of yourself in the outcome of a particular event or in the behavior of another person, you give that event or that person a measure of power over your life. If you can succeed in trimming your personal investment in troublesome areas, your own behavior may help you establish considerable control over predictable stress.

If you have been fretting and worrying about a particular personal or business problem, it may relieve stress to simply deal with that problem. For instance, if you worry that your family will break apart in a bitter fight over your property after you die, call a lawyer and make a will that divides your assets in a way that is fair to everyone concerned.

Here is a useful tool to help you sort out what is—and is not—controllable in your life. It's called "The Serenity Prayer," and it's often employed by twelve-step programs all over the world.

THE SERENITY PRAYER
God grant me the serenity
To accept the things I cannot change,
The courage to change the things that I can,
And the wisdom to know the difference.

Written by world-famous theologian Reinhold Niebuhr, this prayer points out in a simple, concise way that some aspects of your life are simply not within your control, and others are. That you have diabetes is a thing you cannot change. On the other hand, you can find the courage to make changes in the way you live your life, changes of lifestyle that will help you manage and control your diabetes.

Exercise

Remember that the fight-or-flight reflex that accompanies acute distress discharges chemicals such as adrenaline into your blood system. These chemicals prepare your body for physical action—in primitive times, this reflex helped our ancestors choose between grappling with a beast in the jungle or sprinting to safety. It follows that a natural way to relieve stress is to get some exercise. Even a quiet walk around the block when you feel stressed out will probably make you feel better. The benefits of exercise in the self-management of Type 2 diabetes are legendary. Physical activities such as walking, swimming, hiking, skiing, or low-impact aerobic exercise classes will help you throw off the stress hormones that have swamped your bloodstream. Setting aside time each day for exercise will help you work more physical activity into your life. An "exercise prescription" will be a part of your diabetes treatment plan, as Chapter 8 explains.

Good Nutrition

The stress-relieving effects of good nutrition are subtle, and they don't take form immediately. Since stress depletes levels of some essential vitamins and minerals from the body, changing your eating style to include very nutritious foods, and perhaps a multivitamin supplement, may help you deal with and recover from stressful events. If you don't believe that food can affect your stress levels, watch a coffee drinker try to stop drinking coffee for two or three days. As Chapter 7 explains, eating regular, well-balanced meals and faithfully enjoying a small snack in between will help you avoid the stress that comes with quick, erratic meals and a haphazard, fast-food lifestyle that can cause great fluctuations in blood sugar.

Relaxation Exercises

Deep breathing and relaxation exercises are popular ways to deal with stress, and they don't involve strenuous physical activity. Audiotapes, videotapes, and DVDs that instruct you on how to relax are available at bookstores, libraries, drugstores, and video stores and through mail-order houses. Most have soothing music in the background and a pleasant voice instructing you on how to breathe deeply and let your various groups of muscles relax, one group at a time. You can earmark a block of time each day for this calming activity, your quiet time. Even a few minutes of relaxation or breathing exercises here and there will help, particularly if you're under immediate stress and need some quick relief at home or at work.

Meditation

Whether it's the ancient Eastern mode of transcendental meditation or the less formal "relaxation response" popularized by Harvard University physician Herbert Benson, M.D., meditation can help you cope with stress. While physical or emotional stress pumps stress hormones into the body, the relaxation response has a stress-reducing effect. Research has shown that meditation can be useful for many people with Type 2 diabetes and can help lower blood glucose and blood pressure over time. Meditation has been called the other side of prayer because it is a spiritual activity in which the practitioner does not communicate with a higher power but simply coexists with it.

Yoga

Hatha yoga is an ancient Eastern system of breathing and muscle stretching that combines many of the benefits of deep breathing, meditation, and exercise. Many relaxation techniques are spin-offs from yoga. The first written documents of yoga were compiled by a man named Patanjali sometime before the year 300. Legend has it that yoga was passed down orally for many generations, originating perhaps as early as 5000 B.C.

Although the word *yoga* may conjure up images of white-robed, full-bearded religious leaders, yoga is a superb exercise for most people with diabetes because of its stress-reducing benefits. A study involving people with Type 2 diabetes, published in *Diabetes Research and Clinical Practice* in 1993, found that 104 of the 149 subjects showed a "fair to good" response after practicing yoga for only forty days. Yoga improves balance and flexibility and provides an enhanced sense of well-being because it works all the muscle groups in the body. Yoga is a cornerstone of Dr. Dean Ornish's program for reversing heart disease through diet and lifestyle changes.

Yoga classes are available through schools, senior citizens' centers, the YMCA, the YWCA, and sports clubs. Videos, DVDs, books, and other materials can assist in practicing yoga at home. The older hatha yoga is a mild form of exercise that combines stretching with frequent intervals of relaxation and deep breathing. Newer, Americanized forms with names such as "power yoga" are quite different and are more akin to aerobic exercise. Discuss yoga or any other exercise program with your doctor before beginning classes.

Biofeedback

Biofeedback is another mind-body therapy, involving simple machines that can help make you more aware of your body. When properly administered, biofeedback will help you relax groups of muscles that are tense and give you feedback when you succeed. You tell the biofeedback technician what soothes you, and then you practice pulling these thoughts into your mind to help relieve your stress. Once you get it down, you can use biofeedback techniques in times of stress. You can even learn to soothe particular groups of muscles, or to control blood flow to certain areas of the body. In some research studies, more than

80 percent of subjects with Type 2 diabetes used biofeedback to reduce elevated blood glucose levels caused by stress. Biofeedback has also been used to help control neuropathy. To find a clinician trained in biofeedback, consult the Association for Applied Psychophysiology and Biofeedback, which is listed in the "Resources" section at the back of the book.

Imagery and Visualization

Visual-imaging techniques were originally developed for the treatment of serious diseases such as cancer to extend the life spans of terminally ill patients. *Getting Well Again*, by O. Carl Simonton, M.D., Stephanie Matthews-Simonton, and James L. Creighton, is one of the best books on visualization techniques, which may help reduce stress levels and promote healing in people who are chronically ill. Visual imagery is not unlike a system of organized relaxation and daydreaming, in which you regularly place yourself in a quiet, relaxed state and then call up mental images that are healthful and beneficial to you. You visualize images targeted to a particular area of your body to help your body heal. You might visualize a flock of descending birds, for instance, as an image to help lower your blood sugar or decrease insulin resistance. Or you might imagine a globe of healing white light descending into your body, to gently stimulate your pancreas to make more insulin. You can learn imagery or visualization techniques in classes or from a book and then utilize them at home.

Distraction

Plug in anything you truly enjoy doing right here. Distraction can relieve stress if you've been obsessively worrying about your health and you need to get your mind off your problems. Fish-ing, shopping, walking the dog, listening to music, even just watching a soap opera or baseball game on television—all can distract you by taking your mind off your problems for a while. Volunteering to support a worthy cause or helping another person in need can be of immense benefit because such actions not only relieve stress but also make you feel less isolated, powerless, and alone. Local offices of the American Diabetes Association and other health organizations often need volunteers.

Think Positively

There's accumulating evidence that thinking positively is beneficial for your health. In some research studies, just laughing or forcing oneself to smile regularly were proven to strengthen the immune system. Are you too hard on yourself? Try being your own loving parent, treating yourself as gently and with as much tenderness and consideration as you might treat your child. Reward yourself with small, appropriate gifts when you've done something important for yourself, such as learning to test your blood glucose or preparing a favorite meal with healthier ingredients. If you are down in the dumps and thinking negative thoughts, try reversing those thoughts and considering the possibility that the opposite is true. Take a deep breath and then turn that negative thought on its head for a moment.

> *Wrong:* "Diabetes has ruined my life."
> *Right:* "Diabetes has not ruined my life."

> *Wrong:* "I'll never be able to control my blood sugar."
> *Right:* "I will be able to control my blood sugar."

> *Wrong:* "I won't ever be happy, because I have diabetes."
> *Right:* "I'll be able to live a very good life with diabetes."

Making this simple attitude adjustment is a trick that can affect your life in a positive way. Lighten up on yourself to relieve stress. Appreciate what you have. Although it's easier said than done, work to see the goblet of your life as being half full, rather than half empty. When something good happens to you, tell another person the news.

Counseling

Working with a good psychologist or religious counselor can benefit anyone who's under significant emotional stress. Seek the services of a mental health professional when you are depressed or when your problems are overwhelming your life. Identify your most pressing problems and concerns during counseling, and work to cope with them in a positive way. Professional counselors will listen carefully to you and help you sort out your personal issues. Talking with your rabbi, priest, or minister can be comforting too. Support groups can also be useful in dealing with the most emotionally stressful aspects of diabetes, which your medical team may not have the time to address.

Outside the ranks of professional counselors, don't forget to keep in touch with your friends; they know you and care about you in a unique way. Many times, your friends may be able to see when you're under stress before you do because the effects are often more visible to other people than to you. Ask your friends to tell you if you seem upset or under stress. Friends are valuable assets. Research shows that people who are not isolated from others generally live longer, happier, healthier lives.

Prayer

It's not for everyone, but prayer can help relieve stress. Since the beginning of time, human beings have prayed for the health of themselves and their loved ones, turning to a higher power in an intimate, intuitive way. Praying is similar to meditation in its biochemical effects, according to Herbert Benson, who has written several books on meditation and healing. He argues that a belief in a higher power is a part of human nature, useful in countering our uniquely human ability to think about—and dread—our own mortality. As an example, Benson cites the so-called placebo effect, a false positive response that colors almost every medical experiment. The placebo effect occurs when research subjects receive no medicine or treatment, but show a positive response anyway. Benson calls this common response "remembered wellness," an example of the power of the mind and faith in medical treatment to bring about physical healing.

Some proof exists that prayer has a direct connection with physical health. One ten-month study of the effects of prayer on two groups of heart patients at San Francisco General Hospital found that members of the group of patients that was prayed for by other people were much healthier, required fewer antibiotics, and were less likely to develop complications than the control group. A small, somewhat similar study of people with Type 1 diabetes at Healing Sciences Research International, in Orinda, California, used a combination of therapeutic touch and prayer. Eleven out of sixteen people in the prayer and therapeutic touch group were able to reduce their insulin dosages, although the reductions were so small that they were not considered statistically significant.

Studies conducted over three decades showed that churchgoers have slightly lower blood pressures than do nonchurchgoers. Several other studies have shown that people who are religiously committed also have lower rates of depression and anxiety-related illness.

Write It Down

Writing down some of the stressful circumstances you're experiencing can be beneficial to your health. In a study conducted at Southern Methodist University, researchers concluded that sharing feelings is good for the immune system. In this study, one group of students was asked to spend twenty minutes per day for four days writing about traumatic events in their lives. A second group was asked to write about trivial events. The immune systems of the students who had disclosed their feelings were measurably stronger at the end of the four days. "Failure to confide traumatic events is stressful and associated with long-term health problems," wrote Dr. James Pennebaker, who headed the research team.

You can keep a diary anywhere: buy a lock-and-key model at a stationery store or set up a private file for yourself on your computer. The potential benefits of writing down your feelings and thoughts—including lowering stress—may surprise you.

Alternative Techniques

Some success at reducing stress has been experienced through alternative medicine techniques, such as traditional Chinese medicine involving herbal treatments, massage, and acupuncture and acupressure. Therapeutic touch, a system of smoothing out the energy fields in the body, is popular with some nurses, and it sometimes helps manage pain. Several forms of massage relieve stress by reducing blood pressure and loosening tense muscle groups, even if the process does not directly lower blood sugar. Pet therapy, music therapy, humor therapy, and other alternative therapies are also used to relieve stress among some groups of

Alternative Therapies

Some alternative or complementary therapies may be effective for people with diabetes. In addition to changes in diet and exercise, the most potentially useful therapies to be employed in tandem with appropriate medical treatment include the following:

- Acupuncture, or traditional Chinese medicine
- Biofeedback
- Herbal treatments such as gymnema, bilberry, and hawthorn
- Hypnosis
- Homeopathy
- Magnets
- Meditation
- Therapeutic touch
- Yoga

Source: David Drum, *Alternative Therapies for Managing Diabetes* (New York: McGraw-Hill, 2003).

people who are chronically ill. No alternative therapy can cure diabetes, but some may relieve stress.

Since this list doesn't include every possible stress-relieving technique, don't lose sight of the things that have helped you relieve stress in the past. These can include activities that you simply enjoy doing, that are pleasant, and that are not physically harmful to you. Check with your medical doctor before you try anything new or unconventional, or if strenuous physical activity is involved. If you find something that works for you, share this information with your health-care team.

Self-management is an educational process that involves the use of five concepts or tools to help you control your diabetes. These include blood sugar testing, lifestyle changes, and the use of certain medications. Relieving the high level of negative stress that accompanies diabetes is also a key component of good self-management. Exploring some of the techniques to relieve stress will give you a bit more control over your life. The next chapter features the single most fundamental tool of diabetes management—blood glucose testing. Learning how to test and control your blood sugar will be of immense value to you.

Successful Self-Management

According to Stanford University's Chronic Disease Self-Management Program, to successfully self-manage a chronic disease, a person should take the following actions:

- Set goals.
- Make a list of alternative methods to reach each goal.
- Make short-term plans or contracts to move forward.
- Carry out the plans or contracts.
- Check on progress weekly.
- Make midcourse changes as necessary.
- Use rewards when a job is well done.

6

Testing

Blood Sugar Testing Is the Most
Important Thing You Can Do

BLOOD GLUCOSE TESTING is the single most important self-management tool that you may ever have, because it allows you to know exactly what your blood sugar levels are at any one time. Using this knowledge, you may be able to spot problems and respond to them. This chapter explains the necessity of keeping your blood glucose levels within a normal range and spells out the symptoms and dangers of hypoglycemia and hyperglycemia. You'll also learn the basic mechanics of home glucose testing, the equipment that you will need, the frequency with which you should test, and some precautions to take when testing blood sugar.

One of the greatest breakthroughs in the management of diabetes in the past twenty years is a method of blood sugar testing that is simple enough to be done at home and accurate enough to help the average person manage diabetes from day to day. The first glucose testing meters appeared on the market around 1981. Although the first meters were expensive and cumbersome to use, like pocket calculators, they have been simplified and improved in recent years. Right in your home, or in your office, thanks to major leaps forward in technology, you can obtain test results that are useful in controlling your blood sugar.

Blood glucose levels far above or below normal are worrisome. Glucose testing acts as a thermometer for people with diabetes. Blood sugar testing gives you an instant reading on your diabetes, much as a thermometer allows you to check a child's temperature to see if he or she has a fever. If your blood glucose is higher or lower than the level recommended by your doctor, testing lets you know that you need to bring it back to within the normal range.

Every person's blood sugar levels fluctuate during the day. These fluctuations are somewhat predictable, but they vary from person to person. Over a period of time, blood sugar testing allows you to see patterns of highs and lows that develop as your blood sugar levels rise and fall during the day. Understanding and controlling these fluctuations in blood sugar is called pattern management, which simply means recognizing your normal pattern of highs and lows and then developing a strategy to keep your blood sugars as close to normal as possible. When insulin is used, pattern management becomes more complicated because injections of insulin must be coordinated with meals and activities such as exercise, which also affect the blood sugar.

Although blood glucose testing only measures blood sugar, you can use these results in self-management. When you first test your blood sugars, you are like a new driver who begins to notice red or green traffic lights on the road. Understanding these signals from your body will help you become a better driver.

Good Control

As pointed out in Chapter 2, during the recent United Kingdom Prospective Diabetes Study, people with Type 2 diabetes who maintained tight glucose control (an average result of 7.0 percent on HbA1c tests) significantly reduced their risk of complications. With an 11 percent reduction in HbA1c test results, they achieved a 25 percent reduction in the risk of small-blood-vessel complications, along with a 16 percent reduction in heart attack risk. Tightly controlling blood pressure—a separate aspect of the study—also resulted in a 24 percent reduction in complications and a much lower death rate during the time of the trial. The Diabetes Control and Complications Trial in the United States, involving people with Type 1 diabetes, showed even greater benefits for tight control. Clearly, firm control of blood sugar and blood pressure will help you lessen your likelihood of long-term complications.

Blood Sugar Fluctuations

The body requires some glucose in the bloodstream at all times, but every person's blood sugars fluctuate a little during the day. In the average person without diabetes, blood sugar levels and insulin levels rise in lockstep, to peak about an hour after eating. Blood sugar also rises slightly at night because the liver releases a bit of stored-up glucose into the body during sleep. Most people with untreated Type 2 diabetes have higher-than-normal levels of glucose because insulin isn't secreted and utilized by the body in the customary way.

Think of the average person's blood sugar as a truck pulling a trailer full of insulin. This truck-trailer combination goes up hills and down valleys several times a day, with the linkage almost unnoticed because the blood sugar levels are so closely followed by and perfectly synchronized with the insulin.

For people with Type 2 diabetes, however, it's a different scenario. People with diabetes become extremely aware of the trailer full of insulin because theirs is not well synchronized or attached. At any moment, their insulin trailers may fly up too high, or skid to one side or the other, threatening to pull the truck off the road. Driving their truck-trailer rigs requires them to pay attention.

The salient benefit of blood sugar testing is that it gives you the knowledge you need to synchronize your truck and your trailer. Self-management allows you to bring any perilous situation under control. With proper self-management, you can learn to control blood sugar levels. This control will benefit your health.

Normal Blood Sugar

In the United States, blood sugar levels are expressed in terms of milligrams per deciliter, abbreviated mg/dl. In countries such as Canada and Britain, where the metric system is more commonly used, these measurements are expressed in millimoles per liter, abbreviated mmol/L. To convert mg/dl to mmol/L, simply divide by 18. For instance, 100 mg/dl divided by 18 equals 5.5 mmol/L. In the United States, tests in your doctor's office and on your home blood glucose testing meter will express results in milligrams per deciliter. Laboratories and meters sold in other countries will express results in the measurements used in those countries.

The normal level of glucose in the blood is approximately 100 mg/dl, or 0.1 percent of the blood. This level fluctuates all day long. The normal range is 60 to 140 mg/dl, lower while fasting, with increases after meals that subsequently drop as glucose is absorbed. Over the course of a day, the average person's blood sugar levels will fluctuate a bit above and below the average, usually within a range of 30 to 40 mg/dl.

In the United States, the typical person without diabetes may have blood sugar readings in a range of 70 to 80 mg/dl before a meal, swinging up to 110 to 120 mg/dl about an hour after the meal, when the food breaks down into glucose and enters the bloodstream. Over two to three hours, the action of insulin helps lower blood sugar levels to approximately where they were before the meal. This pattern usually repeats at every meal. Since these are average blood glucose levels, a few points above average is of no particular concern. A variation of 10 points higher or lower than average is considered acceptable by most medical doctors.

In the person with Type 2 diabetes, blood sugar levels can soar to many points higher than normal because the available insulin isn't synchronized with the blood sugar. In most people, blood sugar levels above 150 to 160 mg/dl (8.33 to 8.88 mmol/L) are often a serious concern because that's the point at which physical damage leading to complications is believed to begin. Note, though, that elderly people with diabetes may well have different glucose tolerance levels from those of people who are younger, because the human body changes with age. Fasting blood glucose levels increase by 1 to 2 mg/dl per decade after the age of thirty, and postprandial blood glucose levels after a meal can increase by 8 to 20 mg/dl per decade. At least one expert, Peter Porsham, M.D., a professor emeritus in medicine at the

Blood Sugar

Blood Sugar	Fasting	After Eating
Normal range	> 70 mg/dl (3.9 mmol/L)	< 120 mg/dl (6.7 mmol/L)
Point of action	< 60 mg/dl (3.3 mmol/L) or as advised	> 140 mg/dl (7.8 mmol/L) or as advised
Call your doctor	As advised	As advised

University of California at San Francisco, believes that damage from high blood sugar doesn't usually occur in elderly people unless glucose levels rise above 200 mg/dl (11.11 mmol/L). Other authorities contend that the role of high blood sugar in bringing on complications far outweighs the danger of low blood sugar, which increases the risk of falls and bone fractures in elderly people. No matter what your age, ask your doctor to set appropriate blood sugar level goals for you.

Many people can sense when their blood sugar levels are high. You may experience skin problems, feelings of fatigue, or tingling in parts of the body. A quick blood glucose test can confirm if high blood sugar is the cause of these feelings. With a few exceptions, blood sugar levels above 150 mg/dl (8.33 mmol/L) indicate a need for greater control.

Among the things that happen to your body when blood sugar is high, somewhere around 180 mg/dl (10 mmol/L), is that the kidneys begin to unload excess glucose into your urine, a process known as glycosuria. Diabetes is sometimes called sugar diabetes because the urine of a person whose blood sugar is elevated smells and tastes like sugar. *Diabetes mellitus*, the medical term for all types of diabetes, is a combination of *diabetes*, the Greek word for "filter" or "siphon," and *mellitus*, the Latin word for "sweet tasting." In the Middle Ages and for most of human history, the smell or taste of sugar in the urine was used to diagnose this disease.

Blood sugar levels can soar when you are sick, when you are healing from surgery or an infection, or when you are under extreme stress. Special precautions will be needed at these times. More about caring for yourself on sick days may be found in Chapter 11.

Both short- and long-term risks are associated with unbalanced levels of blood sugar. The short-term risks are high or low blood sugar. The long-term risks are the many complications of diabetes. Avoiding these risks is why you must learn to check your own blood sugar levels, much as a good parent frequently checks a child's temperature when the child has a cold or the flu.

Immediate Risks

The two immediate problems associated with blood sugar are unusually high and unusually low blood sugar. Although neither is fatal, both are serious. Unusually high or unusually low blood sugar is a call to action, because either one will affect the brain, creating moments of memory loss, irritability, or depression. When you recognize your symptoms, you can take action to bring your blood sugar up or down.

Know when to call your doctor. Always ask the doctor who treats your diabetes to tell you at exactly what point you should consider your blood sugar levels to be dangerously high or dangerously low. Ask about the normal range for you, and request guidelines as to when you should call. Early on, write down exactly how many test results in a specified high or low range indicate that you should immediately call your doctor.

The medical term for high blood sugar is *hyperglycemia*. With very high blood sugar, you may have a number of sensations that can warn you of the danger. The medical term for low blood sugar is *hypoglycemia*. With excessively low blood sugar, which is much rarer in people with Type 2 diabetes, you may feel it coming on or may even faint in your tracks.

In this book, hyperglycemia is usually referred to as high blood sugar, and hypoglycemia is referred to as low blood sugar. The medical terms look and sound so much alike that it's easy to confuse the two, especially in the beginning, but everybody can understand high and low.

Down the river of self-management, high and low blood sugar are the two health hazards through which people with diabetes must steer their little boats. Learn what these hazards are and how to recognize their symptoms in you. Share this information with your spouse or a trusted friend.

High Blood Sugar

High blood sugar is the greatest single danger for people with Type 2 diabetes because, over time, the presence of too much sugar in the blood is linked with long-term complications, such as heart disease, kidney failure, and blindness. Your power to raise and lower your blood sugar is the greatest reason to check your blood sugar levels on a regular basis.

If you need another reason to control high blood sugar, note that you will continue to gain weight if blood sugars run high. The excess sugar in your blood will be stored in your body, with some of it being converted into potentially dangerous fats called triglycerides. A feeling of depression may occur after several days of high blood sugar; this will affect the way you look at yourself and those around you, and it will probably also hamper your efforts at self-management.

Unfortunately, many symptoms of high blood sugar are subtle and may easily be confused for something else, such as simply having a bad day at work or another minor health problem. This is why you should become attuned to your body and why you should test your blood sugar. Learn to recognize the symptoms that you experience when your blood sugar is high.

One frequent symptom of high blood sugar is a stuffed, Thanksgiving-afternoon feeling. Some people feel a buzzing sensation in their bodies. Slowly healing cuts, sores, or infections likewise can be warnings of high blood sugar. According to Richard Bernstein, M.D., author of *Diabetes Type II: Including Dramatic New Approaches to the Treatment of Type I Diabetes*, other symptoms of high blood sugar may include confusion, headache, trembling hands, tingling in the fingers or tongue, buzzing in the ears, elevated pulse, unusual hunger, a tight feeling in the throat or near the tongue, clumsiness, less ability to detect sweetness in taste sensations, irritability, stubbornness, nastiness, pounding the hands on tables and walls, blurred vision, visual spots, double vision, visual hallucinations, visual impairments, lack of physical coordination, tiredness, weakness, sudden awakenings from sleep, shouting while asleep, rapid and shallow breathing, nervousness, light-headedness, faintness, feelings of unusual warmth, cold and clammy skin, restlessness, insomnia, nightmares, paleness, nausea, slurring of speech, and a condition called *nystagmus*, in which the eyes involuntarily jerk when sweeping from side to side. For some people, blood sugar is elevated when the letters of the alphabet begin to look as if they're written in Russian or Chinese. Other people walk into walls when their blood sugar is high. Some people become intensely angry and upset for no apparent reason. According to Bernstein, the symptoms of high blood sugar may occur either in clusters or alone without other symptoms. Sometimes, you may feel nothing at all.

Since your symptoms will be unique to you, try to identify them with the use of home blood sugar tests. If it will help you remember, tell someone else or write down how you feel at the moment when a test shows that your blood sugar is unusually high for you. Ask your spouse or family members to alert you if they spot any symptoms of high blood sugar in you. Symptoms are distinctive to each individual—pay attention to your body and learn to spot high blood sugar whenever you can.

If your blood sugar does become elevated, practice good self-management to reduce your stress, become more physically active, or adjust your eating patterns to bring it back under control. Medications can also help you accomplish this.

In exceedingly rare and extreme instances of high blood sugar, such as when you have been ill for a long time, you may go into a *diabetic coma*, falling into unconsciousness for no apparent reason to those around you. In this case, you must be taken to a hospital emergency room for treatment.

Don't ignore high blood sugar. All the long-term complications of diabetes are believed to result from prolonged periods of high blood sugar or poor blood sugar control.

Low Blood Sugar

It's rare for people with Type 2 diabetes to experience low blood sugar reactions, which can include fainting at unfortunate moments, such as while driving a car. Repeated episodes of hypoglycemia can affect mental functioning. Low blood sugar occurs much more frequently in people with Type 1 diabetes, whose bodies don't produce any insulin.

Exceptions to this may include people with Type 2 diabetes who are taking hypoglycemic agents, and particularly those who are taking insulin. These people need to be aware of the possibility of low blood sugar, especially when skipping a meal or during bouts of strenuous exercise, which can rapidly lower blood sugar levels. You can raise blood sugar by eating a snack. However, if you faint and go into insulin shock, you'll need an injection of glucagon to snap you out of it, or even medical attention in a hospital emergency room.

Striving for tight blood sugar control can increase episodes of low blood sugar. The possibility of low blood sugar reactions is one reason to take your diabetes medications as prescribed and to never double up on doses if you miss one. If you're taking diabetes pills or insulin, skipping a meal can cause low blood sugar, which is another reason you should hew to your regular meal-and-snacking schedule as closely as possible. Timing of meals is particularly important if you are taking insulin.

Unusually long, strenuous bouts of exercise may cause blood sugar levels to fall quickly, which is why people who strenuously exercise should carry a snack with them when they work out. Drinking alcohol without eating, and taking aspirin, barbiturates, and certain prescription drugs, such as those that thin the blood, can also lower blood sugar.

Symptoms of low blood sugar vary from person to person. They may include a feeling of being "out of sorts," sudden mood swings, loss of concentration, irritability, grumpiness, weakness, paleness, poor coordination, sweatiness, headache, and a feeling that something is wrong with the way that you're thinking. On the other hand, some people experience no symptoms at all when their blood sugar levels drop.

You can easily prepare for and prevent problems with low blood sugar. If you feel low blood sugar coming on, if you anticipate a sudden drop in your blood sugar, or if you test unusually low, just eat something sweet that contains carbohydrates. Glucose tablets or gel, hard candy, raisins, and orange juice or other fruit juice all work beautifully to lift and normalize blood sugar (see the sidebar "Treating Low Blood Sugar"). The tablets and gel products have the advantage of being smaller and easier to carry, and you probably won't be tempted to snack on them.

Treating Low Blood Sugar

If you test below 70 mg/dl (3.89 mmol/L) or whatever level your doctor has set, or if you feel such symptoms of low blood sugar as confusion and shakiness, snacks containing carbohydrates can bring up your blood sugar quickly. Here are some recommended snacks that contain 15 grams of carbohydrates, which is the appropriate amount to raise low blood glucose approximately 40 mg/dl:

- ½ cup apple juice or orange juice
- ½ cup carbonated soft drink (not diet)
- 1 small box of raisins
- 5 small sugar cubes
- 6–7 small pieces of hard candy (not sugarless)
- 3 glucose tablets or 15 grams of glucose gel
- 1 cup milk
- 1 tablespoon honey
- 1 tablespoon sugar

If you have low blood sugar and don't respond to it right away, you may need the help of another person, because untreated low blood sugar can make you confused—and may eventually cause you to lose consciousness. If this is even a possibility, such as when you are working out, let your exercise partner or trainer know how to recognize the signs of low blood sugar.

If you faint, that person should know that you need an injection of glucagon, a hormone that raises blood sugar. Glucagon comes in a kit containing a syringe and a special bottle of pow-dered glucagon; kits may be purchased with a doctor's prescrip-tion. It is not possible to overdose on glucagon. If you are at risk of experiencing low blood sugar, you need to be prepared by showing family members or friends in advance how to give you a shot of glucagon, perhaps letting them practice by giving you an insulin injection. People who have never administered a shot may not be able to do it in an emergency. Also, to prepare for the possibility of glucagon not being available when you pass out, ask another person to call the paramedics in such cases and to explain to them that you have diabetes and may be suffering from low blood sugar. Stress that no one should ever try to pour fruit juice or any other liquid down your throat while you are unconscious.

To repeat, low blood sugar is rarely a concern for most peo-ple with Type 2 diabetes. Still, the off chance that this or another medical emergency may happen when you are traveling is reason enough to take precautions, such as wearing a medical ID bracelet and making sure your companions know that you have diabetes. Blood testing before you exercise, drive a car, or fly a plane will alert you to any potential problems. Again, your spouse or significant other should understand how to help you in case of a medical emergency.

Good self-management and blood glucose testing will help you prevent excessively high or low blood sugar.

Testing Yourself

To achieve good blood sugar control, you must periodically check your blood glucose levels to see how well you are doing. Your medical team will probably ask you to record your test results and will help you analyze them on a regular basis. Checking your blood glucose level periodically will give you and your doctor a sense of the fluctuating blood sugar rhythms of your body. Home hemoglobin A1c tests are also now on the market.

If your doctor asks you to keep written records of your test results, make an effort to keep them accurately. Some people are inclined to cook these numbers, using trickery or stretching the truth in an attempt to please their doctors, delude themselves, or avoid a lecture. Falsifying test results is not productive.

Although your home tests are important, the results you get may not be quite as accurate as the blood tests or laboratory tests given at your doctor's office. In some cases, test results may vary by as much as 20 percent. Given this variability, you should view your home test results with a grain of salt, particularly the first reading that seems way too high or low. In such cases, simply repeat the test. Make sure that you have clean hands when you administer the test. Make sure your glucose meter meets all quality assurance criteria. Call the manufacturer's toll-free number if you have complaints or questions, or if you need help in checking your meter's accuracy.

Each regularly scheduled visit to the doctor who treats your diabetes should include a check of your blood glucose test results against the laboratory blood sugar results taken at the doctor's office. Make it a practice to administer your home blood test at the same time of day that the doctor's office does its test, because if you don't, the comparison won't be accurate.

Portable blood glucose testing meters have been a boon to self-management. But don't be excessively hard on yourself over the results of home tests, which may be higher or lower than you expect. As a general rule, anyone's blood sugar levels will be lower before the person has eaten than it will be after a meal because the ingestion of food triggers a rise in glucose. Ask your medical doctor to recommend blood sugar goals for you. When practicing self-management, aim for the best you can do at the time rather than an impossible standard of perfection.

Meters

To test your blood sugar, you'll need a small inexpensive blood glucose testing meter, disposable lancets to prick your finger, and disposable blood testing strips for the machine to read. You may never enjoy pricking your finger, but you'll test like a trooper after a few tries.

Meters that can give you an accurate reading on your blood glucose without your having to prick your finger are in development but are not yet available. No-stick glucose meters are

Testing Blood Sugar

Here are the basic steps to test blood sugar with the aid of a home glucose testing meter. The sequence and steps may vary according to the meter—use your meter as directed.

- Collect the materials you need, including blood glucose meter, lancet, strips, and record book.
- Wash your hands.
- Stick your finger to obtain a drop of blood.
- Put the drop of blood on the strip, and insert the strip into the meter as indicated.
- Read and record the results.

expected to be expensive when they first appear on the market, but prices will drop just as they did for today's testing meters. For instance, one new meter, recently approved for home use, uses a laser as a lancet and results in "nearly painless" tests, according to the manufacturer. Other prototypes use laser beams to attempt to read blood sugar levels through the fingernail or wrist; others use different technology to attempt a reading through skin patches. Some new meters do tests on the forearm and on other areas of the body that have fewer nerves than the fingertips, resulting in less pain during testing.

Perhaps the most advanced technology involves a continuous glucose-monitoring sensor, approved in 1999, which allows a sensor to be placed under the skin for as long as three days. This sensor is connected by a wire to the glucose meter and can record glucose levels every few seconds and store them as frequently as every five minutes—producing hundreds of readings per day—perhaps the first step in continuous glucose control. Connecting the probe with an insulin pump itself could allow very tight control of blood sugar levels—even an alarm system that signals if glucose drops too low.

Dozens of blood sugar testing meters are now on the market, including models sold by LifeScan, a Johnson & Johnson company; Bayer; Roche Diagnostics; and Abbott Diabetes Care. Check several before you buy. All newer models provide a digital readout. Most are battery operated and are no larger than a pack of playing cards. A few models have the lancing device built into the meter. Several include booklets in which to record your meter readings. A few come with a built-in memory that holds several dozen past readings, and some provide ways to enter information on insulin injections and exercise. Some meters can be connected to a personal computer through a special cable, allowing readings to be turned into easily read charts or graphs by using companion software. A few meters have oversized, illu-minated, or "talking" readouts, which are especially useful for elderly people or for people with limited vision. One meter gives oral instructions for its use and can read the labels of certain insulin bottles aloud. Some can even be hooked up to e-mail your test results to your doctor's computer prior to your appointment. Note that many older meters test and report glucose levels in whole blood, while newer meters and tests at your doctor's office test blood plasma. If you have an older meter, remember that whole-blood readings are roughly 12 percent lower than plasma readings.

Your doctor normally won't advise you on which meter to buy. Your diabetes educator or nurse educator can tell you what's on the market or direct you to reliable sources of information. Some pharmacists, particularly those who have many customers with diabetes, may be able to explain the pros and cons of dif-ferent models. Most mail-order houses specializing in diabetes supplies carry blood glucose testing meters.

Before you buy, consider how you will use your meter. Do you need to carry it to work or to meetings in your briefcase or handbag? Do you need it to help you remember your read-ings, which you may not have the time or inclination to record after every test? Do you prefer a certain color? When you add the cost of the meter, lancets, and strips, which model best fits your budget? Check the costs that your health insurance will cover, and see if your selection is limited in any way. The cost of a meter and some portion of the daily supplies may be reim-bursable. Medicare, for instance, will now pay for a meter if you are taking insulin and if your doctor gives you a written prescription for the meter as part of your treatment plan. More information on the financial aspects of diabetes can be found in Chapter 15.

Most manufacturers are eager to sell you one of their meters, just to guarantee a customer for their strips. The most you should pay for a meter is about $150. Many manufacturers offer some type of rebate; sometimes they'll even give you the meter for free. You'll purchase the blood test strips and lancets as needed, with the test strips usually supplied by the same company that manufactured your meter. The cost of the strips adds up—they're between 50¢ and $1 apiece. You use one strip each time you test, and more than one if you don't do it right the first time.

Lancets are short, fine needles that should pierce the skin with minimal discomfort. They should be easy for you to hold and use. Some fit into a device that looks like a fountain pen, which pricks your skin with a spring-loaded snap. Since you're the only one using them, you may experiment with reusing lancets to save money, but remember that most get dull fairly quickly, and when they are dull, the pricking is painful.

How to Test

You may be clumsy at first, but you'll get the hang of it. The basic procedure is to wash your hands, insert the strip into the meter, prick your finger with a lancet, place a droplet of blood on the test strip, and read and record the results. Read and follow the instructions for testing that come in the package with your meter. Once you're comfortable with the procedure, testing will take less time each day than brushing your teeth.

When you begin, you may unfortunately have to prick your finger more than once to get blood for the test. Don't be discouraged. You'll get better and faster as you go along.

To test, you'll need a sufficient amount of blood. Each meter's requirements are different. If you don't get a good drop, "milk" your finger by rubbing it down away from your palm with the fingers of your other hand and releasing it, as you would the teat of a milk cow. If you can't get a good droplet from one location, try another. You may have to rub down your finger a few times to get a good droplet. Or, you may be one of those fortunate people who bleed easily.

Your choice of fingers to prick will depend on your manual dexterity and on whether you're right-handed or left-handed. Make it as easy as possible on yourself. Pricking too far back on your finger can make it difficult to get the droplet of blood onto the test strip. Many people prefer to prick only the side of the finger, rather than the more sensitive fingerprint pad, where you have more nerve endings. Techniques vary. Some people choose a couple of fingers that they use for testing each time. Some make several sticks into the same location because the callus that builds up also blunts the slight pain of injecting a lancet. If you do it this way, eventually the callus will stop you from getting the proper amount of blood, and you'll have to move on to another location and perhaps create another callus.

Selecting the right lancing device is also helpful. Some are less troublesome than others. Some will stick too deep and some not quite deep enough, because skin thickness varies from person to person. It's worth trying another type of lancing device if you have trouble with your first one—your diabetes educator or nurse may be able to offer guidance. If you find a lancing device that's a bit more expensive but easier and more comfortable to use, it's probably worth the extra money to buy it.

Blood glucose meters usually work well for a long time. However, because they're mechanical devices, few work perfectly. Most manufacturers have a procedure for testing their meters' accuracy. They also have toll-free numbers to call if you experience problems with their products, and service people to walk you through the testing procedure.

Remember that meter manufacturers want to keep their customers happy so that they can continue to sell them supplies. The majority will listen to your complaints or problems and will attempt to rectify them.

When to Test

The doctor who treats your diabetes should recommend a blood glucose testing schedule for you and should ask to see your results during your regular visits. The more frequently you test your blood sugar, the more likely you are to achieve the desired control. But don't go overboard.

Testing your fasting blood sugar before you eat anything in the morning gives you a reading on your sugar levels without any food, but it still includes the small amount of glucose that your liver pumped out during the night, while you slept. Testing after meals tells you how the additional glucose generated by your meal is being assimilated. Blood sugar levels are often highest about an hour after you eat, when easily digested sugars and starches surge into your bloodstream and peak, before declining. If you test after eating and your blood sugars are lower than before you ate, your meter or your testing technique may be faulty. If you use insulin before you eat, you could also experience a low reading.

The number of tests your doctor recommends will depend on several factors and may vary from what is considered standard. In *A Touch of Diabetes*, authors Lois Jovanovic-Peterson, M.D., Charles Peterson, M.D., and Morton Stone recommend that people controlling Type 2 diabetes through diet and exercise alone test before breakfast and an hour after each meal every other day, or about three days a week. They recommend that people using diet, exercise, and diabetes pills test before breakfast and an hour after each meal every other day. For people using multiple insulin injections, they recommend testing before each meal and an hour after each meal every day.

Some doctors recommend that patients with Type 2 diabetes test a minimum of four times per day, one day a week. Others recommend two tests per day every day.

Testing before meals may be recommended by your physician if you're on medications such as diabetes pills or insulin, because these tests can help tell you how well the medications are working. If you are taking diabetes pills or insulin, of course, you should also test your blood sugars any time you experience the recognizable symptoms of low blood sugar—feeling confused, sweaty, shaky, nervous, or weak. It will greatly help you to know the level at which you get these symptoms. If you really need to eat a snack, do so. The first rule of self-management is to take good care of your health.

Whatever your doctor's recommendations, your results may be kept in a record book, on forms provided by your health-care team, or in a file in your computer that you can print out and take to your doctor. If you've been testing as directed, an examination of your test results may yield clear, general patterns of high and low blood sugar, which may be modified through changes in eating patterns, stress-reduction techniques, increased physical activity, or other means.

If your doctor doesn't recommend blood testing at home, ask why not. If your doctor says blood testing is not necessary, this physician has not kept up with the times. Blood glucose testing has been an accepted part of good diabetes care for several years, for both Type 1 and Type 2 diabetes.

Remember that a glucose meter reads blood sugar levels only at the moment at which they are taken. As the Greek philosopher Heraclitus observed, you never step into the same river

Blood Glucose Goals

Every person's blood sugar levels rise and fall during the day in response to food consumption, stress levels, and other factors. Your blood sugar levels will probably not be low when you begin blood sugar testing, particularly if you are either young or elderly. Listed here are some general blood glucose targets that people can aim for over the long term. However, always check with your medical doctor for blood sugar goals that are appropriate for you.

Time	Ideal Range	Acceptable
Fasting	70–110 mg/dl (3.9–6.1 mmol/L)	60–120 mg/dl (3.3–6.7 mmol/L)
1 hour after a meal	90–150 mg/dl (5–8.3 mmol/L)	80–180 mg/dl (4.4–10 mmol/L)
2 hours after a meal	80–140 mg/dl (4.4–7.7 mmol/L)	70–150 mg/dl (3.9–8.3 mmol/L)
3 hours after a meal	60–110 mg/dl (3.3–6.1 mmol/L)	60–130 mg/dl (3.3–7.2 mmol/L)
Pregnancy— fasting	60–95 mg/dl (3.3–5.3 mmol/L)	
Pregnancy— 2 hours after a meal	< 120 mg/dl (< 6.7 mmol/L)	

twice. Accept that your blood glucose levels rise and fall. Unless you're a fortune-teller, you won't be able to predict all your test results. Some blood glucose tests will be higher than you expect, some lower. Try to be philosophical. Don't fall into the trap of getting upset over tiny variations in test results. Try to look at these numbers as a scientist would look at raw data, rather than taking them as personal messages from the oracle about whether or not you're a "good diabetic." You're a good diabetic if you test, no matter what the results.

Again, high blood sugar levels don't mean that you've suddenly become a bad person. Stress, certain foods, sickness, and many other conditions and circumstances can jack up blood sugar levels. If you get too upset over your test results, you will further elevate your blood sugar. Look at blood sugar testing as a tool you can use to achieve control, rather than as a series of verdicts on whether you've been naughty or nice.

Every person's blood sugar levels are in constant flux, and each test that you administer reflects only that one moment in time. Always follow your doctor's recommendations on how many times to test, as well as when to test. Record the results as directed. Test your blood sugar more frequently when you are ill, and anytime you feel unusual.

Lifestyle Issues

Your doctor should recommend a glucose testing schedule that takes your work schedule and lifestyle into account. There should be some element of convenience in your testing schedule. You don't want to take on additional stress trying to test your blood sugar when you're pressed to do other things that are important to you, such as taking your children to school. Whether you're a farmer who spends long hours in the field on a combine during harvest season or a businessperson with a long commute to the office, you should test at times that fit comfortably into your schedule. Remember, too, that testing is a means of preventing low and high blood sugar. Testing yourself before you operate machinery is a good way of ensuring your safety and that of others.

Since your body chemistry is unique, you may react to some foods different from the way other people react, even other people with diabetes. You can track your particular reactions to foods using blood sugar testing. Do you suspect that a four-cheese, pepperoni, and sausage pizza will unduly affect your blood sugar? Testing before and an hour after eating it will tell you how dramatically the pizza affected your blood sugar. When you learn something meaningful about your blood sugar, share this information with your health-care team.

If you're exercising, especially strenuously, your doctor may advise you to test before your workout, because aerobic exercise lowers blood sugar. Before you begin exercising, you may want to eat a light snack if your blood sugar tests low for you—around 80 mg/dl or whatever level your doctor or exercise physiologist has set for you. But try not to use the possibility of low blood sugar as an excuse to pig out.

As a general rule, aim for blood sugars as close to normal as possible; that's where the human body functions best. As directed by your doctor, you may be able to safely aim for blood glucose levels between 90 and 100 mg/dl (or 5 to 5.56 mmol/L) before eating, and 150 to 180 mg/dl (or 8.33 to 10 mmol/L) an hour or so after meals. Your medical doctor will help you set realistic goals for your tests.

Use common sense. If you test at 200 mg/dl (or 11.11 mmol/L) before lunch, don't eat a big, rich, carbohydrate-laden lunch. Take a short walk or do some exercise instead. Drink some water. Or you may modify your lunch to include only protein (such as a piece of chicken) and eliminate most of the carbohydrates (such as fruit, milk, sugars, and starches) to see if that helps bring your blood sugars back down. This is a situation in which it can help to know your reaction to particular foods.

Blood glucose testing is a self-management tool. Blood sugar levels will fluctuate. Your home test results can help you manage these fluctuations. Find a glucose meter that suits you, and test yourself as directed by your doctor and health-care team. You can use the results in many ways, such as fine-tuning your eating style, which is the subject of the next chapter.

7

Food

Changing Your Style of Eating
Helps Control Diabetes

WHAT YOU EAT directly affects your weight and blood sugar levels. Controlling what you eat and when you eat is a central part of your self-management, whether your goal is to drop some pounds or merely to control blood sugar. A registered dietitian or nutritional consultant, often a key member of your health-care team, may work with you to help you change your eating style in a way that suits your life. The basics of nutrition and a few possible dietary strategies are set out here, as are tips to get you going and keep you going, as well as help get you through the hazardous holiday periods when temptation often appears.

We all need food to live, but food has both physical and psychological meanings for most people. Eating well, and in moderation, has long been recognized as integral to good health. During the time of the Roman Empire, the poet Horace wrote in his *Satires*, "Now learn what and how great benefits a temperate diet will bring along with it. In the first place, you will enjoy good health."

About Your Weight

Approximately 56 percent of all Americans between the ages of twenty and seventy-four are overweight, and 30 percent of those are technically obese, according to the Department of Health and Human Services. When people with Type 2 diabetes are considered as a group, an even greater proportion, more than 80 percent, are overweight. If you are within this group, your blood sugar levels may return to normal if you can return to your normal or recommended weight. This is particularly the case if you have had diabetes for less than ten years.

Blood sugar levels may drop significantly with just a small reduction in weight. Even if you are overweight, a loss of only 10 to 15 pounds will substantially lower your blood glucose levels and reduce your risk of heart attacks. Almost instantly, you'll feel better with lower blood sugar. A decade or two from now, you'll have limited your chances of serious complications. Adopt a more physically active lifestyle along with some reduction in body weight, as every medical expert recommends, and you'll feel better and reduce your risk of future complications even more.

Losing weight is not an easy thing, given our sedentary lifestyles. Losing weight can be stressful, especially for older people. Most obese people have been overweight for years. If you are overweight and have diabetes, you also have a metabolism that is out of kilter. Overweight people almost always eat more of certain types of foods than they need to maintain a normal weight. Obesity can have a psychological dimension, too, which also must be considered if changes in eating patterns are to be maintained over time.

It's heartening that many people diagnosed with diabetes have been able to throw away their diabetes pills or insulin syringes simply by modifying their diets and becoming more physically active. True, you won't get a gold medal when you avoid wolfing down an extra-large piece of birthday cake or switch to more nutritious foods. No one will hand you an Academy Award for taking a walk or participating in an exercise class on a regular basis. But in the long run, changing your lifestyle to include a healthy, nutritious, well-balanced diet will increase the quality—and probably extend the length—of your life.

Optimum Weights

Listed here are some optimum weight ranges for women and men, according to the U.S. government's Dietary Guidelines for Americans, released in 1995. Of course, women typically are shorter and have less body mass than men. The lowest end of these ranges is appropriate for women with small frames, while the upper limits are for men with larger, heavier frames. In the treatment of diabetes, your doctor or dietitian will help you determine a weight goal that is appropriate for you.

Height	Weight in Pounds	Height	Weight in Pounds
4'10"	91–119	5'9"	129–169
4'11"	94–124	5'10"	132–174
5'0"	97–128	5'11"	136–179
5'1"	101–132	6'0"	140–184
5'2"	104–137	6'1"	144–189
5'3"	107–141	6'2"	148–195
5'4"	111–146	6'3"	152–200
5'5"	114–150	6'4"	156–205
5'6"	118–155	6'5"	160–211
5'7"	121–160	6'6"	164–216
5'8"	125–164		

After all, thin people generally live longer. Actuarial tables prepared by insurance companies associate longevity with below-average weight. Amazing research studies conducted at UCLA and the University of Texas found that laboratory animals can extend their average life spans by as much as 50 percent if they consume fewer calories. It's well established that people who are overweight have much higher rates of not only diabetes but also heart disease, cancer, and other diseases. According to the U.S. Centers for Disease Control and Prevention, poor dietary habits and a lack of physical activity are associated with an estimated 300,000 deaths per year, ahead of every other known risk factor except the use of tobacco.

Nobody knows all the answers about obesity, which is epidemic in the United States among both adults and children. Sedentary lifestyles and high-fat, low-fiber diets are obvious suspects. Stress is another contributor. Genetics may be a factor in some cases. Research published twenty years ago in England found that people who are obese tend to eat two to three times the amount of food eaten by lean people, and eat it two to three times as fast. This may be because overweight people don't allow themselves to enjoy the food they eat. As surprising as it may seem, many overweight people probably don't often give themselves permission to savor and enjoy their food.

Eating more food than your body uses is the root cause of being overweight. Reducing your intake of certain foods, increasing your intake of others, and adding more physical activity to your life will help you control your weight. Maintaining a healthy lifestyle produces significant health benefits over time.

Nutritional Support

After being diagnosed with diabetes, you should be referred by your medical doctor to a registered dietitian or a nutritionist to help educate you about foods and help you plan meals. This is now called medical nutrition therapy or diet therapy. Medical nutrition therapy is integral to diabetes management, according to the American Diabetes Association (ADA), and ideally it takes account of your food intake, your lifestyle, your culture, and your finances and prepares you to set goals and make necessary dietary changes. According to an ADA study, people with Type 2 diabetes saved an average of $1,994 apiece just from reduced expenditures for oral agents and insulin as a result of diet therapy. Helenbeth Reynolds, a registered dietitian affiliated with the University of Minnesota, says diet therapy often involves an average of two or three visits with a registered dietitian, who should have laboratory test results from your doctor in hand. The first visit may be in a group setting to cover basic nutritional care and set goals. This is often followed by one or two individual sessions or follow-up visits to examine and individualize meal plans.

A registered dietitian or nutritionist may work with a particular doctor, have a professional affiliation with a clinic or hospital, or even have his or her own office. Your nutritionist should get to know you and tailor recommendations to you.

Since your body is unique and reacts in a distinctive way to food choices, you must use what you already know—and what you can still learn from a nutritional specialist—to choose what you eat. Think of yourself as an athlete in training, advises Los Angeles dietitian Diane Woods, R.D. An athlete in training looks at food as an essential aspect of achieving physical goals. If you plan nutritious meals for yourself and keep nutritious food in your home, you are on your way to a life of sensible, appropriate food choices that can help you control your blood sugar.

Even if you are not overweight, you may not be aware of all the food you eat, especially if your eating style includes snacks while watching television. For this reason, a registered dietitian or nutritionist may ask you to keep a written record of everything you eat for a few days. Once you know where you've been, planning your meals can take you where you'd like to go. You may change your eating style on your own, but consulting an expert can save you a lot of time and help you to succeed.

As stated at the beginning of this section, your first appointment with a nutritional consultant should be set up by your doctor after you are diagnosed with diabetes. If your doctor does not recommend that you see a dietitian, act on your own. If you are in a health maintenance organization, ask your doctor to refer you to a dietitian even if he or she does not routinely do so. Remind your primary care physician that the American Diabetes Association recommends that you work with a knowledgeable registered dietitian experienced in treating people with diabetes, because nutritional therapy is integral to good diabetes care. Another way to locate a registered dietitian is to call the American Dietetic Association's toll-free telephone number, which is listed in the "Resources" section at the back of the book.

A registered dietitian might charge $75 to $125 per hour, with sessions ranging from half an hour to an hour. Medicare now covers diet therapy, also known as medical nutrition therapy, if it's prescribed by a physician, but most health insurance companies still approve it only on a case-by-case basis.

Look for a dietitian who frequently works with people who have diabetes, and who understands current principles of nutrition. When you locate one, make an appointment for yourself.

The Role of a Nutritionist or Dietitian

In a nutshell, you and your dietitian should review your current food choices and figure out how to make them better. One meeting is not enough to do more than learn a few essential principles. So learn what you can, work to apply it, and go back for follow-up appointments as recommended. Also, try using the telephone to seek help with problems.

As a first step in this process, your dietitian or nutrition specialist may take a diet history, which will involve interviewing you about the foods you eat and writing down this information. You may also write a diet history yourself, as preparation for an interview with a diet professional or simply to make yourself more aware of your eating patterns. If you're one of those people who can recall every meal and snack eaten for the past two weeks, then write down what you've eaten for the past few days and take it with you to your first appointment.

Another way of tracking your eating patterns is to keep a food diary of everything you eat for a set period. You can estimate the quantities, but don't fudge on the details by leaving out a piece of candy here or a bag of potato chips there. Strive for total honesty and accuracy. A food diary is as good a place as any to begin thinking about the quantity of food you eat and to start estimating the weight of some food items as you eat them. You may not be able to do this at every meal—if you're rushing to catch a commuter train after breakfast or having lunch with the members of your garden club—but most meals will allow you time to begin your measuring. As your self-management progresses, you may be asked to track several aspects of your care.

A food diary covering three days is a good way to begin examining your eating style. It may help to think of yourself as a detective, out to discover vital clues that will solve the mystery of why you're overweight. If you don't already have a food scale, buy one and begin weighing those hamburgers and steaks. Take out your measuring cups and begin measuring portions of fruits and vegetables. Count those slices of bread, count how many slabs of butter you spread on each slice, and so on. Sure, it's a lot of arithmetic, but counting and measuring even a few food items

Treatment Plan record for the week beginning Monday, _____ January 13th _____ (date)

Diet Log

Goal: 2,000 calories/day

Date	breakfast	lunch	dinner	snacks	Exercise type/duration	Glucose Monitoring blood/urine time/result	Rx time	Notes
Mon.	1-ww bagel lt. cream ch. 1/2 orange w/ nonfat yogurt	ham sand. on ww bread 1/2 c. chicken soup 1 apple 8 oz. 1% milk	4 oz. fl. steak green beans mushrooms 1/2 c. corn 1/2 cantaloupe	8 1/2 animal crackers-9:30 _____ 1/2 banana	10 A.M. walk	8 190 / 5 172	✓ / ✓	cut on toe-called nurse-no problem
Tues.	1/2 c bran flakes 8 oz. 1% milk 1/2 banana	turkey sand. w/ mustard 1 oz. potato chips 1 1/4 c. melon	4 oz. baked chicken brown rice 1 c. carrots green salad	X —— 2 slices cake!!!	yoga class	8 177 / 5 194	✓ / ✓	Sorry-it's my husband's 50th birthday!
Wed.								

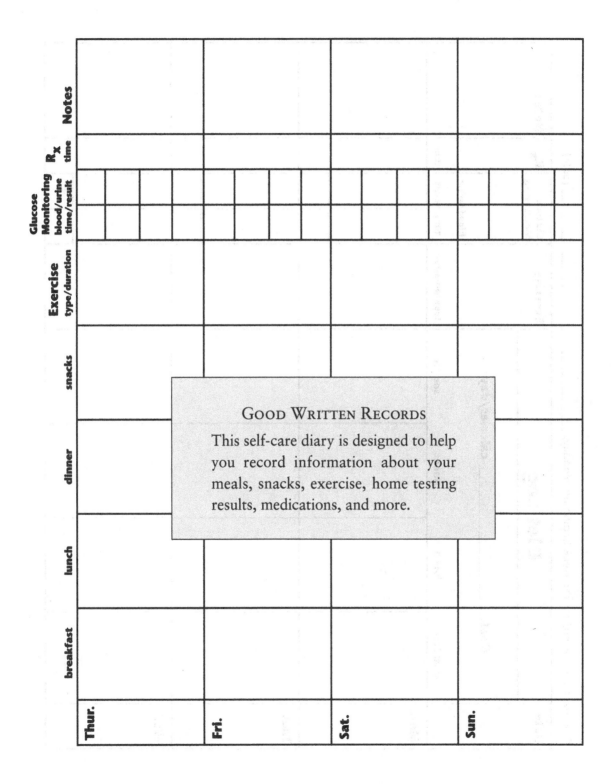

	breakfast	lunch	dinner	snacks	Exercise type/duration	Glucose Monitoring blood/urine time/result													R$_x$ time	Notes
Thur.																				
Fri.																				
Sat.																				
Sun.																				

GOOD WRITTEN RECORDS

This self-care diary is designed to help you record information about your meals, snacks, exercise, home testing results, medications, and more.

Treatment Plan record for the week beginning Monday, _____ (date)

Date	**Diet Log** Goal: _____ calories/day				Exercise	Glucose Monitoring		R_x	Notes
	breakfast	lunch	dinner	snacks	type/duration	blood/urine	time/result	time	
Mon.									
Tues.									
Wed.									

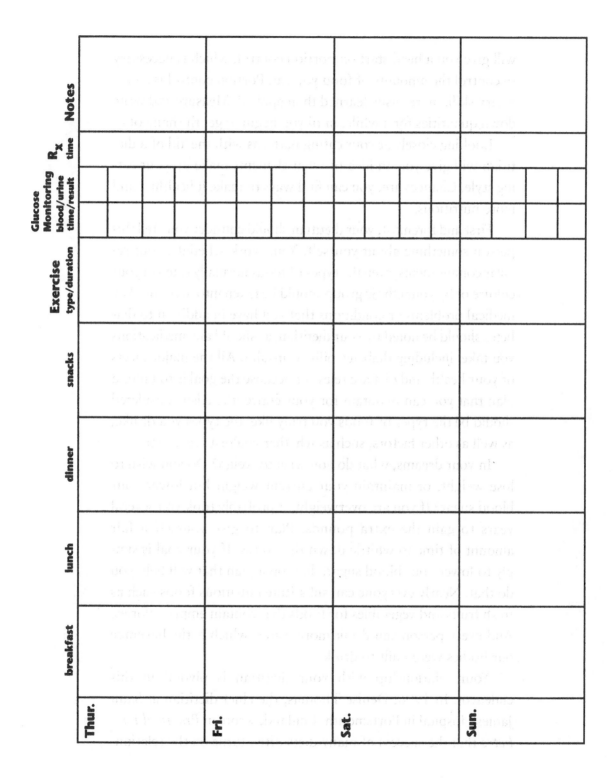

	breakfast	lunch	dinner	snacks	Exercise type/duration	Glucose Monitoring blood/urine time/result								Rx time	Notes
Thur.																
Fri.																
Sat.																
Sun.																

will give you a head start on portion control, which is necessary to control the amounts of food you eat. Portion control is a necessary skill, more easily learned than applied. Measure and write down quantities for a while, until you begin to get the hang of it.

Looking closely at your eating patterns with the aid of a dietitian will give you an idea of what elements make up your eating style. Chances are, you can find ways to make it healthier and more nutritious.

First and foremost, your dietitian should consider you. Tell this person something about yourself. Your work schedule, your regular commitments, even the types of foods normally eaten in your culture or by your ethnic group should be taken into account. Any medical problems or conditions that you have in addition to diabetes should be noted by your dietitian, as should any medications you take, including diabetes pills or insulin. All the major facets of your health and diet are relevant because the goal is to tailor a plan that you can maintain for your entire life. Also considered should be the types of foods you truly like, the types you dislike, as well as other factors, such as whether you're a vegetarian.

In your dreams, what do you wish to weigh? Do you wish to lose weight, or maintain your current weight but lower your blood sugar? If you are overweight, it probably took you several years to gain the extra pounds. Plan to give yourself a fair amount of time to whittle down the excess. If your goal is simply to lower your blood sugar, develop a plan that will help you do that. Nearly everyone can substitute nutritious foods such as fresh fruits and vegetables for foods that contain empty calories. And every person can drink more water, which is the beverage our bodies were built to drink.

Your relationship with your dietitian is pivotal in this endeavor. In 1996, Denise Thomas, the chief dietitian at Saint James Hospital in Portsmouth, England, wrote in *Practical Diabetes* that the success of many diets often turns on the relationship between dietitian and patient. Many times, she observed, the dietitian's recommendations will fail if they are not appropriate to that patient. Many diets fail because they are too restrictive or strict for the individual, causing the person to first break the diet and then feel guilty and eat even more.

A Lifelong Effort

Usually, the more you know and the more you participate, the more you wisely choose appropriate foods for yourself and the greater the benefit you will receive. Look at a change in eating style as a lifelong effort. You may choose to modify your diet following a few general guidelines and then fine-tune it later through something like an exchange-group plan, which gives you a method of measuring and controlling the calories you eat.

Changing what you eat is the safest method ever devised for controlling blood sugar. If you eat well and in moderation, a healthy eating style can survive an occasional mistake.

As time goes by, you will learn through experience and blood sugar testing what foods raise your blood sugar. Avoid foods that jack up your blood sugar, or eat them only in minimal amounts, as part of an otherwise healthy meal. Chinese food, pizza, and pretzels can send blood sugars soaring for some people, as can candies sweetened with sorbitol. A consistent rise in your blood sugar levels after you eat a particular food indicates a strong blood sugar response to that food. If you suspect that a particular food is a culprit, try cutting it out for a while or substituting something healthier—for instance, thin-crust vegetarian pizza for deep-dish pepperoni pizza—and see what effect that has on you. Foods affect us all differently. Even some people who eat the often-recommended bedtime snack of air-popped popcorn wake up with high blood sugar, because most people need a combination of foods to slow their glucose release.

If you have already begun blood sugar testing, you'll be happy to know that controlling your food intake for just a day or two can reduce your blood sugar levels and be reflected on home glucose tests. The results may be even better if you also adopt a more active lifestyle, especially one that incorporates a little aerobic exercise. You will do yourself and your family a big favor over time if you adopt a healthier, happier lifestyle.

The Joy of Eating

Eating and drinking are topics fraught with pleasure and pain for the human race. Eating food and drinking fluids are primitive, sensual, life-sustaining pleasures. For us, food has social and psychological importance. "You are what you eat," quipped the French gastronome Jean Anthelme Brillat-Savarin, memorably expressing the undeniable bond between good food and a good life. However, in our weight-conscious society, eating can also be a guilty pleasure, since even a small weight gain can be humiliating, particularly for women.

We are prisoners of evolution. For thousands of generations, tribes of human beings spent much of their time hunting, gathering, storing, and preparing food, activities that required the continuous use of the leg and arm muscles. Certain foods were not always available. To survive in this environment, the human body developed the ability both to maintain a fairly constant level of glucose and to store great quantities of fats. In our sedentary culture, we have taken most of the physical labor out of gathering and preparing food. In industrialized societies, we can buy almost unlimited quantities of even the foods that our bodies require only in tiny amounts and then eat too much of them. In all of the animal kingdom, only human beings and their domestic animals suffer from obesity.

On the most primal level, eating produces a feeling of comfort, filling the stomach and drawing blood from the brain and other parts of the body to help with digestion. Food provokes the release of the neurotransmitter serotonin, which produces in the brain the sensation of being full. Since the production of serotonin slows when people diet, mood changes and periods of carbohydrate craving can appear in people who have problems synthesizing this chemical. This chemically induced craving for carbohydrates is one reason why many people fail to stay on crash diets, which do not incorporate the beneficial changes in eating style necessary to stabilize weight over the long term.

Only a small percentage of people who try fad diets achieve long-term weight loss. In the National Weight Control Registry, a database of individuals who lost 30 pounds or more and kept it off for more than a year, most of the people surveyed said they needed not only a desire to eat less and exercise more but also the ambition and willpower to do so. Many people trying to lose weight can relate to a memorable couplet written by Samuel Hoffenstein, who may have set pen to paper in a moment of great gastric unhappiness:

> *"My soul is dark with stormy riot,*
> *Directly traceable to diet."*

The psychological aspects of dieting are complex, as are our society's attitudes about food.

Mixed Messages

In this society, we give each other mixed messages about food. Women are expected to provide nourishing, comforting food to their families while remaining slim and beautiful as they presumably deny food to themselves. Men take candy to their sweethearts but are stricken with horror if their sweethearts gain weight. Your mother might have told you that sweets were "bad for you," yet your grandmother rewarded you with special holiday sweets, homemade cookies, or other carbohydrate-laden surprises.

In many families, food becomes a reward, an inexpensive and tangible symbol of affection or love. Food can be a bribe, a seduction, even a weapon. Too many of us reward (or punish) ourselves with sweet, succulent, forbidden food treats, even though the damage to the waistline is predictable over time. In the worst case, food can actually become an addiction, in which case self-help support groups such as Overeaters Anonymous or Weight Watchers may be of help.

Old rituals involving food are embedded in contemporary culture, where echoes of harvest festivals and successful hunts for game may still be present. After a year of competitive sports, athletes traditionally have an awards banquet that involves a meaty feast as part of their reward. Religious and secular holidays, weddings, births, and deaths are often accompanied by huge banquets, with food a centerpiece of the event. Marketers of food and drink products capitalize on these old associations, producing glossy advertisements and television commercials that show trim, beautiful models rewarding themselves with beer, sweet soft drinks, and junk foods.

"I've been a diabetic for too long and cheated too often," confessed a woman who has been managing Type 2 diabetes for twenty years and who now receives support and encouragement from her family in the area of food choices. "My whole attitude now is just to ask myself, 'Is it worth it?'"

It's not easy to lose weight. In 1986, according to a consensus statement issued by the National Institutes of Health, only about 25 percent of people with diabetes who needed to lose weight were successful in losing 20 to 40 pounds. Only 5 percent were successful in losing more than 40 pounds. While strategies for changing eating patterns have evolved and may be more effective, these statistics point out the difficulties inherent in weight loss. Measured against these statistics, any weight loss is a victory. And keeping that weight off is a huge success.

Some obesity may be genetic. The first evidence of this was when researchers at the Howard Hughes Medical Institute, in New York, examined a strain of obese mice, which they named ob/ob mice, that carried the same mutant gene. This was the first evidence of a gene linked to obesity. Subsequent studies reported in the *New England Journal of Medicine* in 1995 theorized that some overweight people with diabetes may have a type of genetic flaw on the receptors of their fat cells that causes them to burn calories more slowly than do normal people. This flaw, which research scientists believe may be due to a defective beta 3 receptor, has been correlated with incidences of diabetes and obesity in studies of Pima Indians and with a study of obesity in Finland. Although these findings are preliminary, they suggest that losing weight may be a lot more complicated than simply summoning a little willpower.

There's always more to learn when it comes to food. People who prepare their own food are more likely to succeed in changing their eating styles than those who don't cook at all. The reason for this may be that cooks have more control over the ingredients that they use, as well as a direct physical connection with what they eat.

Remember that food is neither moral nor ethical. Hershey's Kisses are not intrinsically "bad," and carrot sticks are not intrinsically "good." All items may be reduced to calories and therefore to numbers, says registered dietitian and diabetes educator Debbie Solomin, a diabetes nutrition specialist at Encino-Tarzana Hospital, in Tarzana, California. Understanding and working with these numbers (expressed as calories) can help you change your eating style. Slow and steady permanent changes in eating

style, rather than crash dieting, allow you to take weight off—
and keep it off—over time.

Different Strokes

Choose your own approach to changing your eating style,
because many approaches may work. The degree of sophistication that you put into fine-tuning your eating style is up to you.

The truth is that healthy eating is no longer much different
for people with diabetes than for people without diabetes. In
recent years, the American Diabetes Association, the American
Cancer Society, the American Heart Association, and other
health organizations have advised people to eat a variety of foods
that provide necessary nutrients, particularly high-fiber foods
such as fresh fruits and vegetables, and to cut down on consumption of saturated fats, trans-fatty acids, sugars, and salts.
Alcoholic beverages are OK, they say, but always in moderation.
And of course, most health organizations recommend that you
maintain a desirable weight, which a healthy style of eating will
help you achieve if accompanied by regular physical activity.

"Whoever was the father of a disease, an ill diet was the
mother," observed the writer George Herbert, about four hundred years ago. Herbert could have been writing about diabetes,
because the link between this disease and diet is fundamental.

Your Eating Style

Many people already know what a healthy diet entails. However,
too many of us blithely ignore what we know is in our best interest. Instead, we eat too many junk foods, convenience foods, fast
foods, greasy foods, rich foods, fattening foods, and sweet and
salty foods whose seductive flavors and convenience blind us to

their nutritional shortcomings. Processing robs food of nutrients and often adds nutrient-challenged sugar, white flour, fats, and chemicals to provide flavor. One theory about why so many people are overweight in the United States is that people eat greater quantities of processed foods than they do unprocessed foods in an attempt to consume the vitamins, minerals, and other nutrients that are in such short supply in processed foods. And it's no secret that the typical American's eating style contains an unhealthy high percentage of fats, leading many men and women to become overweight.

Changing your style of eating is one of the challenges you may face in controlling diabetes. Bad habits can be broken. An unhealthy eating style can be changed. This is not a quick process. Even if your intentions are good, you won't wake up tomorrow morning looking as great as you did in high school. But you can improve. Think in terms of small steps, taken one at a time, rather than a single dramatic leap into the evening gown or tuxedo that you wore years ago to the senior prom.

The average American eats a diet consisting of 40 percent to 50 percent fats, 25 percent to 35 percent carbohydrates, and 25 percent protein. Fats contain more calories than carbohydrates or protein do, and eating a lot of them packs on the pounds. New government dietary guidelines recommend that you keep your total fat intake to between 20 percent and 35 percent of calories, and that most of these come from sources such as fish, nuts, and vegetable oils, which contain unsaturated fats. Saturated fats, such as those in butter and meat, should be held to below 10 percent of total calories, and the consumption of trans fats such as those found in fried food and some processed food should be kept as low as possible. The way you approach this is up to you. Many people benefit from keeping written records during a period of weight loss because it helps them to see and track their progress. A study of people with

Type 2 diabetes on weight-loss programs conducted at the University of Pittsburgh medical school showed that the people who kept meticulous written records lost an average of 37 pounds, while those who kept less meticulous records averaged a weight loss of only 10 pounds.

Time Is on Your Side

A healthy style of eating is not a magic pill or a quick fix, but over time it will make you a healthier person. A good eating style doesn't rely on a tasteless diet of health foods. Instead, it should contain a nutritious balance of all types of foods—even, with moderation, the occasional savory sweet.

A healthy eating style for most people with diabetes is about the same as what is recommended for any person growing older, if that person hopes to avoid medical problems such as high blood pressure and heart attacks. A good eating style combined with regular aerobic activity can actually slow the physical degeneration that accompanies aging.

What should we eat? Almost always, the answer is a balanced diet. A balanced diet comprises a good mix of foods, all of which contain nutrients such as carbohydrates, proteins, and fats, and all the vitamins, minerals, and other food elements that we need to remain alive. A quick look at the U.S. Department of Agriculture's new Food Guide Pyramid, pictured in this chapter, will help you understand the mix of foods that constitutes a balanced diet.

New Food Guide Pyramid

The following are recommended amounts of food to be eaten in the five major categories of the USDA Food Guide Pyramid, which was updated in 2005.

Source: U.S. Department of Agriculture (USDA) Center for Nutrition Policy and Promotion

- Grains: 6 ounces per day, including at least 3 ounces of whole grain cereals, breads, crackers, rice, or pasta. An ounce is about one slice of bread, or a ½ cup of cooked rice or pasta.
- Vegetables: 2½ cups per day, especially dark green or orange vegetables.
- Fruits: 2 cups per day, from a variety of fruits, including fresh fruit, and go easy on fruit juices.
- Milk: 3 cups of low-fat or fat-free milk, yogurt, or other dairy products per day.

- Meat and beans: 5½ ounces per day, particularly of fish, beans, peas, nuts, seeds, and low-fat or lean meat and poultry portions that are not fried but rather baked, broiled, or grilled.

The new Food Guide Pyramid is designed to give you an easy-to-understand guide to healthy eating. It explains simply the types and quantities of food choices that contribute to a healthy diet. Note that grains, fresh fruits, and vegetables are in greatest quantities: the message is that we should consume many more servings of plant products than we do of all other types of foods. To get in the swing of this, try to think of yourself as a vegetarian who occasionally eats animal products. Thinking of fish, chicken, or meat as a side dish rather than a main course will help. The USDA warns against eating foods and beverages that contain a lot of added sugar, such as most soft drinks, which contain empty calories with no nutrients. It also advises limiting your intake of solid saturated fats, such as butter and shortening, and recommends fish, nuts, and vegetable oils as better sources of fats. It advises checking food labels to limit intake of saturated fats, trans fats, and sodium.

For the first time, the USDA also recommends physical activity as part of a healthy eating strategy. It recommends finding a balance between food and physical activity, since calories that aren't burned off remain in the body to form fat. For most people, the recommendation is thirty minutes of physical activity most days of the week. In addition, guidelines specify that an hour a day of activity or moderate exercise may be needed to prevent weight gain. The USDA advises children and teenagers to engage in an hour of physical activity every day, for most days of the week.

Food Facts

Human life can be sustained on a mixed diet containing many types of plant or animal foods. In fact, the body requires a mix of food items to survive—ideally, a balanced diet. The three basic macronutrients are carbohydrates, proteins, and fats. Many foods contain all three. All three macronutrients work differently in the body. Some of each is essential for good health.

All macronutrients contain calories, which are units of potential food or heat energy. A calorie is the amount of energy needed to raise the temperature of 1 kilogram of water 1 degree centigrade. Since people have different energy requirements depending on their age, sex, weight, activity level, and lifestyle, most diets are expressed in terms of calories consumed per day, as in 1,200 calories per day, 1,600 calories per day, or 2,000 calories per day.

For the person with diabetes, the most essential thing to understand is that all three macronutrients convert at least partially into glucose, but carbohydrates, proteins, and fats convert into glucose in different proportions and at different rates of speed, as shown in the following table. Excess quantities of carbohydrates, proteins, or fats are stored as various types of fats, or triglycerides, in the body.

Facts About Macronutrients

Nutrient	Calories/Gram	% to Glucose	Maximum Glucose
Carbohydrates	4	100	1–1.5 hours
Protein	4	60	2–2.5 hours
Fat	9	10	5–6 hours

Carbohydrates

Carbohydrates are used for quick energy. Sugars are the simplest form of carbohydrates. Starches, or complex carbohydrates, are more chemically complex, as the name suggests. Complex carbohydrates are more nutritious than simple sugars, especially the sugars in sweet junk food. Since carbohydrates are smaller molecules than proteins or fats, they are more easily absorbed into the bloodstream, where their glucose reaches its high point an hour or so after eating. Sugars include sucrose, as in white table sugar; fructose, or fruit sugar; lactose, or milk sugar; maltose, or beer sugar; and the sweetener dextrose. Although the average American eats about 20 teaspoons of sugar per day, the equivalent of 320 empty calories, most people don't realize the quantity of sugar they consume because it's added to processed foods. Starches, or complex carbohydrates, include potatoes, corn, peas, pasta, rice, bread products, and legumes. Carbohydrate consumption is recommended at 50 percent to 60 percent of total food intake, which is higher than the typical American diet. Of this, it is suggested that a maximum of 10 percent of the total calories be in the form of sugar.

Proteins

Proteins, sometimes called the building blocks of life, are needed for the growth of cells such as hair and hormones, in many organs of the body, and in a number of complicated chemical processes such as the repair of cells. The metabolism slows with age, reducing the need for protein. The American Diabetes Association has recommended that people with diabetes limit their protein intake to between 10 and 20 percent of their total diet, lower than the typical American diet. Animal products such as chicken, fish, meat, milk, and eggs contain protein, as do some plant foods such as grains, rice, and legumes. Some research shows that soybean products such as tofu, which is a complete protein, can help lower cholesterol and triglycerides when substituted for animal foods and can help prevent bone loss in women because of its plentiful amounts of calcium and other minerals. Proteins convert more slowly into glucose than do carbohydrates, reaching their high point between two and two and a half hours after a meal.

Fats

Fats are the most concentrated source of calories, which is why most diets advise people to cut the amount of fats that they eat. Too many fats can make you fat. However, fat from foods such as fish and nuts supplies the essential fatty acids used in the body to insulate us against heat and cold, and to carry fat-soluble vitamins such as vitamins A, D, E, and K. If your cholesterol or triglyceride levels are elevated, try to reduce the percentage of total calories you receive from saturated fats and trans fats, which are listed on food labels. Less harmful are the monounsaturated or polyunsaturated fats, which include olive oil, canola oil, and corn oil. Although fats are concentrated calories that contribute greatly to weight gain, the good news is that only a small percentage of fats converts to blood sugar. Glucose from fats peaks very slowly, five to six hours after eating, and then slowly disappears from the bloodstream.

Learning which foods contain calories in the form of carbohydrates, proteins, and fats and planning meals to create a balanced diet are a great leap forward in making any fundamental change in eating style.

Your Plan

Medical doctors and dietitians are nowhere close to agreement on the proportions of carbohydrates, proteins, and fats that should appear in the diets of people with diabetes. This is probably as it should be, since each person's body is different; any changes you make in your diet should be appropriate for you.

As a general rule, people who need to lose weight will need to develop a diet that gives them fewer calories to eat than they burn off each day. If you can cut 250 to 500 calories per day from your diet by reducing portion sizes, particularly of the most fattening items, some of your weight will disappear. Losing about a pound a week is a reasonable goal, and losing weight gradually will help you keep it off. The reason many crash diets fail over the long run, some experts believe, is that the body has a natural set point, like a thermostat, that slows the metabolism when calorie intake is drastically reduced and makes it almost impossible to keep the weight off. Participating in a weight-loss diet that you've helped design, especially one that aims at a slow reduction in weight, should result in significant weight loss over time, particularly when combined with a more physically active lifestyle.

One way to choose items that are low in calories and fats is to read food labels. For instance, comparing the standardized labels that must appear on the backs of milk cartons, and other food items, will show you that regular milk gets 30 percent of its calories from fat, while low-fat 2 percent milk gets 20 percent, 1 percent milk gets 10 percent, and nonfat milk gets negligible calories from fat.

Most dietitians recommend three meals plus two or three snacks at regular intervals during the day for all people with diabetes. This is because spreading out your meals and snacks helps even out fluctuations in blood sugar. For the same reason, do not miss a meal. Skipping breakfast is associated with being over-weight. It may surprise you to learn that people who always eat breakfast tend to be thinner than average.

A Choice of Plans

Exchange lists, food points, and constant carbohydrates as well as fat and carbohydrate counting are the approaches that are most commonly used by dietitians in menu planning. All of these approaches work for some people. One may suit you. The ADA recommends that people with diabetes receive medical nutrition therapy that tracks both total grams of carbohydrate and the type of carbohydrate, perhaps in conjunction with the glycemic index, which is discussed later in this chapter. Although the ADA no longer recommends a particular diet for people with diabetes, it cautions against diets restricting carbohydrates to 130 grams or fewer a day, such as in the first phase of the Atkins diet.

All weight-loss diets require time, thought, and effort to learn and implement. All involve planning, being aware of the differences among foods, selecting food items, and measuring portions. Even experienced cooks don't think naturally in terms of individual portions of food. Could you identify a 3-ounce steak on the meat rack in your supermarket, or place exactly 1 cup of green beans onto your plate? Measurements such as these are integral to diet plans. A greater awareness of the weight and volume of various portion sizes comes from simply reading the backs of food packages to size up the portions inside. The most accurate method is to use a scale and cups to measure what you eat.

In order to control what you eat, you need to know the precise servings or portions of various foods and their caloric values. If you aim for a particular number of calories each day, a knowledge of serving portions and the caloric values of foods gives you all the information you need to plan your meals. As you plan, you need to add these numbers until they reach 1,600 calories per day or whatever goal you have developed with your dietitian or nutritionist. Then you need the discipline to shop correctly and stick with the plan.

All dietary approaches restrict total calories. Whether the aim is to lower blood sugar or to eventually reduce your weight, any basic change in eating style should strive to provide all the nutrients you need for good health.

Systems to Use

The exchange list system is one system recommended by many dietitians. This strategy centers on planning servings based on lists of foods that have approximately equal calorie, carbohydrate, and fat content. Exchange lists allow a variety of food choices each day and provide the option of substituting foods for others of equal exchange-point value. The idea is that you can exchange, for example, a serving of complex carbohydrates for a serving of a sugar or fruit at the same meal because they're of equal value in the exchange list tables and have a similar effect on blood sugar. The exchange list system is flexible, giving it more appeal to most people than following a rigid meal plan every day.

Milk, vegetable, fruit, bread/starch, meat, and fat exchange categories are included in the exchange lists, with exchanges limited to foods of approximately the same caloric value. Books explaining the exchange list system are available from your dietitian, doctor, or diabetes educator, or from the American Diabetes Association or the American Dietetic Association. Exchange lists have been developed for ethnic foods and fast foods and come in English or Spanish versions. The original Weight Watchers program is similar to the exchange list plan.

Another option, the constant carbohydrate strategy, involves setting a goal of so many servings and grams of carbohydrates per day, and counting the grams of carbohydrates in each food item. Fat gram counting methods do a similar thing with fats. Fat gram counting aims to reduce the intake of fats at each meal to certain levels. Fat gram counters are used to show you how many grams of fat are contained in various foods. Cutting the grams of fat you eat each day will help you lose weight, which in turn helps you better utilize your available insulin. Recent research has shown that for some individuals, cutting down their total fat intake is more effective than cutting calories when the goal is to lose weight.

The food points system assigns points to various foods, using the equivalent of 75 calories for 1 food point. This makes 22 calorie points the rough equivalent of 1,600 calories per day, while 40 calorie points is roughly equal to 3,000 calories per day.

It can't be overemphasized that all weight-loss programs work best when done in tandem with a program of daily physical activity or exercise, which also helps reduce blood sugar and blood pressure levels.

Always use moderation and common sense in your diet.

Glycemic Index

Although it doesn't have much to do with weight loss, the glycemic index does relate to blood sugar. Glycemic indexes seek to quantify the rate at which various foods convert to glucose and enter the bloodstream.

In 1981, David J. A. Jenkins, D.M., and his associates at the University of Toronto published the first carbohydrate glycemic

The Glycemic Index at a Glance

This glycemic index, developed at the University of Toronto, measures the rate at which various foods convert to glucose, which is assigned a value of 100. Higher numbers indicate a more rapid absorption of glucose. This is not an index of food energy values or calories.

Sugars
Glucose   100
Honey   87
Table sugar   59
Fructose   20

Dairy Products
Ice cream   36
Yogurt   36
Whole milk   34
Skim milk   32

Snacks
Candy bars   68
Potato chips   51
Sponge cake   46
Fish sticks   38
Tomato soup   38
Sausages   28
Peanuts   13

Root Vegetables
Parsnips   97
Carrots   92
Instant mashed
  potatoes   80
New boiled potatoes 70
Beets   64
Yams   51
Sweet potatoes 48

Cereals
Cornflakes   80
Shredded wheat 67
Muesli   66
All bran   51
Oatmeal   49

Pasta and Rice
White rice   72
Brown rice   66
White spaghetti 50
Whole wheat
  spaghetti   42

Breads		Legumes	
Whole wheat	72	Frozen peas	51
White	69	Baked beans	40
Buckwheat	51	Chickpeas	36
		Lima beans	36
Fruits		Butter beans	36
Raisins	64	Black-eyed peas	33
Bananas	62	Green beans	31
Orange juice	46	Kidney beans	29
Oranges	40	Lentils	29
Apples	39	Dried soybeans	15

index, measuring how quickly sixty-two different foods raised blood sugar. Under the Jenkins system, 100 is the top figure, assigned to glucose. Beans and dairy products are generally low on the glycemic index, and interesting variations occur within food categories that lend weight to the idea of eating more whole grain foods. Among the grain products to which Jenkins assigned an index value, for instance, whole wheat pasta is 42, white pasta is 50, brown rice is 66, and white rice is 72.

In a more recent glycemic index, which uses white bread as the standard of 100, one of the lowest index values is given to chan dal, an Indian food similar to chickpeas, which gets a 12 on the glycemic index. Nopal, the prickly pear cactus, gets a 10 and is the lowest known food on a glycemic index.

Each person's body chemistry is different, as noted earlier, since we all convert foods into glucose at our own pace. Nevertheless, the glycemic index can be a good way to start thinking about the effects of various foods on blood sugar.

Carbohydrate-Restricting Diets

Some doctors still recommend the use of very low-carbohydrate diets, which were popular in treating diabetes during Victorian times. Some of these employ quick, severe carbohydrate restrictions as a first step in changing the eating style, a strategy designed to quickly bring blood sugars under control. A few use medically supervised low-carbohydrate diets as a long-term strategy for weight loss.

Doctors and dietitians at the Presbyterian Diabetes Center, in Albuquerque, New Mexico, sometimes recommend the Fast Fast to bring blood sugars under control. Not a complete food fast, the Fast Fast is actually a fast from sugars and starches for three to five days. It's given under a doctor's supervision and requires testing blood sugars at least twice a day. People with Type 2 diabetes undergoing a Fast Fast eat a small serving of meat each day, plus all the salad with low-fat dressing and all the sugar-free gelatin they want, as well as unlimited sugar-free soda, coffee, and tea. The Fast Fast requires the person to drink at least eight large glasses of water per day, according to nurse educator Virginia Valentine, coauthor of the book *Diabetes Type 2 and What to Do*, along with June Biermann and Barbara Toohey. After a few days, people coming off a Fast Fast begin adding low-carbohydrate vegetables such as broccoli and green beans, one at a time, while testing and observing each food's effects on the blood sugar. People taking diabetes pills or insulin who do the Fast Fast need special attention and coaching from their health-care teams.

Yehuda Handelsman, M.D., a diabetologist and an instructor at the University of Southern California, recommends that his new patients fast from food for twenty-four hours and then go on a high-protein diet for a week or two to bring their blood sugars under control. After that, his patients add carbohydrates and fats. Among other things, Handelsman says that protein induces the production of insulin, a reason why every meal eaten by a person with diabetes should contain a bit of protein. After patients have achieved blood sugar control, Handelsman recommends a diet of 25 percent to 30 percent protein, 40 percent to 45 percent carbohydrate, and 35 percent to 40 percent fat. Monounsaturated fats such as those found in olive oil, canola oil, and walnuts are preferred. Handelsman cites a research study published in the *New England Journal of Medicine* in which eleven patients substituted olive oil for carbohydrates and experienced a significant improvement in blood sugars. Garlic is another good food to include in the diet, he adds, because some tests show it can reduce cholesterol levels 8 percent by reducing cholesterol production in the liver.

Other recent studies have affirmed the value of the low-carbohydrate Atkins diet for people with diabetes. At least nine published studies of the Atkins diet showed it could result in drops in both blood sugar and blood pressure and could lower insulin resistance. Another low-carbohydrate diet, by Los Angeles endocrinologist Calvin Ezrin, M.D., strictly limits carbohydrates over the long term, producing some remarkable losses of weight when followed under a doctor's supervision. According to Ezrin, severely limiting carbohydrates forces the body to burn fats, the body's preferred fuel. The Ezrin diet calls for a very low intake of 20 to 35 grams of carbohydrates per day for the first two weeks, increased in increments after that. Ezrin's diet and the Atkins diet do throw the body into a state of "beneficial" ketosis, causing ketones produced by the utilization of fat to be excreted in the urine. However, Ezrin says that this mild ketosis is not medically dangerous when the diet is supervised by a doctor. People following the Ezrin diet take vitamin and mineral supplements, including vitamins C and B complex as well as calcium and salt. Dieters are advised to exercise to their natural limits, drink lots of water, and take other precautions as recommended by the doctors supervising their weight loss. The Ezrin plan is spelled out in *The Type 2 Diabetes Diet Book*, cowritten with health writer Robert Kowalski.

Vegetarian Diets

Vegetarian diets can be extremely beneficial when properly supervised, because fruits and vegetables contain almost all the vitamins and minerals you need, plenty of fiber, and no saturated fat, trans fat, or cholesterol. Vegetarian diets can help control heart disease and may help people lose or control their weight. They also contain hundreds of beneficial phytochemicals not found in animal foods. While the average American eats about three and a half servings of fruits and vegetables per day, from five to nine servings is the current recommendation, particularly of dark-colored foods, which contain the most phytochemicals.

Although our stomachs can handle both plant and animal products, some anthropologists believe that humans are primarily plant eaters, because the human intestinal tract is much longer than that of animals that mainly eat meat. A longer digestive tract has evolved, this theory goes, because of the greater amount of time that it takes to digest and pass plant foods, which contain fiber. Short digestive tracts are more often found in meat-eating animals because the digestion of meat produces toxins that need to be quickly expelled from the body for the organism to survive. In addition, human teeth resemble the teeth of animals that primarily eat plants, a difference you'll notice by comparing your teeth with those of carnivores, such as cats and dogs, and with plant-eating animals such as horses and cows. And from an ecological point of view, because the supply of land is limited, it's much more efficient for farmers to grow edible plants than to grow plants to fatten up farm animals. You can grow 10 tons of potatoes on an acre of land, for instance, but the same acre can produce only 165 pounds of beef.

Special precautions must be taken by vegetarians, who need to make a concerted effort to replace nutrients such as the calcium they might get from dairy products, or the iron and protein they might get from meats, even though vegetarians may require less of these vitamins, minerals, and nutrients than do people who eat animal products. Vitamin B_{12} levels sometimes drop in vegetarians, making B_{12} shots or supplements necessary. No single plant food has the complete protein found in animal products, containing all the essential amino acids, although many common food combinations, such as rice and beans, do equal a complete protein. For these reasons, the guidance of a registered dietitian or nutritionist is recommended for anyone beginning a vegan diet—in which no animal products are eaten. Lacto-vegetarians have an easier time eating a balanced diet because they allow themselves to eat dairy products. Lacto-ovo vegetarians eat dairy products as well as eggs.

In 2003, the American Dietetic Association and Dietitians of Canada released a position statement on vegetarian diets that included the following remarks:

> It is the position of the American Dietetic Association and Dietitians of Canada that appropriately planned vegetarian diets are healthful, nutritionally adequate, and provide health benefits in the prevention and treatment of certain diseases. . . . Well-planned vegan and other types of vegetarian diets are appropriate for all stages of the life cycle, including during pregnancy, lactation, infancy, childhood, and adolescence. Vegetarian diets offer a number of nutritional benefits, including lower levels of saturated fat, cholesterol, and animal protein as well as higher levels of carbohydrates, fiber, magnesium, potassium, folate, and antioxidants such as vitamins C and E and phytochemicals.

Vegetarians have been reported to have lower body mass indices than nonvegetarians, as well as lower rates of death from ischemic heart disease; vegetarians also show lower blood cholesterol levels; lower blood pressure; and lower rates of hypertension, Type 2 diabetes, and prostate and colon cancer. . . . Vegetarian diets can meet guidelines for the treatment of diabetes, and some research suggests that diets that are more plant-based reduce risk for Type 2 diabetes. Among the possible explanations for a protective effect of vegetarian diet are the lower BMI of vegetarians, and higher fiber intake, both of which improve insulin sensitivity.

Adding More Fiber to Your Diet

Fiber may help you lose weight, because it produces that satisfied feeling of being full. Fiber helps move food through your body and may prevent other diseases. Here are a few simple ways to add fiber to your diet:

- Eat more fresh fruits and vegetables—at least five servings per day are now recommended by major health organizations.
- Cook vegetables and fruits such as potatoes and apples with their skins on whenever possible, and eat the skins.
- Choose whole grain bread and whole grain cereals instead of food products made with refined flour.
- Add a spoonful of unprocessed bran, wheat germ, or oat bran to food items such as salads and hot cereals.
- Drink more water, because water helps you to use the fiber more effectively.

James Anderson, M.D., a physician from Lexington, Kentucky, now champions high-fiber diets, especially for overweight people who have Type 2 diabetes. His high-carbohydrate and high-fiber nutrition plan features very low-fat meals; he says that if the diet is followed, it will help lower weight, blood sugar, and cholesterol. Anderson recommends that people with diabetes eat up to 70 grams of fiber per day, more than four times the average American's consumption of 10 to 15 grams of fiber per day. He believes improved glucose control and lower cholesterol levels result from a greater consumption of foods containing soluble fiber, such as oat bran, beans, peas, potatoes with skin, brussels sprouts, corn, zucchini, prunes, apricots, bananas, blackberries, and barley. Anderson observes that replacing 6 ounces of meat with 1½ cups of beans will reduce total calories by 200, reduce dietary fat by 10 percent, and add 10 to 15 grams of fiber. This is explained in his book *Diabetes: A Practical New Guide to Healthy Living*.

The program that Dean Ornish, M.D., developed in San Francisco for reducing heart disease involves a diet that is basically vegetarian, with a few exceptions such as fish and yogurt. Ornish's program is said to reduce deposits of plaque in the blood vessels, partially by permitting only 10 percent of total calories to be drawn from fats, with almost all of those in the unsaturated form. In addition to diet, Ornish employs a multidisciplinary approach to heart disease that includes yoga, meditation, and communication training, along with other stress-reduction techniques that can work together to reduce heart disease without surgery or drugs.

About Fiber

Whether or not you think of yourself as a vegetarian, fiber is important for good health. Increasing your consumption of fiber is recommended by the American Diabetes Association, the

American Heart Association, and the American Cancer Society because high-fiber, low-fat diets help prevent heart disease and cancer. Since heart and vascular problems are among the most deadly complications of diabetes, this is reason enough to include plenty of fiber in what you eat. Although 25 to 30 grams per day are recommended for most people, even this amount of fiber can cause intestinal discomfort and bothersome flatulence in some people.

Unfortunately, small increases in fiber consumption won't make much short-term difference in your blood sugar. The current consensus is that although certain types of soluble fiber may delay the absorption of glucose, fiber in itself doesn't have much effect on blood sugar. Fiber does have the great benefit of making you feel full, so increasing your fiber intake may help you lose weight. Since fiber is found in healthy foods such as grains, fruits, and vegetables, adding fiber may help you change your eating style from a hodgepodge of junk food and empty calories to healthier, balanced meals that make you feel that you've eaten something. Eating more foods that contain fiber may also benefit people with diabetes in more subtle ways. A 1990 study published in the *American Journal of Clinical Nutrition* showed that a high-carbohydrate, high-fiber diet increased insulin sensitivity and lowered cholesterol.

When it comes to how you feel after eating, a calorie is not necessarily just a calorie. A study published in the *Lancet*, a prestigious British medical journal, measured the effects of meals of apple juice, applesauce, and apples on patients at the Royal Infirmary, in Bristol, England. Each apple dish contained identical calories. Subjects ate the food and were tested. Blood sugar levels rose about the same for each form of apple but fell or rebounded quickly after the juice, with less rebound for the applesauce and none at all for the patients who ate the apples.

Respondents reported that apples were the most satisfying and filling, followed by applesauce, and the apple juice was the least satisfying and filling of the three. It took research subjects more time to eat the apples. Juice was consumed eleven times faster than the apples and four times faster than the applesauce.

Essential Vitamins

Vitamins and minerals are essential micronutrients, needed in very small amounts to keep our bodies functioning properly. Most people get enough of the thirteen vitamins and minerals such as iron and calcium when they eat a well-balanced diet. The catch is that many people still don't eat a balanced diet.

People with diabetes who are cutting their calorie intake to below 1,200 calories per day to lose weight or control blood sugars are frequently advised to take vitamin and mineral supplements because it's difficult to meet the average daily requirements with severely restricted food choices. However, few dietitians recommend diets below 1,200 calories. Many dietitians advise people who are restricting their food intake to take one multivitamin tablet per day, simply as insurance against not getting adequate supplies of all vitamins in their food. High blood sugar causes the body to excrete vitamins in the urine, particularly the water-soluble B and C vitamins.

Consult your doctor before you begin taking large doses of vitamin supplements. Tell your doctor what vitamins you take, just as you tell him or her about your medications. Vitamins are foods, not medicines. Megavitamin supplements will not cure diabetes and are not a substitute for nutritious food, medical treatment, or physical activity, although supplements can be helpful in some cases. The use of vitamin supplements remains controversial, although the use of certain vitamins is more accepted now than in years past.

A survey of vitamin-related research by Daniel E. Baker, Pharm.D., and R. Keith Campbell, of Washington State University, published in *Diabetes Educator* in 1992 concluded:

> Some degree of supplementation with certain vitamins (e.g., vitamin C and vitamin E) and minerals (e.g., magnesium) may be beneficial to prevent long-term complications of diabetes. Daily supplements of vitamin C, vitamin E, and magnesium ultimately may do some good, and unless the patient has a severe renal dysfunction, probably will do no harm to the person with diabetes.

A few vitamins, such as niacin, taken for other health conditions can slightly raise blood sugar levels; their use should be monitored in people with diabetes. Niacin is sometimes prescribed at a level of 50 to 100 milligrams per day, to lower fat and triglyceride levels. Before you take niacin supplements, check with the doctor who is treating your diabetes.

People with diabetes often have unusually low levels of certain vitamins, particularly two antioxidant vitamins, vitamin C and vitamin E. The American Diabetes Association cites "theoretical reasons" in favor of antioxidant supplements but does not recommend them, because it says the benefits have not been confirmed.

Vitamin C levels in the blood are low in people with diabetes compared with people without diabetes who have similar diets. The reason for this is unclear. A large study of the diets of Finnish and Dutch men over several decades showed a relationship between low vitamin C intake and glucose intolerance, a precursor to Type 2 diabetes. Supplementation with vitamin C is believed to help prevent or reduce incidences of some complications, such as cataracts and nerve disorders. One study showed that 1,400 mg per day of vitamin C improved the results of HbA1c hemoglobin tests. On the downside, vitamin C supplementation can throw off the results of a urinary test. Vitamin C is found in many fruits and vegetables, including citrus fruits, berries, tomatoes, lettuce, green peppers, potatoes, and cantaloupes, and it's sometimes used as an additive in other foods. Vitamin C and vitamin E are antioxidants, which can help repair cell structures damaged by oxidation and high blood sugar.

Vitamin E has well-known beneficial effects on the heart and the circulatory system. Ensuring that vitamin E intake is at least up to daily requirements can reduce the chance of complications involving the heart and blood vessels, including cataracts and other problems involving the small blood vessels of the eyes. Adequate vitamin E may inhibit the production of a blood-clotting chemical called thromboxane, which can damage blood vessels. Vitamin E is found in wheat germ, whole grain cereals, soybean and canola oil, green leafy vegetables, and egg yolks. There is some evidence that folic acid, one of the B vitamins, can aid in preventing vascular disease in people with diabetes.

Supplements of antioxidants at reasonable levels may help you, but it's probably better to get most of your antioxidants directly from food. Food contains complicated mixtures of not only vitamins and minerals but also thousands of other beneficial substances that activate various processes in the body. Vitamin supplements are chemically different from food, and they don't contain fiber. You may not want to place all your faith in individual supplements. All the antioxidants work best as a sort of biochemical team—what Lester Packer, Ph.D., of the University of California, calls the "antioxidant network."

Magnesium, a mineral concentrated in the organs and skeleton, is rarely depleted in the general population. However, some recent studies have found that as many as 25 percent of people with diabetes have a magnesium deficiency. Magnesium is believed to play a role in the release of insulin from the pancreas and in blood pressure control. Magnesium may be depleted by high blood sugar and by diuretics such as coffee. Significantly, some low-calorie diets given to people with diabetes to help them lose weight may not meet the recommended daily allowance for magnesium. If your magnesium levels are low, supplements at the recommended daily allowance may improve glycemic control. Magnesium supplements are not recommended for people with kidney problems. Foods containing magnesium include spinach, broccoli, whole grain and bran cereals, cashew nuts, peanuts, almonds, soybeans, whole wheat, rice, dried fruits, dry beans, peas, potatoes, milk, shrimp, fish, and even chocolate. Almost all unprocessed foods contain some magnesium, but food processing depletes it.

Claims are made for another trace mineral, chromium, which in the chromium picolinate form may increase insulin sensitivity and slightly lower blood sugar. Chromium is a mineral needed by the body in tiny amounts, but even those amounts are difficult to get from eating a typical diet, because processed foods have basically been robbed of chromium. Brewer's yeast, organ meats, mushrooms, and broccoli are good natural sources but scarce in most diets. Taking between 200 and 1,000 micrograms of chromium per day has been shown in some tests to slightly lower blood sugar, HbA1c levels, and blood fat levels. A study conducted in China on people newly diagnosed with Type 2 diabetes showed significant reductions after supplementation at the rate of 1,000 micrograms per day for two months, and greater reductions at four months. Lesser levels of improvement were achieved with daily supplements of 200 micrograms. Dr. Yehuda Handelsman recommends chromium picolinate supplements, 200 micrograms twice a day, as part of an overall program that includes diet, exercise, and medications. Chromium picolinate should be taken under a doctor's supervision, with monitoring of blood glucose levels to determine if levels of diabetes medication or insulin should be adjusted as a result. Some nutritionists recommend a supplement containing chromium

Some Useful Supplements

Here are some vitamins and minerals that may be useful for people with diabetes if levels are low. All of these are also available in food, although food processing removes some of them from natural sources. Newer tests of red and white blood cells, rather than blood serum, provide the most accurate readings of deficiencies or low levels of particular vitamins or minerals.

- Vitamin A in beta-carotene form, unless liver function is poor
- Vitamin B complex, often recommended by doctors
- Vitamin C
- Vitamin E
- Calcium
- Chromium
- Manganese
- Magnesium
- Potassium
- Vanadium
- Zinc, less than 50 mg per day

Source: David Drum, *Alternative Therapies for Managing Diabetes* (New York: McGraw-Hill, 2002).

picolinate and magnesium for people with Type 2 diabetes. Vanadium is another trace mineral that may prove to increase insulin sensitivity. The amounts of these minerals required by the body are small, and deficiencies are difficult to even measure. Zinc supplements have been touted as a way to improve insulin utilization, but this has not been proved (although zinc has a general role in healing).

Among the other supplements, coenzyme Q-10, a protein molecule found in every cell in the body, is widely used in countries such as Japan to manage heart problems. As reported in *Alternative Therapies for Managing Diabetes*, some studies have shown that it lowers blood pressure and may have beneficial effects on insulin production and blood sugar. Alpha-lipoic acid has reduced fasting glucose levels in some studies, and gamma linolenic acid (evening primrose oil) has been shown to improve nerve function in animal studies.

The omega-3 fatty acids found in fish and canola oil lower triglyceride levels but have little effect on glucose levels, according to some research. However, new government dietary guidelines note that consuming two servings of fish a week can reduce the risk of heart disease, and that fish oil supplements may reduce the risk of dying from a heart attack in people who have already experienced one. Government dietary guidelines also recommend increasing the consumption of foods containing potassium to help reduce blood pressure. Leafy green vegetables, fruits from vines, root vegetables, and some fish contain good amounts of potassium.

Motivation

Strategies to change eating patterns vary by individual. Thinking this through will take some brain work and perhaps a bit of trial and error. You can change your eating style, but you must keep yourself motivated, especially at the outset.

Because making food choices can raise questions, you may work best with a dietitian, who will guide you and answer your questions as you go along. It's also possible that you are a person who is able to change your eating patterns only with the help of a group such as Weight Watchers, which can offer lots of positive reinforcement and group support. Or, you may be able to wake up one morning, decide to change, and pull it off single-handedly.

Changing your eating style is a long-haul proposition. Think of it as planning for a series of small vacations. Most things you'll be able to anticipate; planning will help you enjoy yourself. On the other hand, no matter how carefully you plan, you won't be able to anticipate every little twist and turn in the road.

You need to set both short-term and long-term goals for yourself and then move forward at your own pace. Don't rush yourself. If you achieve a goal, treat yourself with small gifts and rewards, such as a trip to the movies, or simply tell someone about your success. Don't set unrealistically high goals for yourself—such as losing 20 pounds a week—and then fall into the oldest diet trap of all: feeling guilty and hating yourself because you can't do the impossible. Remember that a little improvement every day or every week is preferable to none. The idea is to always make progress, not to achieve perfection. If you can get it right about 80 percent of the time, many professionals say you're on the right track. First you learn, and then you use what you've learned to make sensible and flavorful food choices that fit into your life and even make it more exciting.

Changing your eating style may be easier if you haven't already tried a lot of crash diets and fallen into the mind-set that you can't possibly succeed with any diet. Most crash diets are so restrictive that the great majority of people who attempt them fail. However, anyone can slowly change his or her eating style. Even grizzled diet veterans can succeed, especially if they are motivated by something such as controlling their blood sugar or improving the course of their lives. Sometimes newcomers to these concepts, such as men, can even do better.

Your probability of success increases if you have a strong motive for changing your eating habits, such as having seen a favorite overweight relative or friend (who may even have diabetes) barely survive a heart attack, or suffer complications. Still, being diagnosed with diabetes may be motivation enough for you. Psychological research has shown that you're most likely to adjust your behavior if you have a strong reason to do so. If you're looking for a way to motivate yourself, a desire to improve your health for the rest of your life may be sufficient incentive to change.

The Joy of Cooking

It's easy to fall into the TV dinner diet trap. This is the trap in which you eat the TV dinner but don't really feel full, so you eat some more.

If you cook for yourself, according to registered dietitian Diane Woods, you're often ahead of the game. If you cook, you have control over all the ingredients in your meals. You can substitute healthier ingredients, use less sugar, control the portions that are served, and experience the fun of actively moving around the kitchen with the fragrant smell of good food in the air and perhaps some relaxing music on the radio. Cooking a quick meal can take as little as ten minutes of your time. Many recent highly rated cookbooks emphasize quick, delicious, easy-to-prepare meals. You may not be able to cook every day and every night, but you can spend ten to fifteen minutes every now and then preparing your own meals and savoring the experience.

If you eat slowly and relish each bite, and if you give your-self permission to enjoy the experience of eating, you may find yourself eating a bit less food but enjoying it more. The late gourmet chef Julia Child observed that many Americans think of food much as they think of medicine, rather than seeing a meal as the sensual experience and social catalyst that it ought to be. For goodness sake, enjoy your food.

In the minds of many overweight people, the guilt associated with eating has taken the pleasure away from the activity. No matter what your weight, consider it important that you give yourself permission to eat slowly, chewing each bite a few times. Try to spend at least twenty minutes eating each meal. Believe it or not, this helps change destructive eating patterns. Horace Fletcher, a nineteenth-century nutritionist, recommended that every person chew each bite of food thirty-two times, matching the number of teeth we have. Fletcher's advice may be overstated, but taking a moment to savor each mouthful is an excellent idea simply because you'll not only taste every bite of your food but also take longer to eat it. A well-known medical doctor has a trick that works for him: because the first and last bites are always the best, he allows himself one and only one bite of the richest, most gooey, and most fattening desserts.

Be your own friend in self-management, especially when it comes to food. Working to like—or love—yourself and to cher-ish and celebrate each small success will compound the positive aspects of your changes in eating style. If, instead, you become your own worst enemy and focus only on your mistakes, you'll find that the guilt, depression, and horrible feelings of failure will also compound. Work to forgive yourself if you slip, because you are human, but work just as hard to reward yourself when you succeed.

Be aware that changing your eating style may create battles within your family. Know who your friends are in this area, as well as those who might want to sabotage your meal plan. In the battle of the bulge, your first mission is to take care of yourself. Situations that pose risks for some people include being depressed, frustrated, or under stress; having a normal schedule suddenly disrupted; being pressed for time; feeling deprived or left out; and even attending social events with family or friends.

"Diabetes is such an individual thing. For instance, we all react so differently to different foods," one woman says. "I've learned that I have to watch myself. When I'm not in a good spot, that's when I'm weak. Sometimes, there are people out there who will try to sabotage you."

Some of your so-called friends may say, "Oh, you can get away with eating an extra piece of wedding cake just this one time." If you reply that you're on a diet, they may try to pull you off the wagon. However, if you simply refuse the second piece of cake with a polite, "No, thank you; I'm full," the discussion should end, because few people will try to give you food when you clearly don't want it. A 1990 study of women who successfully lost weight and maintained the weight loss showed that they devised strategies and plans to do so that fit their lives. The most successful women had a tendency to confront rather than avoid problems and to distract themselves by exercise, work, or shopping, rather than by eating, smoking, sleeping, or wishing the problem would magically disappear. They were more likely to exercise and less likely to try "quick-fix" solutions such as diet pills or fad diets. Women who maintained their weight loss allowed themselves to eat their favorite foods occasionally in moderation and were a little more likely to have support from friends or family members.

Bring your family members into the picture, if you can. They can help a lot, not by lecturing incessantly about what you should and shouldn't eat, but by giving you a pat on the back when you achieve a personal goal. If your family members are supportive, tell them when you lose your first 2 or 3 pounds, or whenever you feel that you have accomplished a little something. If you're comfortable doing so, ask for a reasonable amount of help when you feel other people might support your efforts.

When you make a shopping list and go to the market, be sure to choose healthy, nutritious foods such as fresh vegetables and fruits. Keep healthy foods in your home at all times. If needed, make a special list to get started; you may even wish to make a trip to a farmers' market or a health food store. Integrate the foods into your life that you know are healthy and nutritious and that will help you control your blood sugar. Buy whole grain foods, fresh fruits and vegetables, fish, low-fat milk, diet sodas, low-fat ice cream, sugar substitutes, and whatever else is on your list. Unprocessed foods are generally healthier than processed foods. Make a list. Planning will help you succeed.

Practical Tips

Here are a few quick, practical tips to help you change your eating style and control your weight and blood sugar:

- Make it really easy to eat healthy foods and difficult to eat unhealthy foods. Keep fresh fruits and vegetables handy. Remove temptation from your refrigerator and workplace. Leave yourself written orders on the refrigerator to eat nutritious snacks when you're hungry. Hide the cookies or cookie jar. If you can't stop with a single cookie, don't eat the first one. Ask family members to work with you.
- Drink a glass of water before you eat.
- Spread calories around throughout the day, and don't eat all your carbohydrates at the same meal.
- Eat salad first, and wait half an hour to eat the rest of the meal.

- Make yourself aware of portion sizes for particular items. This will give you better control both at home and when eating out. On exchange lists, for instance, one serving of rice is ⅓ cup; if you eat at a Chinese restaurant, where a normal serving is 1 cup of rice, ask for less rice. A portion size means, for instance, ½ cup of yams, 1¼ cups of strawberries, or half an apple. What do you do with the other half of the apple? Dip it in citrus juice to stop oxidation and prevent it from turning brown, and then wrap and refrigerate it.

- Unsweeten sweetened fruits. With canned fruit, pour out the juice; if it's packed in syrup, rinse the syrup off.

- Satisfy your hunger by snacking on high-fiber, low-calorie items such as salads and vegetables. Vegetables have fewer calories than fruits, and fruits have more fiber than fruit juice. Graham crackers, whole wheat bread, and bran cereal are all high-fiber snacks.

- Read food labels. Some foods labeled "no fat," such as no-fat mayonnaise, are made with carbohydrates substituted for fat; the extra carbohydrates may equate to an additional serving of starch or fruit. Reading food labels will tell you much of what you need to know to work a particular food into your eating plans.

- When eating out, eat half the entrée portion (which is often too large); request doggie bags to take the rest home for another meal, or request a half serving. An alternative is splitting part of your meal with a dinner companion, which also saves money.

- Use smaller plates to make portions appear larger.

- Don't reward yourself with food. Instead, call a favorite relative or old friend and chat, buy yourself a bouquet of flowers, rent a sexy video, or treat yourself to a trip to a museum or the zoo. The same recommendations apply to people who punish themselves by eating more food.

- Instead of eating, exercise. Even just a short walk around the block will help get your mind off eating and put your feet back on the ground.
- Don't assign moral values to foods. Celery sticks, chocolate éclairs, eggs Benedict, or any other food can be reduced to its numerical essence: calories. If you eat the "bad" cheesecake in a moment of weakness, simply calculate the calories, add them to your list, and get back on track as soon as possible.
- Don't beat yourself up for more than twenty-four hours if you slip and happen to eat something forbidden. Slap your wrist, forgive yourself, vow to do better, and move on with your life.

Diet Pills and Surgery

Most of us would like to go to a doctor and get a magic pill or have a little operation that makes all our problems go away. In a society that values instant gratification, diet pills may seem like the answer. Diet pills work as long as you take them, but they are not a panacea for losing weight. Diet pills containing amphetamines have had a sinister reputation for years, due to side effects that can include psychosis. The newer diet pills are said to be more benign, even though their use is restricted in many states to a period of weeks. The new diet pills do suppress appetite, and people do lose weight, but they gain the weight back when they stop taking the pills.

Many diet pills typically produce an initial loss of 20 to 25 pounds, after which you feel good and gain back 10 to 15 pounds, to wind up with a 10- to 12-pound loss. This pattern

Holiday Diet Tips

Among all the holidays that we celebrate with food feasts, the winter festivities are sometimes the most perilous for people with diabetes. In some families, the main holiday event is a big meal of high-fat, high-calorie food. The holidays are often stressful, and many people handle stress by nibbling on food. Plan your approach. Therese Farrell, R.D., asserts that planning can help keep your holiday eating under control as well as help in other situations involving the perils of rich, overabundant food.

Just maintaining your current weight is often the best goal during the holidays. Set reasonable weight-loss goals, and don't beat yourself up for too long if you slip or gain an extra pound. Before Thanksgiving dinner, remember the last Thanksgiving that you overate and how bloated and uncomfortable you felt afterward. In all cases, moderation is advised, because almost anything can be enjoyed in small amounts.

Here are a few tips for handling some of the perilous situations you're likely to encounter over the holidays:

- Eat what you like, but take smaller portions of foods that you know are rich, and eat them slowly to savor each mouthful.
- Do some additional exercise or physical activity to compensate for the extra food you may eat. Going for a short walk after dinner will help you relax and lower blood sugars.
- If you have a choice, choose low-fat items over high-fat ones, and skip the food items you don't really need or want, such as extra butter on bread.

- Keep a supply of light foods such as fruits, vegetables, and prepared salads on hand for eating between parties and when you're on the go.
- Plan how much food you will eat at a party, and tell your significant other about your plans if that will help. Snack before the party, arrive fashionably late, and take only a small plate to the buffet table.
- Give fruit baskets or low-calorie cookbooks rather than boxes of candy.
- If you receive a high-calorie gift, exercise your generosity and give away that box of candy to someone else, or even to a needy family or homeless person who truly needs the calories.
- If you're throwing a dinner party, try to make it a potluck, and provide suggestions for low-fat, low-calorie dishes if people ask.
- If you're baking cookies or other treats, experiment with lower portions of fat ingredients, or reduce the amount of sugar you use. Cooking does involve some beneficial exercise, but try to control your tasting. Give away any extra baked items as soon as possible, or if you're giving cookies as gifts, store them in sealed containers and place them in hard-to-get-to locations to keep the Munching Demon at bay.
- If you drink alcohol, drink in moderation and avoid sugary mixed drinks. When you drink, eat a little something too.
- If you ruin your game plan by overindulging, admit your mistake, and then immediately forgive yourself and get back to work. Don't wait until New Year's Day to resume watching what you eat.

applies to people on the once-fashionable phen-fen diet, or Redux, as well as other substances that can result in weight loss, such as Prozac and cigarettes. A few new drugs target people who are seriously obese, but these medications are not suitable for all people and should be used only under a doctor's supervision. One, sibutramine (Meridia), was approved in 1997 and prolongs the "full" feeling you have after eating a meal. Another drug, orlistat (Xenical), was effective in a study of 254 obese patients with Type 2 diabetes, who lost more weight (6.2 percent of their body weight, versus 4.3 percent) than the control group and also lowered the amount of diabetes medication they required. Xenical is a lipase inhibitor, blocking the absorption of fat in the intestine, but also unfortunately blocking the absorption of fat-soluble vitamins such as vitamins A, D, E, and K. The drug is recommended only for people who are very obese. Both Meridia and Xenical must be taken indefinitely, and like all other drugs, they have side effects. Side effects of Meridia can include constipation, dry mouth, insomnia, and increased blood pressure. Orlistat can cause oily, liquid, or loose stools; flatulence; and abdominal pain. If you do take these medications, remember that any weight-loss program is most effective when combined with lasting changes in diet, exercise habits, and lifestyle.

If you took diet pills such as the once popular phen-fen diet pill combination, or Redux, your doctor should check you for signs of damage to your heart or lungs as a precaution, because these drugs have been shown to produce heart valve damage in some patients. An echocardiogram test, which is painless, can aid your doctor either in locating heart valve problems or in giving you a clean bill of health. If you do have heart valve damage, you may need to receive antibiotics before teeth cleanings, tooth removal, and a few other similar procedures, as a precaution.

Medical science has begun to view obesity as a condition that needs to be treated for life. Since pills are a quick fix, with temporary benefits and unknown long-term effects, think about changing your eating style slowly enough to have a lasting beneficial impact on weight, and a lowering effect on blood sugar.

In some extreme cases, surgery may be employed to aid weight loss. Weight-loss surgery basically reduces the capacity of the stomach to hold food. The two main types of weight-loss surgery are gastric bypass surgery, which reroutes food to the small intestine, and restriction surgery, which restricts the amount of food in the stomach. Any surgery is risky, and infections can occur from leaks in the stomach or intestines.

Most people lose a lot of weight after these types of surgery, which usually causes glucose and blood pressure levels to drop as a result of the weight loss. According to guidelines from the American Obesity Association, stomach surgery is a medical option when a person is at extremely high health risk from being overweight. People with eating disorders or unstable medical or mental conditions are not good candidates for bariatric surgery.

Although the benefits of such surgeries are obvious, complications can include the stomach's stretching to allow more food in after surgery. Also, staples placed in the stomach can leak. Vomiting is the most frequent side effect, but lactose intolerance, ulcers, vitamin deficiencies, mineral deficiencies, and even malnutrition can occur. In summary, while drugs and surgery can help some people, for most, a basic strategy of healthy diet, regular exercise, and perhaps medications is the preferred route to good control.

Sugar, Salt, and More

People with diabetes are sometimes advised to decrease their intake of sugar, dietary cholesterol, salt, and even alcohol.

About Artificial Sweeteners

Since sugars are pure carbohydrates that move quickly into the bloodstream to become blood sugar, some dietitians recommend the moderate use of calorie-free sugar substitutes to cut calories and carbohydrates. These sweeteners are all much sweeter than sugar—saccharin (brand names include Sweet'n Low, Sucaryl, and Sugar Twin) is 375 times sweeter than regular sugar. Sucralose (brand name Splenda) is 600 times sweeter, and aspartame (brand names Equal, Sweetmate, and Spoonfuls) is 180 times as concentrated as sugar. In the little packets, these products are so concentrated that manufacturers use other sugars such as dextrose as bulking agents. Scientific controversy exists over these three artificial sweeteners, saccharin being the oldest of the three. High amounts of saccharin have apparently caused cancer in lab animals (this is printed as a warning on the labels of saccharin products). The U.S. Food and Drug Administration (FDA) doesn't consider aspartame harmful, because it doesn't cause cancer in lab animals. However, serious questions have been raised about aspartame, which in liquid form breaks down into formaldehyde and another carcinogen when heated to more than 85 degrees. More than ten thousand complaints have been filed about aspartame with the FDA, mostly for central nervous system and gastrointestinal problems. Sucralose appears to be safer, but it is chemically constructed by attaching chlorine atoms to the sugar molecule to make an artificial sweetener that is not digested. Long-term effects of consuming this product are unknown. The herbal sweetener stevia, used widely in Latin America for more than a century and popular in Japan, is probably a safer alternative for reducing calories.

Food companies can play games with food labels, trying to advertise fewer carbohydrates than their products actually contain. The food labeling terms "net carbs," "active carbs," and "impact carbs," introduced by food companies, are misleading in that they don't count sugar alcohols such as sorbitol and mannitol or the carbohydrate in fiber. Sugar alcohols such as sorbitol are chemically altered alcohol molecules that can raise blood sugar and have a laxative effect. For a more accurate measure of carbohydrates, use the label's standard FDA-approved listing of carbohydrates on the back of the package.

If you have a sweet tooth and want to keep sweetness in your meals, cut back on the amount of sugar that you use. Reduce the amount of sugar added to recipes a bit each time you make them, or substitute nutmeg, cinnamon, almond extract, or vanilla for sugar. Fresh fruits are sweet snacks and have the added health benefit of fiber.

About Cholesterol

Much confusion exists about cholesterol because high cholesterol levels in the blood are a well-publicized precursor to heart attacks. Cholesterol is a form of fat that contributes to the development of such sex hormones as estrogen and testosterone, and it's needed by cell membranes. Most of the cholesterol you need to survive is manufactured in your liver. Dietary cholesterol is present in all animal products that contain saturated fats. Saturated fats elevate your blood cholesterol, also known as serum cholesterol. The average American eats foods containing 400 mg of cholesterol per day but needs to consume almost none. Cholesterol levels typically rise a bit in the winter and fall a bit in the summer. Cholesterol is tested as part of a lipid profile, one of the tests covered in Chapter 10. A desirable cholesterol level is less than 200.

About Sodium

Sodium, or salt, is another essential element, and it's a big factor in fluid retention, which can add weight. Although in ancient times salt was so scarce that it was used as a substitute for money, most of us today have way too much salt in our diets. Americans typically consume 6,000 to 10,000 mg per day, much more than we need. Health authorities recommend between 2,400 and 3,000 mg of sodium per day for most people. Sodium is loaded into most TV dinners, snack foods, hot dogs, and canned soups as a preservative and flavor enhancer. Sodium is now listed on food labels, expressed in milligrams and as a percentage of the 2,400 mg recommendation. People with high blood pressure or other complications of diabetes are often advised to cut their salt intake to normal or below-normal levels to help lower their blood pressure. New government dietary guidelines advise people seeking to lower their blood pressure to also eat more foods rich in potassium, since potassium blunts the effects of salt on blood pressure. As a rule of thumb, look for 500 mg or less of sodium per serving in processed food items.

About Alcohol

Alcohol lowers blood sugar, but it does contain empty calories, which should be included in calorie counting. Some doctors believe that it's OK to have a drink or two every day because of alcohol's relaxing qualities and because alcohol raises the "good," or HDL (high-density lipoprotein), cholesterol. If you are taking medication for your diabetes, talk to your doctor before imbibing, since the alcohol you drink passes immediately into the bloodstream, persists for up to 36 hours in the blood, and can interfere with the action of some medications. Alcohol increases your risk of experiencing hypoglycemia, or low blood sugar, so prepare for this possibility by having a quick-acting carbohydrate snack on hand if you drink, and don't drink after vigorous exercise. To help prevent causing low blood sugar when drinking alcoholic beverages, always eat a meal or snack with your drink. Make sure the mixed drinks you consume don't contain extra sugar—shy away from those cute, sugary, tropical-type mixed drinks that come decorated with little cherries and umbrellas. Even light or low-calorie beer contains calories—and about the same amount of alcohol as regular beer.

Check Your Medicines

It's normally not a problem, but many prescription and over-the-counter medicines contain a bit of sweetener to give tablets a more palatable taste. Even those labeled "sugar free" should be checked to ensure that they don't contain dextrose, fructose, or sorbitol, which are forms of sugar. Get in the habit of reading the labels of medicines as well as foods. People who are ill or under stress should monitor their blood sugar levels frequently; during those situations, avoid medicines that contain a bit of sugar. Some medicines also contain alcohol, which you'll discover when you read the label.

Yes, You Can Succeed

When you bring about a change in your eating style, you help yourself control your blood sugar levels and perhaps lose weight. Talk with a registered dietitian or a reliable nutritional consultant and follow the expert's recommendations. Select a personal approach to eating. A balanced diet—one that guarantees you of adequate nutrients of all types—is always best. When combined with a more physically active lifestyle, the subject of the next chapter, changing your eating style will dramatically change the way you feel today and promote the benefit of better long-term health tomorrow.

8

Exercise

How You Benefit from a More
Physically Active Lifestyle

BECOMING MORE PHYSICALLY active is another lifestyle choice
that will help you lower and control your blood sugar. This
aspect of self-management may also help you lose weight and
achieve better health. Activity comes in many forms, of course,
and all deliver both physical and emotional benefits. Your medical doctor or an exercise physiologist may work with you in
developing a program of activity or exercise, particularly if you're
making a dramatic change from your current lifestyle. Becoming more physically active may be based on a specific strategy to
work more physical activity into your life, or even to join sports
clubs or exercise classes. Any activity that you choose should be
enjoyable—and sustainable—for you. Some special precautions
exist, particularly for older people or people with complications.
As with all aspects of self-management, a new physically active
lifestyle should first be tailored to fit your interests.

The two major lifestyle changes that can control your blood
sugar are adjusting your eating style and increasing your physical activity. Every person needs to use his or her body, particularly the larger groups of muscles and the lungs, at least a little

bit every day. It's a sad truth that Americans are getting lazy. In 2002, the U.S. government reported that 26 percent of all adult Americans do not participate in any leisure-time physical activities at all. Meanwhile, approximately 38 percent of American high school students watch more than three hours of television every day. It's well established that sedentary lifestyles increase the risk of obesity, heart disease, high blood pressure, osteoporosis, and many types of cancer, in addition to diabetes. New U.S. government dietary guidelines now strongly promote regular physical activity for all age-groups, including older people. The government calls for at least thirty minutes of moderate physical activity most days of the week, and more to manage body weight or prevent weight gain. For children and adolescents, an hour of physical activity most days of the week is suggested. Older adults are advised to engage in regular physical activity in order to minimize the effects of aging.

Physical activity has long been recognized as a key to good health and well-being. A study of Harvard University graduates published in the *New England Journal of Medicine* claimed that for every hour most people spend exercising, they actually add an hour to their lives.

"No less than two hours a day should be devoted to exercise," declared the third U.S. president, Thomas Jefferson, a gentleman farmer who was physically active until his death in 1826. More than 150 years later, President John F. Kennedy cited Jefferson when he urged Americans to become more physically active, by observing, "If the man who wrote the Declaration of Independence, was secretary of state, and twice president could give it two hours, our children can give it ten or fifteen minutes."

New benefits of exercise are still being discovered. Keep in mind that physical activity should not be hazardous; it should be enjoyable. Begin adopting changes slowly, and don't overdo it.

Once you find a physical activity that you enjoy, you can have fun and firm up your body at the same time.

The doctor who treats your diabetes may write you an exercise prescription or refer you to an exercise physiologist, a specialist in the effects of physical activity on the body. The person you see should help you develop a program that matches your physical needs with your interests and abilities. Any exercise prescription will involve a choice of physical activity, along with recommendations for both the intensity and frequency of exercise. Many exercise physiologists are also certified diabetes educators who can explain how particular exercises affect your blood sugar. This is not usually true of personal trainers at health clubs, who often have degrees in physical education but are not up to speed on diabetes.

Before making any exercise recommendations, your doctor or exercise physiologist must consider your medical history as well as any complications that you may have. Foremost, this person should look at how you have been doing recently with blood sugar control. Heart disease risk factors, physical characteristics, age, weight, physical condition, and the results of pertinent diagnostic tests should all be taken into account. Also considered should be your lifestyle, any limitations that you have, and any medications that you take. For instance, medicines called beta-blockers, often prescribed for cardiac problems, can slow your heart's normal response to exercise and can mask low blood sugar.

Certain medical tests are useful before any program of physical activity is undertaken. For instance, the American Diabetes Association now recommends a graded exercise, or stress, test for people over the age of thirty-five with diabetes and for people over the age of twenty-five who have had diabetes for more than 10 years. This test allows a physician to gauge your exercise tolerance to see if your body can handle additional physical stress. The presence of any additional risk factors for heart disease such as high blood pressure should be considered, given that heart disease is the leading cause of death for people with diabetes. Electrocardiograms also are frequently given. Ideally, your doctor or exercise physiologist should recommend a safe, enjoyable program that can be sustained and be of continuing benefit to you.

Always check with your doctor before beginning any new exercise program. Special limits on exercise apply to people with diabetes who have complications such as microvascular or macrovascular disease. Exercises that are most appropriate to people with particular complications are included in Chapter 16.

Big Benefits

Most programs of self-management contain a certain level of physical activity or regular exercise. Exercise has many benefits when done carefully and regularly.

If exercise were a pill, every doctor alive would prescribe it to patients with Type 2 diabetes because of its miraculous effects. While exercise yields broad short-term and long-term physical and mental benefits, it has almost no detrimental side effects if properly done. This is why a medical doctor's recommendations for exercise are often called an exercise prescription. Exercise is known as the "other insulin" because of its direct beneficial impact on lowering blood sugar.

Your muscles can use at least 95 percent of the glucose that your body produces. If you don't use your muscles very much, they don't use much glucose. Inactivity is part of the reason that glucose backs up in your blood, elevating blood sugar. It stands to reason that working your muscles more often will cause them to utilize more glucose and, hence, lower your blood sugar. Aerobic exercise will always produce an immediate drop in your blood sugar. Research published in the *Lancet* established that two to three hours of rhythmic exercise three times a week can lower blood pressure as much as hypertensive drugs can.

Since blood sugar levels rise and fall, the best times to get physically active or to exercise are usually when blood sugars are the highest. These times are frequently about an hour after meals and first thing in the morning. Blood sugar testing at various times of the day will tell you when your blood sugar levels are highest. Whenever your blood sugar is high, that's the ideal time to do some physical activity.

How Exercise Works

Perhaps the most obvious benefit of exercise is its ability to accelerate weight loss. When you become more physically active, you burn more calories and use insulin more efficiently. You also build your overall health, stamina, and vigor. Exercise makes your heart pump faster, which strengthens your heart and all the other muscles that you use. As you engage in physical activity, your body burns fat and cholesterol. Your muscle tone improves, reducing any muscle atrophy that has occurred. Regular exercise also helps prevent the onset of diabetes—something you may want to discuss with your children, grandchildren, or other relatives if diabetes runs in your family.

Physical activity will help you improve the quality of your life. This is partially because exercise combats depression and relieves physical and emotional stress. Strenuous exercise releases "happy" chemicals called beta-endorphins into your bloodstream, creating euphoria and relieving pain. Even moderate exercise causes your body to release mood-altering chemical substances that perk up your spirit.

As explained, physical activity helps the body utilize glucose. For most people, a half hour of moderate physical activity will cause blood sugar levels to drop 20 to 25 percent. This drop is a result of the combination of a greater burning of sugars by muscle cells during exercise, a lesser production of glucose within the body, and the creation of new insulin receptors on your cell membranes. If your blood sugar levels are too high, exercise will make them drop, sometimes for more than twenty-four hours after one exercise session.

When combined with changes in eating style, physical activity results in even better control of blood sugar. Even if you completely change your style of eating for the better, when dieting is done along with exercise, you will achieve greater weight loss, greater insulin sensitivity, and lower blood sugar than you would with only your improved eating pattern. Exercise helps your body burn fat alone, rather than the combination of fats, proteins, and lean muscle tissue that are burned when you simply diet. Weight-bearing exercise reduces the risk of osteoporosis in women. Exercise relieves stress, distracts you from your problems, stimulates your brain, and reduces mental depression by both giving you an immediate psychological lift and releasing chemicals such as serotonin and norepinephrine into the brain. All these responses are beneficial to your physical, mental, and emotional health.

Obesity

Obesity and being overweight are serious health problems in industrialized countries. According to the U.S. Centers for Disease Control and Prevention, approximately 26 percent of all

A Few Well-Known Benefits of Exercise

Benefits for the Body
- Lowers blood sugar as a result of increased insulin sensitivity
- Burns calories to help weight loss
- Burns off harmful fats and cholesterol
- Lowers blood pressure
- Strengthens the heart and lungs
- Increases muscle strength and endurance
- Increases bone density
- Decreases sensations of physical pain
- Improves reaction time
- Improves central nervous system functions
- Reduces physical stress

Benefits for the Mind
- You feel better immediately
- Your self-confidence increases
- Your body image improves
- Helps control depression
- Increases mental flexibility
- Improves memory
- Reduces emotional stress

Americans have a completely sedentary lifestyle, while 54 percent engage in less than thirty minutes of moderate physical activity most days of the week. Excessive body weight can almost always be controlled by a regular program of exercise and diet. In fact, the National Weight Control Registry reports that peo-

ple who lose weight and successfully keep it off do the equivalent of six to seven hours of moderate exercise per week. New research shows that, in addition to exercising, avoiding prolonged periods of sedentary behavior such as hours of television watching can help people prevent diabetes and control weight.

Obesity is defined as "an excessive accumulation of body fat," specifically, fat levels greater than 25 percent of total body weight in men and 30 percent in women. *Overweight*, a more general term, means that a person's total weight is greater than a statistical average, even though that weight could include a substantial percentage of muscle, which weighs more than fat. Of the two conditions, obesity is more hazardous to your health. Whether or not you have diabetes, obesity is harmful because the extra weight puts a heavier burden on the body's normal operations, increasing the risk of heart disease, high blood pressure, hemorrhoids, hiatal hernias, arthritis, and cancer.

Continuing obesity can increase the likelihood of all the known complications of diabetes, because over time it multiplies the negative effects of high blood sugar on the body. According to Dr. Claudia Graham, a certified diabetes educator in Los Angeles who has a doctorate in exercise science, the presence of excessive fat tissue in the body is harmful because it blocks the beneficial effects of insulin. Her ideas about exercise may be found in *The Diabetes Sports and Exercise Book*, cowritten with June Biermann and Barbara Toohey.

The Sedentary Life

Sadly, the average American spends almost five hours a day watching television, according to the Center for Science in the Public Interest. Like surfing the Internet and playing video games, television watching is almost always a passive, sedentary activ-

ity, one that requires the viewer to sit and stare for a long time in one direction—a somewhat unnatural task for the muscles of the human body. Television watching is often accompanied by consumption of sweet or fat-laden snacks. Commercials exhort you to buy more junk food, fast food, beer, and sugary carbonated drinks. Watching television also affects your brain waves, which slow into an alpha state, causing your metabolism to slow as well.

If you watch a lot of television, consider skipping one or two shows and devoting that time to physical activity. You could substitute an exercise class or a leisurely stroll around the neighborhood for your least favorite programs. If there's a conflict, you might videotape or record the programs that you miss. If you can't miss even one program, could you move an exercise machine or stationary bicycle into the room and do something active with your body while you watch the commercials?

Good News/Bad News

Every person's physical prowess declines with age. Research has shown that between the ages of thirty and seventy, flexibility typically declines by 20 to 30 percent, both muscle mass and work capacity decline by 25 to 30 percent, and bone mass declines by 25 to 30 percent in women and 15 to 20 percent in men. This is the basic bad news about aging. Now let's turn back to the benefits of exercise. To combat these effects, exercise strengthens the cardiovascular system, the muscles, the joint structure, and bone composition. More good news is that even a moderate amount of exercise has a correlation with longevity. Most of us know individuals who remain active long past their prime, with minds and hearts fully engaged in their lives and interests. It's not a coincidence that most of these people have led physically active lives.

As one becomes more physically active, the muscles firm, and the body becomes slender and fit. Physical activity improves muscle strength and flexibility, while it lowers blood pressure. Cardiovascular function improves, and fats and glucose in the bloodstream burn away. For the person with diabetes, blood sugar swings become less frequent and dramatic, and therefore less harmful. You may need less medication or insulin when you incorporate physical activity into your life. And a few pounds may melt away.

When you choose to become more physically active, you empower yourself a little bit more each day.

Fitness

A physically active lifestyle doesn't mean you're spending every spare minute in exercise classes, dressed in a designer sweatsuit while waving your arms and legs in a furious, flapping, sweat-drenched workout. It also doesn't mean that you must suddenly begin jogging ten miles to work or pumping iron like a young Arnold Schwarzenegger. Fitness involves you as you are. If you add more physical activity to your life, you will become more physically fit. Selecting an activity that you can enjoy, or at least tolerate, is the heart of the matter, because the primary obstacles to exercise are not physical but psychological.

If you wish to enjoy the known benefits of physical activity, including better blood sugar control and the loss of weight, what you are shooting for is a healthy level of physical fitness. This is a level of activity you can sustain that is adequate to help control blood sugar. According to Claudia Graham, you do not need a level of fitness adequate to participate in team sports, nor the stamina to compete in a ten-mile run and not embarrass your-self. Health-related fitness is all you really need to control blood sugar, and it's enough to help you lose weight.

Think for a while about what you enjoy and don't enjoy doing. Then choose physical activities that appeal to you, whether or not you think of those activities as exercise. Would it suit you to integrate some exercise into your workday, such as taking the stairs rather than the elevator, or parking or exiting the bus a few blocks away so that you can walk to and from the office? Would you derive pleasure from spending more time sight-seeing, traveling, or playing with your children or grandchildren?

Are you the solitary type, who would get a lift in spirits from becoming more active outdoors—chopping wood, shoveling snow, working in your yard, or tending a community garden? Could you find satisfaction in doing more housework yourself, or doing it more frequently? How about finding a frisky little dog and treating your new best friend to a hearty walk a few times a day? If you were to spend a lot of money for home exercise equipment or hand weights, would you be inclined to use the stuff regularly? Would you enjoy a plan that involves the same type of exercise every day, or would you prefer to mix it up with a variety of activities, to avoid boring yourself?

Are you a social person? If so, it might help you to exer-cise with a partner, or in group classes at a sports club, senior center, or local YMCA. You may be an ideal candidate to par-ticipate in the American Diabetes Association's fund-raising Walk for Diabetes or the bicycling fund-raiser Tour de Cure. Would you like to hike or trek in the wilderness with a group of environmentally minded individuals, as in the Sierra Club? Would you go with a group to try cross-country or downhill skiing? Would any exercise program work best for you if it involved a family member or a friend who also enjoys the diversion? Would it help you to keep moving if you simply bribe yourself? Do you need to draw up a legal contract with yourself and sign it? Would keeping written records bolster your resolve or discourage you?

You probably know what can help motivate you and keep you motivated. Schedule physical activity to avoid conflicts with your most important obligations to your job, family, and other facets of your life. Then find a way to work it solidly into your life. Customize the physical activity to match your fascinations and desires, but make it as regular as possible. Don't set your standards so high that you guarantee failure. Remember: daily exercise is best for reducing blood sugar.

Golden Rules of Exercise

Here are the two golden rules of physical activity or exercise:

1. Some exercise is better than none at all.
2. Regular exercise is even better.

The reason that regular physical activity is best doesn't involve just the calorie-burning benefits that last for several hours after you stop exercising. When you exercise regularly, after a few months your metabolism actually changes, and you burn more calories all day long.

If you become more physically active, you may also have less trouble changing your eating style. Certain hormones are released during exercise; these chemicals actually decrease rather than increase the appetite. Studies of laboratory rats reveal that rats eat more and fatten up if they are denied physical activity.

The same is true of beef cattle fattened up on feedlots. While athletes in training frequently eat large quantities of food, they burn most of it off by exercising.

Feel the Difference

After beginning your more physically active lifestyle, you should soon feel some improvement. Your blood sugar levels should begin to fall. With lower blood sugar, you should feel slightly more energetic and a bit less tired and fatigued. In approximately a month and a half, your utilization of oxygen and your heart rate will improve.

From three to seven muscle-using sessions of twenty to thirty minutes per week may be a respectable goal. Sometimes, longer exercise sessions are recommended for promoting weight loss and increasing insulin sensitivity. The intensity and type of exercise or activity employed will vary, with each person encouraged to do what's possible within safe limits to produce a benefit.

Most of us should start exercising gradually and work our way up to longer sessions. Short, moderately strenuous daily exercise is preferable to exercise that is arduous, infrequent, and of high intensity. Remember that running guru and author Jim Fixx dropped dead of a heart attack while jogging. Don't overdo it. Moderate, regular activity is also helpful in losing weight. Ten years ago, 184 overweight Boston police officers went on low-calorie diets, and half also participated in an exercise program involving ninety-minute sessions three times a week. Results of the research published in the *American Journal of Clinical Nutrition* showed that the police officers who dieted and exercised not only lost more weight but also kept it all off for years afterward if they continued to exercise.

Lifestyle Changes

In the beginning, a little bit of physical activity is better than none. In small increments, try to step up the level of physical activity in your life. If fatigue is a problem, be sure to eat breakfast and other meals, drink plenty of water, get adequate sleep, and avoid sleeping pills. Getting a little sunlight in the morning, turning off the TV, and avoiding sitting in one spot for long periods can increase your energy levels.

Studies have shown that great numbers of obese people don't move around much at all. If you are very overweight, simple activities such as vacuuming the house or dusting the furniture may be a sensible, productive way to begin exercising and shine up your home at the same time. If you sit in a cubicle at work, stand up every now and then, take a short walk down the hall, work out with some light hand weights, or do something during your breaks and lunch period that involves moving your body. Using a cell phone or a cordless telephone, for example, allows you to pace back and forth when you talk. Moving further afield, if it won't ruin your image, you might spurn the electric golf cart and walk instead, pulling your bag of clubs around the course.

Some individuals need to trick themselves to get started. Removing the batteries from the remote control for your television or DVD or CD player is a ploy that often works—because it forces you to stand up and walk over to the set and push the buttons. Instead of carrying a heaping plate of snack food into the television area with you, force yourself to walk back into the kitchen every time you want a snack, and try to grab something nutritious. Or if you're at work, force yourself to walk around the block before or after allowing yourself to eat a doughnut. Start walking to the supermarket if that is possible, and make frequent trips. Unplug the automatic dishwasher, the electric egg-beaters, and other labor-saving appliances, and do some of the work by hand, the old-fashioned way. You can begin to lower your blood sugar through modest increases in daily physical activity.

These days, almost all pregnant women are advised to exercise; limited exercise is even recommended for pregnant women with diabetes or gestational diabetes. Pregnant women with diabetes are often encouraged to begin an exercise program early, but exercise sessions are often kept short, no more than fifteen to thirty minutes, to avoid depleting the supply of oxygen to the fetus. Exercises such as walking, bicycling, and swimming are frequently recommended, although some precautions apply to certain pregnancies. You'll find more on gestational diabetes in Chapter 12.

As you become more active, be sure to drink more water or other liquids to replace the body fluids that you lose during exercise. The human body is about 75 percent water, so we all need to drink a supply of it every day. Drinking more water helps your kidneys rapidly flush waste materials out of your system, a natural and healthy benefit to people with diabetes. Drinking plenty of water also prevents dehydration, which runs up the blood sugar. It's not a coincidence that almost every diet advises its practitioners to exercise and drink lots of water every day, because both are crucial factors not only in health but also in weight loss.

As you become more physically active, you may choose to take on a program of exercise that is more structured, so that you can further improve your strength and help yourself.

Blood Sugar Control

For blood sugar control, Claudia Graham recommends taking a fifteen- to twenty-minute walk an hour or so after every meal, and also in the mornings. Mornings are a good time to walk because many people have high blood sugar then. Walking is a pleasurable activity that prevents blood sugar from rising as it normally does after a meal. Graham also emphasizes checking blood sugar levels after the walk. This practice is particularly applicable to people on insulin, who need to coordinate the timing of their injections with meals and exercise.

Unless your blood sugar is unusually high, physical activity should be undertaken when your blood glucose is highest. This will help you manage and control your sugars. Blood sugar peaks and valleys vary from person to person. And unfortunately, most of us can't just drop everything we're doing and exercise at the ideal times. Any time you can exercise is the best time.

If your goal is weight loss, Graham recommends building up to longer sessions of up to an hour of continuous aerobic exercise. Sessions of this length are the most effective in any weight-loss program, she says, because it takes thirty to forty-five minutes of aerobic activity before the body begins burning fat as a fuel.

Aerobic Exercise

Aerobic exercise is an ideal form of exercise for people with diabetes because it directly lowers blood sugar. In addition, exercise physiologists often point out the merits of an anaerobic, or weight training, type of exercise, and muscle-stretching exercises before and after workouts.

"Whenever I give a talk and mention aerobic exercise as the exercise of choice, the men in the audience always get a sort of glazed-over look," Graham notes. "I think they have this image of wearing leotards and dancing to Jane Fonda tapes. The truth is aerobic simply means the exercise requires you to use more oxygen."

Aerobic exercise should be rhythmic and continuous. In addition to pumping more oxygen through the lungs, Graham's definition of aerobic exercise includes any exercise that engages the major muscle groups, such as the arms and legs, that increases the heart rate for at least twenty to thirty minutes, and that is performed at least three times a week. In people with adequate insulin, just thirty minutes of moderate aerobic exercise can pay off in up to a 20 to 25 percent decrease in blood glucose levels, because the body becomes more sensitive to insulin while the muscles burn up glucose.

Always start slowly and work your way up. Mild to moderate aerobic exercise is often preferred. The old rule of thumb is that if you can sing, you're moving too slowly, but if you can't talk, you're moving too fast. Gunnar Borg's Scale for Rate of Perceived Exertion is based on the idea that people can easily identify their own levels of exertion. Ideally, according to Borg's scale, aerobic exercise should be somewhere between exercise we perceive as fairly light and exercise we perceive as hard.

Moderate aerobic exercise can include activities such as walking, jogging, swimming, cycling, roller-skating, ice-skating, and cross-country skiing. All cause air to huff and puff through the lungs, and cause the heart to briskly pump oxygen to every part of the body. Moderate exercise is preferred to strenuous exercise for people with diabetes because moderate exercise burns more fat but does not excessively deplete the glucose stored in the liver or muscles, as can long bouts of strenuous exercise. Water aerobics is a non-weight-bearing exercise that can build strength and aerobic capacity, because water supports the body and can provide plenty of resistance as well.

Walking briskly is a natural, weight-bearing aerobic exercise with many benefits. The 10,000 Steps program, begun in Japan, is gaining popularity in this country as a walking exercise program, as is the American Diabetes Association's ClubPed. Both are programs that encourage regular walking. A study conducted in Australia followed a group of overweight postmenopausal women with and without Type 2 diabetes for three months. Each group was asked to walk an hour five times a week, without modifying their diets at all. The nondiabetic women didn't lose weight, but, on average, the women with diabetes lost 5.3 pounds, their HbA1c levels fell from 7.78 percent to 7.19 percent, their fasting glucose dropped from 167 to 148 mg/dl, and their cholesterol improved. One Los Angeles diabetes specialist estimates that waking twenty-minutes three times a week will add a year and a half of good life, while walking an hour a day adds three good years to the life spans of people with diabetes.

Cross-country skiing is one of the best of all aerobic exercises. Folk dancing, square dancing, or ballroom dancing can be a sexy, social, and pleasurable aerobic activity. Choices abound. However, it may surprise you to learn that running a 50-yard dash is not considered aerobic exercise, because it requires only a short, concentrated burst of energy. Aerobic exercise also does not include activities in which you move only once in a while, such as baseball, golf, and bowling; these are considered anaerobic, a word that means "without oxygen."

Do what you enjoy. Varying your workouts will help avoid injuries by stressing and toning different sets of muscles. Variety may keep you from becoming bored. The expenditure of enough energy to burn 150 calories is a good day's moderate activity, according to *The Commonsense Guide to Weight Loss for People with Diabetes*, by Barbara Hansen and Shauna Roberts. In less than an hour, you can burn 150 calories by gardening, washing windows, walking, dancing fast, washing and waxing your car, or wheeling yourself in a manual wheelchair. Playing basketball for fifteen to twenty minutes or pushing a baby stroller for a half hour accomplishes the same.

Being old—or even bedridden—should not prevent you from exercising. So-called armchair exercises can be a good activity for people who are hospitalized or elderly, or who have limited mobility. Some of these exercises are done by sitting in a chair and performing simple muscle-strengthening movements and stretches. A few incorporate light weights, while others can be done to music. Some senior citizens' centers, hospitals, and YMCAs offer group classes. Or videos may be purchased or rented for exercising at home.

In general, Graham says, the safest exercises for older people are those that support the body weight—aerobics, swimming, cycling, rowing, armchair exercises, and light strength training. More hazardous to older people are running programs, which put more than twice the stress on bones and joints as does walking. Proceed with caution when contemplating heavy weight lifting or isometric exercises, which can raise blood pressure. Exercises that require quick, rapid new movements are not recommended for most older people. Many of these guidelines also apply to people who are extremely overweight.

Other Forms of Exercise

In addition to aerobic exercise, your doctor or exercise physiologist may urge you to work other forms of exercise into your program of physical activity. Stretching and anaerobic exercises add safety and variety to your workouts.

Five or ten minutes of warm-ups and stretching before any exercise is recommended, particularly movements that stretch the leg muscles. Stretching exercises are advisable because the nerve endings in the legs of people with diabetes can become dull, and you may not feel the normal sensation of pain in the ligaments that connect the muscles with the bones. Not noticing this pain can result in torn ligaments or broken bones in the foot. Purely for the sake of safety, it's important to stretch the Achilles tendon behind each ankle, as well as the calf and hamstring muscles. Stretching exercises increase flexibility but are recommended only to the point of regular joint motion, not to the point of searing pain. After exercising, a few minutes of cooldown and stretching exercises are suggested by most doctors. Professional athletes do this to minimize injuries.

Weight training, also called resistance training or anaerobic exercise, is another form of exercise frequently urged for people with diabetes because it can help lower blood sugar. Weight lifting, soccer, and basketball are all anaerobic. Anaerobic exercise rapidly uses up the fuel stored in the muscles and increases insulin sensitivity in muscle cells. Proper techniques of lifting and breathing must be employed to minimize injury, as well as to compensate for any resulting rise in blood pressure. Weight training is not recommended if you have complications involving the eyes or kidneys, or if you have high blood pressure.

Among the benefits of weight training are improved muscle strength, increased lean body mass, increased bone density, and perhaps improved blood sugar control. This form of exercise also strengthens bones and joints and reduces the risks of injury in other types of exercise.

Weight-bearing exercise is particularly beneficial for women because it reduces the risk of osteoporosis, a disease in which calcium and other minerals are depleted from the skeleton, causing brittleness of the bones. Women face more risk for osteoporosis because they lose certain hormones as they age, which contributes to bone loss. Diabetes accelerates bone loss in women and, to a lesser extent, in men. Weight-bearing exercises can help minimize bone loss.

Weight-bearing exercise can be as simple as walking, which an estimated 40 million Americans claim as their exercise of choice. There's a lot to be said for this most natural form of exercise, including the fact that it's almost impossible to injure yourself while walking if you take sensible precautions with your feet. After all, our bodies were built to walk every day, searching for food and adventure. Walking briskly gets the heart and lungs working, but even a leisurely stroll at 3 miles an hour five days a week can raise HDL, or "good," cholesterol levels, according to a study of women walkers published in the *Journal of the American Medical Association*. Walking is inexpensive, doesn't require special equipment or training, and may be done in your neighborhood or in any safe and preferably scenic location, such as a park, or almost anywhere else weather permits. Indoors, walking can be done on a treadmill, if you have one available, or in a mall. As Chapter 11 explains, daily foot care is necessary whether you walk or not.

The weather, the altitude, illness, injuries, smoking, drinking, taking medications, and other factors may require extra precautions, which should be explained to you by your doctor. If your doctor doesn't address these topics, ask about them.

Sports Clubs

Sports clubs are places to get a workout, and many have personal trainers on staff. If you prefer to exercise in the company of others, or if competition inspires you, sports clubs or exercise classes may be the way to go. Select a location that's fairly close to your home, so that it will be easy for you to get there.

Some commonsense precautions apply. The authors of *The Diabetes Sports and Exercise Book* recommend that you check out a club by asking specific questions about diabetes before you join. Will the club permit you to check your blood sugar between exercises, for instance, or do club officials become squeamish at the sight of blood? Will the club let you take a small snack into the workout room to eat if your blood sugar gets low, or is there an ironclad rule against snacking? Before you join, meet with the club's personal trainer, if one is available, and find out if he or she knows anything about diabetes. Not every personal trainer knows the limits that should be placed on exercise for people with diabetes. If you determine that the club's trainer is ignorant about diabetes, and you still join the club, don't let that trainer put you into an exercise program not approved by your medical team. Don't do anything that sounds dangerous to you. For instance, don't do something as reckless and harmful to yourself as hanging upside down in gravity boots if you've got eye problems.

If the club checks out and the price is right, join it and take advantage of its services. In addition to a floor full of exotic-looking exercise machines, which you may enjoy like a kid discovering a new playground, many sports clubs offer interesting exercise and dance classes.

Plain old community exercise classes are another alternative that will help you become more physically active, and they're less trouble than joining a sports club. Classes are offered by many schools and community colleges and through organizations such as the YMCA and YWCA. Senior citizens' centers sometimes sponsor classes in more exotic disciplines such as tai chi and yoga as well as in aerobics, square dancing, swimming, and gymnastics. The YMCA offers exercise classes for people with arthritis.

If you enjoy socializing while you exercise, you may want to see if your town has any mall-walking clubs, which offer group physical activity with the added distraction of high-speed window-shopping in a cool, safe place. Mall-walking clubs typically meet early, before the mall opens its doors. They're a nice way for businesses to share their facilities with the public. These clubs sometimes reward members who achieve certain personal milestones, such as walking their first thousand miles.

Precautions to Take

The benefits of exercise outweigh the risks in almost every person, but consult your doctor about any precautions you should take before you suit up. Certain types of exercise are taboo with certain complications of diabetes and with some medications. Of course, never exercise when you are sick, a topic covered in Chapter 11. High blood sugar should not stop you from exercising, unless it is accompanied by ketosis.

If you exercise vigorously, don't forget to take a day off now and then to allow your body to recover. If the opposite is the case, and you have taken a break from your exercise program for quite a while, your body will know it. After only a few weeks of bed rest and limited motion, you'll lose some of your muscle mass, oxygen-consuming capability, improvement in heart rate, and even calcium to a slight degree. You'll likely feel stiff and tired; you may be somewhat depressed. You may regain weight and may lose some control of your blood sugar. When you return to a more physically active lifestyle after being sick or bedridden, begin gradually and slowly build back your strength over a month or two.

Although low blood sugar is rarely a problem for people with Type 2 diabetes, exercise can occasionally cause low blood sugar in people who take diabetes medications, particularly insulin. In consultation with your doctor, you may reduce your insulin dosage prior to exercising. As a precaution, inject insulin in sites other than the muscles you'll be using for exercise: if you plan to jog, for instance, don't inject insulin into your legs. Carry a snack with you. Test your blood sugar. If your blood sugar is low, eat some quick-acting carbohydrates such as Life Savers, Skittles, or glucose tablets. Avoid low blood sugar by snacking before or during your exercise period, or by planning exercise during periods of peak blood glucose, such as early morning hours or sixty to ninety minutes after eating a meal. Do not drink alcohol right after exercising, because it further lowers blood sugar. And if your exercise lasts all day, as in a wilderness hike, you'll need to eat something every hour.

If you take insulin or other diabetes medications, be on guard for immediate symptoms of low blood sugar such as shakiness, weakness, sweating, nervousness, dizziness, or hunger. Also watch for symptoms that can come on more slowly, such as irritability, confusion, drowsiness, headache, and poor coordination. Some symptoms of low blood sugar often accompany exercise— for instance, a quickly beating heart, or sweating. A quick blood sugar test will tell you for sure. Since some symptoms of low blood sugar are unique to the individual, keep your own history in mind. If your exercise or activity lasts much longer than an hour, check your blood sugar during exercise.

People who exercise frequently are at a slightly higher risk for a rare condition called postexercise, late-onset hypoglycemia, or PEL. PEL may occur after long periods of exercise, or exercise of particularly high intensity. PEL is more likely to occur if you have been sedentary and suddenly begin an exercise program. PEL occurs because the exercise causes your body to become more sensitive to insulin, increasing your metabolism and causing sugar to be pulled out of storage in the liver and muscles. PEL can occur up to twenty-four hours after exercising. Extreme heat or cold weather can cause your body's insulin levels to fluctuate more than normal, so pay attention to how extremes in weather affect your blood sugars. If you exercise frequently, ask your doctor about PEL. Although the condition is rare, it's wise to test your blood sugars after exercise in order to help avoid it.

It's Your Life

Some people know the benefits of physical activity but still find it difficult to work more exercise into their lives. It's estimated that half the people who begin an exercise program drop out within the first year. It's hard to find time for exercise, some people say. They're too busy. They're too old. They're too sore. They're too fat. They're too embarrassed. They're too afraid that exercise might hurt. Consider the possibility that these are unacceptable excuses.

The choice you have is between becoming more active and refusing to change.

It's tough, but not impossible, to change your behavior. Make the decision to become more physically active. Look at it as a job, if that works for you. Every day, motivate yourself. Plan ahead, and exercise on time. Figure out tricks—and treats—that keep you motivated. Don't allow yourself too many lazy days off, and don't buy your own transparent excuses. One woman who has continued to exercise uses the "five-minute rule": If she doesn't feel like exercising on a particular day, she forces herself to exercise for only five minutes. After the five minutes, if she still doesn't want to exercise, she allows herself to stop.

To succeed, you must fit the physical activity to yourself. Start slowly and build up to longer and more challenging sessions. Exercise at home, if that suits you. Join a club or exercise class if that spurs you on. Be as active as possible as regularly as possible. Don't chastise yourself if you miss one session, or if you're sick or busy and happen to skip one day. Miss what time you absolutely must, and then go back to living a more physically active lifestyle as soon as you can. If you must take a pass on one session, immediately schedule another in its place. Set realistic goals that can be achieved by you.

Most of all, permit yourself a moment or two after each exercise session to savor how good you really feel. Almost every human being feels better after exercising. The long-term rewards that you may not even notice should include greater physical strength, easier breathing, a better attitude toward yourself and your life, and perhaps even better sleep.

Along with these valuable lifestyle changes, medications may have a place in your self-management strategy. The next chapter looks at the medications that your doctor may prescribe in treating diabetes.

9

Drugs

A New Look at
Diabetes Pills and Insulin

IN ADDITION TO the lifestyle changes discussed in previous chapters, several drugs can be useful in the treatment of Type 2 diabetes. This chapter discusses the types of drugs that may be prescribed by your doctor, including diabetes pills and insulin. It explains what these drugs are, what benefits and side effects may occur, and how each drug may be employed in treating diabetes alone or in combination with other drugs. Precautions regarding each medication are also discussed.

At some point in your treatment, your doctor may suggest that you try one of the medications available to keep blood sugar at acceptable levels. Oral hypoglycemic medications, often called diabetes pills, are frequently used in tandem with diet and exercise to control blood sugar.

Diabetes pills may be prescribed when your treatment begins, at certain points along the way, or when lifestyle changes alone do not sufficiently lower blood sugar. Prescription drugs have side effects. Ask your doctor to tell you both the risks and benefits of diabetes pills or of any other medication he or she prescribes. Do understand that the side effects of a medicine that is properly used in the treatment of diabetes will do less harm to your body than prolonged levels of high blood sugar.

In more than three out of four cases of Type 2 diabetes, the body produces adequate insulin, but this insulin cannot be properly utilized by the body. In these cases, lifestyle changes may be enough to achieve blood sugar control. However, if you have the form of Type 2 diabetes in which your body does not produce adequate insulin, you will not be able to control diabetes through lifestyle changes alone. In this event, your doctor will prescribe either diabetes pills or insulin. In addition to lifestyle changes, you will need medication to keep your blood sugars under control.

When you begin taking most diabetes pills or insulin, one unfortunate side effect is that you may gain weight. This is because blood sugar rushes into your cells. Even though you might have been eating a lot of food, your body has actually been in a fasting state, with excess glucose backed up in your bloodstream. Rather than being absorbed and metabolized for energy, this circulating sludge of glucose couldn't reach your body's cells. Medications help release your body from this state of artificial fasting and produce weight gain. Sugar will rush into your cells for several days after you begin taking these medications, and some of it will be stored as fat. One exception to this phenomenon among diabetes drugs is metformin, which normally causes a small amount of weight loss. Other drugs that do not promote weight gain include acarbose (Precose) and the newly approved exenatide (Byetta).

Remember that diabetes medications work best within a coordinated program of lifestyle changes encompassing modifications in eating style, efforts to reduce stress, and increased physical activity. This approach produces the quickest improvements in blood sugar.

Using Diabetes Pills

Two primary precautions apply to people taking oral hypoglycemic agents, or diabetes pills:

1. Take each pill before or with meals, as directed.
2. Do not double up pills if you miss a dose.

Diabetes Pills

Diabetes pills help people with diabetes utilize their own insulin more effectively. According to the Centers for Disease Control and Prevention, about 53 percent of people with Type 2 diabetes are prescribed diabetes pills. When diabetes pills are first taken, blood glucose levels frequently drop 15 to 20 percent.

Diabetes pills are normally not the first choice to get blood sugars under control. Most physicians prefer to initially try lifestyle changes centered around diet and exercise in order to bring blood sugars under control without medications. A few physicians do prescribe the oral agents first; then, after blood sugars are under control, they add lifestyle changes to further reduce weight and blood sugar levels. Both strategies work. In the latter situation, if your body manufactures adequate insulin, and if you are vigorously pursuing lifestyle changes to lower your blood sugar and are making progress, you can ask your doctor for a little more time to get your blood sugar under control before you begin taking insulin or pills.

Diabetes pills are not a cure. Most of them work for a while, usually several years, and then slowly lose their effectiveness. If the pills no longer provide adequate control of blood sugar, you are then started on insulin.

Side effects depend on the medication and the patient. Diabetes pills can cause unusually low blood sugar, or hypoglycemia. Hypoglycemia has occurred approximately 1 to 2 percent of the time with some medications in clinical trials. Other possible side effects from oral hypoglycemic agents include stomach upset, appetite diminishment, rashes, and itching. Many of these side effects are normal when you begin taking a particular medication but gradually disappear as your body learns to tolerate the drug. However, certain precautions are in order when diabetes pills are combined with other medications.

New Medications

Several experimental medications to treat diabetes are being developed by pharmaceutical companies, and the U.S. Food and Drug Administration (FDA) will probably approve a few for use within the next few years. In fact, the first incretin mimetic, exenatide (Byetta), was released in 2005. Scientists believe incretin mimetics have the potential to actually help restore beta cells in the pancreas, as well as lower blood sugar and blood pressure and encourage weight loss. Another new drug approved in 2005, pramlintide (Symlin), is an analog, which is structurally similar to the pancreatic hormone amylin. Other analogs of this type may appear.

The newer medicines act differently on the body from the oldest class of diabetes pills, the sulfonylureas, which are still prescribed to help control diabetes. The sulfonylureas stimulate the pancreas to produce more insulin, and they have helped millions of people with Type 2 diabetes keep their blood sugar levels under control for periods of time.

Doctors often suspend the use of hypoglycemic agents, or replace them with insulin, during periods when a patient is experiencing extreme physical or mental stress, such as pregnancy, surgery, severe infections, or major trauma. Also, precautions are advised with these medications for elderly people of normal weight, who can have incidences of low blood sugar. Pregnant women and women with diabetes seeking to become pregnant should not take sulfonylurea medications, because they increase the chance of complications during pregnancy. People allergic to other sulfa drugs rarely react to sulfonylureas, but just in case, you should tell your doctor if you have a sensitivity to sulfa drugs or any other medication.

Since most diabetes pills lose their effectiveness over time, new medications are increasingly being prescribed to supplement older ones. Combination therapy may extend the benefits of diabetes pills for a significant time.

As with any other medications, diabetes pills should be taken as directed. This is almost always before meals or with meals. If you skip a pill, never try to make it up by taking two pills the next time. Simply go back on schedule by taking the prescribed dose at the next appropriate time.

If you're working to change your eating style, become more physically active, and reduce negative stress, you should not abandon those parts of your self-management program just because you've begun taking diabetes pills or insulin. Medications help, but they are not powerful enough to do the job by themselves. If your doctor has prescribed diabetes pills as a first step in a comprehensive strategy to assist you in controlling your blood sugar, you may be able to lower your recommended dose, or stop taking medications altogether, once you've made appreciable progress through lifestyle modifications.

Available Hypoglycemic Agents

The following is a rundown of drugs that are prescribed for the treatment of diabetes, listed with the scientific name first and then brand names in parentheses. These hypoglycemic agents lower blood sugar. The following listings summarize how particular medications work and specify normal dosage levels and the most common side effects. The newer medications metformin, exenatide, acarbose, and troglitazone are listed first, followed by the sulfonylureas and the oldest effective drug for diabetes, insulin.

Metformin (Glucophage, Riomet, Glucophage XR)

Metformin is a derivative of the French lilac, a traditional herbal remedy for diabetes in parts of Europe. It is often the first line of drug therapy for many people with diabetes, including children. Although relatively new to the United States, metformin has been used in Europe and Canada for several years. Unlike the sulfonylureas, metformin does not stimulate the pancreas to produce more insulin. Instead, it reduces the liver's normal production of glucose, which is about a gram or two a day in most people. It also improves the body's response to insulin, increases the body's uptake of glucose, and reduces the absorption of sugars in the intestine. All of these effects usually lower blood sugar. One research study of metformin showed an average blood sugar decrease of 53 mg/dl. Metformin can also reduce levels of triglycerides and other fats such as LDL (low-density lipoprotein), or "bad," cholesterol in the blood. Metformin works as an appetite suppressant in many people, so it is sometimes used as a diet pill.

Metformin cannot cause hypoglycemia, or low blood sugar, when taken alone. However, it may be used in combination with sulfonylurea drugs, which can cause low blood sugar.

Metformin pills are white and are available in either 500 mg or 850 mg tablets. Typically, daily doses begin at one 500 mg tablet and increase gradually to about 1,500 mg. The maximum effective dose is 2,000 mg per day. As noted, metformin may be used in combination with other diabetes drugs.

Side effects: In 10 to 30 percent of users, Metformin may have such side effects as loss of appetite, nausea, stomach upset, and diarrhea. These effects frequently subside over time, but if not, the dose can be lowered. Metformin can also cause a slight lowering of vitamin B_{12} levels.

Precautions with metformin: Do not take metformin if you have a kidney problem, use alcohol excessively, or have severe congestive heart failure. The use of metformin under any of these circumstances can result in a serious and potentially fatal side effect, lactic acidosis, which develops when body tissues don't get enough oxygen. Lactic acidosis can occur if metformin is taken by people with plasma toxemia or if it is taken before surgery or before receiving dye for imaging procedures.

Exenatide (Byetta)

Exenatide, the first of a new class of drugs called incretin mimetics, stimulates the secretion of insulin when blood sugar is high and restores the first-phase insulin response that is often lost in patients with Type 2 diabetes. It lowers blood glucose levels by stimulating insulin secretion only when blood glucose is high, resulting in lower hemoglobin A1c levels. Exenatide slows the release of the hormone glucagon after meals, thus slowing the rate of food intake. In clinical trials with exenatide, most patients lost weight.

At the time of this book's publication, exenatide was approved for use in combination therapy with metformin and the sulfonylureas. The possibility was open that exenatide or another drug in its class not yet approved would be approved as stand-alone therapy in the future. Several pharmaceutical companies are working on new drugs of this type.

Exenatide is injected subcutaneously (under the skin) with an injection pen device in the thigh, abdomen, or upper arm up to an hour before morning and evening meals. It is available in doses of 5 to 10 micrograms.

Side effects: Can include nausea, vomiting, diarrhea, jittery feelings, dizziness, and headaches. Some patients experience reduced appetite or weight loss, which is not a cause for concern.

Precautions: Exenatide can cause low blood sugar when used in combination with sulfonylureas, or with metformin and sulfonylureas. No increase in incidences of low blood sugar was noted in trials when it was used in combination with metformin alone. Medications that need threshold concentrations in the blood, such as antibiotics and birth control pills, should be taken at least an hour before exenatide injection, or at another meal. Do not administer after a meal.

Acarbose (Precose)

This drug works in the small intestine to slow the breakdown of carbohydrates, particularly complex carbohydrates, thereby holding down the so-called postprandial blood sugar rise that normally occurs after eating. Technically an alpha-glucosidase inhibitor that does not act within the endocrine system, acarbose blocks the action of several enzymes such as glucomylase and sucrase, which help break down complex carbohydrates for absorption in the small intestine. Acarbose slows the natural breakdown of starches, dextrins, maltose, and sucrose to absorbable monosaccharides. When taken alone, it can lower blood sugar without the risk of hypoglycemia, hyperinsulinemia, lactic acidosis, or weight gain. Since acarbose inhibits the blood sugar rise after eating, it is most effective in people who have their greatest problems with high glucose levels at that time.

The benefits of acarbose are proportional to carbohydrate intake—if you eat a lot of carbohydrates, acarbose has a more pronounced effect. Acarbose is FDA approved as a combination therapy with a sulfonylurea. It has been used in combination with metformin and insulin.

Acarbose is taken just before meals, or with the first bite of each meal. Tablets are white to yellow-tinged. Use typically begins with 25 mg doses, or half a 50 mg tablet. The maximum dose is 50 mg to 100 mg per day, depending on the weight of the patient.

Side effects: Can include abdominal pain, diarrhea, and flatulence, all of which can diminish after a month or two. However, some patients cannot tolerate these effects.

Precautions: Acarbose is not to be used by patients who have inflammatory bowel disease, colonic ulceration, or partial intestinal obstruction. There is a danger of low blood sugar reactions when acarbose is used in combination with sulfonylurea drugs.

Miglitol (Glyset)

Miglitol also prevents the breakdown of carbohydrates in the intestines by inhibiting the action of certain enzymes, resulting in lower blood sugar levels after eating. Miglitol may be employed as monotherapy or in combination with sulfonylureas. It can cause a slight weight loss and can block or reduce a sulfonylurea-induced weight gain. The pills are white and are available in 25 mg, 50 mg, and 100 mg strengths. The starting dose is 25 mg; the typical dose is 50 mg at mealtime.

Side effects: Can include flatulence, diarrhea, abdominal pain, and occasionally skin rash or lowered iron levels. Miglitol is not recommended for patients with renal dysfunction, inflammatory bowel disease, obstructions of the colon, or a predisposition to chronic intestinal diseases.

Repaglinide (Prandin)

Repaglinide is a chemical derivative of benzoic acid, which stimulates the beta cells in the pancreas to make more insulin, assisting glucose uptake. The first of a new group of diabetes drugs called the meglitinides, it acts quickly and dissipates quickly to suppress the glucose rise after a meal. It is taken before meals and can be used as needed by people whose meals come at unpredictable times. Repaglinide may be taken by people with kidney disease. The starting dose is 0.5 mg; the maximum dose is 4 mg per day. It is available in white 0.5 mg tablets, yellow 1 mg tablets, and red 2 mg tablets. This drug may be used in combination with metformin but not with the sulfonylureas.

Side effects: Repaglinide can cause low blood glucose reactions and sinus or breathing problems. It carries a slightly higher risk of heart-related problems than some other diabetes medications.

Precautions: Repaglinide can interact with other drugs, including troglitazone and drugs used to treat fungal or bacterial infections. Do not take a pill if you skip a meal.

Nateglinide (Starlix)

Nateglinide, like repaglinide, stimulates the pancreas to release insulin faster after the person has eaten. It is an amino acid derivative and can be taken a half hour or less before meals. Nateglinide can be used in combination therapy with many other diabetes medications such as metformin. It may be prescribed in 60 mg yellow tablets or 120 mg pink tablets, with the lesser dose for people who are near their blood sugar testing goals. The maximum daily dose is 360 mg. Nateglinide may be used three times per day, alone or in combination with metformin, but not in combination with sulfonylureas.

Side effects: The drug may cause low blood sugar reactions if no meal is eaten after the pill is taken, or in amounts larger than prescribed. Low blood sugar reactions can occur when nateglinide is used with nonsteroidal anti-inflammatory drugs, salicylates, MAO inhibitors, and beta-blocking drugs.

Precautions: Corticosteroids, thyroid products, thiazides, and other drugs may reduce the blood glucose lowering effect. Do not take nateglinide if you skip a meal.

The Glitazones

The glitazones work against insulin resistance by allowing cells to "open up" and take in more glucose. They also decrease the production of glucose by the liver. The first of these was troglitazone (Rezulin), followed by rosiglitazone (Avandia) and pioglitazone (Actos). Troglitazone caused a scandal several years ago when some patients experienced liver damage that was not reversible, and it was taken off the market. The two newer glitazones, rosiglitazone and pioglitazone, have not been shown to permanently damage the liver, but manufacturers recommend periodic testing as a precaution against the reversible liver inflammation that occasionally can occur. A heart disease study conducted by Policy Analysis, Inc., of Brookline, Massachusetts, found that patients taking glitazones had a slightly increased risk

for developing heart failure, perhaps because the drugs sometimes cause the body to retain more fluid.

Rosiglitazone (Avandia). Rosiglitazone acts by increasing
insulin sensitivity, particularly in muscle and adipose tissue and
in the liver. It reduces levels of free fatty acids and increases HDL
and LDL cholesterol levels. It is taken once or twice daily, with
or without meals, either in the morning or in the morning and
the evening. The usual starting dose is 4 mg per day, which may
be increased to 8 mg after three months if advised. It is available
in 2 mg, 4 mg, or 8 mg pink, orange, or brown tablets. The maximum daily dose is 8 mg. Rosiglitazone may be used alone or in
combination with metformin. It is approved for combination
therapy with insulin, in doses of 4 mg per day or less.

Side effects: Can include a slightly greater chance of upper
respiratory tract infections, anemia, and edema. Some trials have
shown an increase in total cholesterol. Rosiglitazone can cause
resumption of ovulation in women who have insulin resistance
and have stopped ovulating; in these cases, birth control measures are prudent.

Precautions: This drug is recommended to be used with caution by patients with edema, heart failure, or liver problems.
Although rosiglitazone is believed to have no liver toxicity, periodic monitoring of liver enzymes is recommended by the
manufacturer.

Pioglitazone (Actos). First manufactured in Japan, pioglitazone
acts to lower blood sugar primarily by decreasing insulin resistance, which enhances the effects of circulating insulin in the liver
and elsewhere in the body. It may be taken once a day, with or
without meals. It achieves peak concentration within about two
hours, or a bit longer if food is ingested, and usually reduces

triglyceride levels and increases HDL, or "good," cholesterol levels in the blood. It can result in weight gain. It may be used in combination with sulfonylurea, metformin, and insulin (in doses of up to 30 mg of insulin per day). It is available in white to off-white 15 mg, 30 mg, and 45 mg tablets. The maximum dose is 45 mg per day as monotherapy and 30 mg per day as part of combination therapy.

Side effects: Like other agents, pioglitazone can increase the incidence of hypoglycemia. It causes an average 2 to 4 percent decline in hemoglobin and hematocrit in blood. It can make birth control pills less effective, indicating additional birth control methods for women. It can also cause increased possibility of mild to moderate edema, upper respiratory tract infections, headache, sinusitis, myalgia, and tooth disorders. Patients should immediately report unexplained nausea, vomiting, abdominal pain, fatigue, anorexia, or dark urine to their doctors.

Precautions: Pioglitazone should not be used by patients with liver disease or hepatic insufficiency. It should be used with caution by patients with edema.

Sulfonylurea Drugs

The first diabetes pills, the sulfonylureas, were discovered by accident during World War II. Researchers at work on sulfa antibiotics noticed that this particular class of sulfa drugs lowered blood sugar in the research subjects. This finding was soon applied to people with diabetes, who benefit from the side effect of lower blood sugar.

Sulfonylureas stimulate the pancreas to make more insulin, overcoming either a shortage of insulin or insulin resistance. At the end of their natural cycle, sulfonylurea drugs break down in the liver and are excreted. They can be safely taken for long periods and often work effectively for years. Beginning these medications can produce a weight gain of 5 to 10 pounds.

Sulfonylurea compounds include the first-generation drugs tolbutamide, acetohexamide, tolazamide, and chlorpropamide, and the second-generation drugs glipizide, glyburide, and glimepiride. Several pharmaceutical companies make brand-name sulfonylurea drug products, but almost all of these drugs are now available in generic form. Among the exceptions, glimepiride's patent is set to expire in 2005, but the extended-release form of glipizide is still under patent.

Sulfonylurea drugs are listed on the following pages, with the most frequently used agents listed first. Most sulfonylureas may be used in combination with insulin, but this increases the risk of low blood sugar.

Side effects: Can include occasional incidences of low blood sugar, or hypoglycemia, as well as headache, nausea, flushing of face, dizziness, diarrhea, skin rashes, and increased urination. The second-generation sulfonylureas do not have the side effect of increased urination, but they are a bit more likely to cause low blood sugar because their active ingredients are more concentrated and therefore more effective. If you are just beginning to take these diabetes pills, watch out for symptoms of low blood sugar such as sweating, shakiness, dizziness, difficult or slurred speech, hunger, blurry vision, nausea, mental confusion, and irritability. Low blood sugar may occur after or during strenuous exercise, or when you skip a meal. If you suspect low blood sugar at any time, test yourself. If your blood sugar is too low, simply eat a carbohydrate snack and you'll be fine.

Second Generation (Most Commonly Used). Glipizide (Glucotrol, Glucotrol XL)—Action begins an hour after ingestion, and the drug remains in the body for twelve to sixteen hours.

Glipizide is to be taken on an empty stomach, about thirty minutes before a meal. This drug can even out blood sugar levels during the day. It can be used effectively in combination with insulin: one study found that subjects taking glipizide with insulin used only 48 units of insulin, compared with 77 units by subjects using insulin alone. Glipizide is available in 5 mg and 10 mg white tablets. It is taken one or two times per day. A maximum dose for most forms of glipizide is 40 mg per day, but for Glucotrol XL, the maximum is 20 mg per day.

Precautions: This drug is not normally prescribed for elderly patients.

Glyburide (Micronase, DiaBeta, Glynase PresTabs)—An intermediate-acting oral agent, glyburide begins to take effect in about an hour and a half, and it remains in the body for a maximum of twenty-four hours. It is available in 1.25 mg, 1.5 mg, 2.5 mg, 3 mg, 5 mg, and 6 mg tablets. The smallest available doses for each brand are white tablets; larger doses have pink, blue, or light green tablets, depending on the manufacturer. It is taken one or two times per day. The maximum dose is 20 mg per day.

Precautions: Caution is urged for the use of this medication by elderly people.

Glimepiride (Amaryl)—This drug may be taken once a day, to even out blood sugar over the course of a day. It is taken with breakfast or the first main meal of the day, usually beginning with a dose of 1 mg to 2 mg. The usual maintenance dose is 1 mg to 4 mg. It is available as 1 mg pink tablets, 2 mg green tablets, and 4 mg blue tablets. The maximum dose is 8 mg per day.

First Generation (Not Commonly Used). Tolbutamide (Orinase)—This short-acting medication starts working in an hour and is gone from the body within six to twelve hours. The only short-acting diabetes medication, tolbutamide comes in 250 mg and 500 mg white tablets, usually taken two or three times per day. Doses range between 500 mg and 3,000 mg per day.

Acetohexamide (Dymelor)—This medication starts working within an hour and remains in the body for ten to fourteen hours. Available in 150 mg and 500 mg tablets, it is usually taken one or two times per day. The maximum daily dose is 1.5 grams, or 1,500 mg.

Special precautions: This drug is not to be used with patients having kidney problems.

Tolazamide (Tolinase)—This medication is prescribed for people who absorb their food very slowly; its onset is from four to six hours after ingestion. Tolazamide comes in 100, 250, and 500 mg white tablets and is usually taken one or two times per day. The maximum recommended dose is 1 gram, or 1,000 mg, per day.

Chlorpropamide (Diabinese)—Action starts in about an hour, but the drug stays in the body about seventy-two hours, making it the longest-lasting of the sulfonylureas. It is available in 100 mg and 250 mg blue tablets. The maximum recommended daily dose is 500 mg, and it is taken once a day.

Side effects: Can include frequent urination; vascular problems, with symptoms such as headache or flushing of the face; and an Antabuse-type reaction when taken with alcohol.

Precautions: Chlorpropamide is not recommended for anyone with kidney problems or for elderly people.

Secondary Failure

For approximately one in five people with Type 2 diabetes, treatment with oral sulfonylureas may be effective for longer than ten years—occasionally for as long as twenty or twenty-five years. For all the others, the results are typically less long-lived. The average time that these medications work to their full effect is between five and seven years, at which point their effectiveness dims.

For some reason that doctors still don't understand, diabetes pills do not work at all on approximately one-third of the people who try them. These so-called primary failures happen both in the beginning and after a period of time. In other cases, diabetes pills slowly lose their effectiveness for about 5 to 10 percent of the people taking them each year, a phenomenon called secondary failure.

Primary and secondary failures are sometimes temporary, brought on by illness, stress, or an infection. Under such circumstances, doses of insulin may be prescribed to get you over the physical or mental stress that instigated the failure, after which you may start taking the diabetes pills again. Secondary failures may also be permanent; researchers speculate that they may occur because the body becomes more resistant to its own insulin.

When a certain drug doesn't work or stops working, one possibility is to switch to another type of diabetes pill. For instance, your doctor might begin with a sulfonylurea and then switch you to metformin. Another physician facing the same situation might choose to combine medications, prescribing a sulfonylurea and metformin, or a sulfonylurea and acarbose, but in lower doses for each. Such switches or combination therapy can often extend the period of effectiveness of drug treatments.

When medications begin to lose effectiveness, some physicians prefer a period of time with the diabetes pills plus insulin injections in the evening, rather than switching immediately to multiple insulin injections and abandoning the diabetes pills. This can be an effective halfway step because lower doses of insulin are required when diabetes pills are taken. Another strategy is to begin insulin injections and abandon the pills when the diabetes pills fail.

On the horizon are a few promising new oral hypoglycemic agents, currently in clinical trials throughout the world. Some, including newer formulations of sulfonylurea drugs, may ensure a more consistent level of blood glucose all day long on just one dose per day.

Drug Combinations

Doctors may ask patients to try combinations of various diabetes drugs, which can extend the benefits of the drugs over a longer period. However, one problem with this approach is that it gives patients a lot of pills to take and coordinate. To help address that problem, there are now three standardized combinations on the market: Avandamet, Glucovance, and Metaglip.

Avandamet is a combination of metformin (Glucophage) and rosiglitazone (Avandia). It comes in five dosing combinations, combining from 1 mg to 4 mg of rosiglitazone and 500 mg to 1,000 mg of metformin.

Glucovance is a combination of a sulfonylurea (Glynase) and a biguanide (Glucophage). It comes in three dosing combinations, combining from 1.25 mg to 5 mg of glyburide and 250 mg to 500 mg of metformin.

Metaglip is a combination of metformin (Glucophage) and the sulfonylurea drug glipizide (Glucotrol). It combines between 2.5 mg and 5 mg of glipizide with between 250 mg and 500 mg of metformin.

Generic Drugs

Several diabetes drugs, including most of the sulfonylureas and metformin, are now available in generic form. Generic forms of drugs are much less expensive than drugs that are still protected by a twenty-year exclusive patent or a patent extension. The FDA estimates that the average brand-name prescription costs $72, as opposed to $17 for a generic version, although discounts on diabetes pills are often less than average. Your medical doctor may specify on a prescription that a brand name rather than a generic drug is to be dispensed, by writing the words "Do Not Substitute" on the prescription. However, there's now a trend toward the use of less expensive, generic drugs whenever they are available. Many health-care providers now encourage the use of generic drugs, sometimes by offering the incentive of a lower co-payment if you choose a drug in its generic form. Using generic drugs is not quite the same as buying the house brand at the supermarket, although there are similarities. Pharmacists can be helpful in explaining the differences between brand-name and generic drugs. Since profit margins are actually higher on generic drugs, if your pharmacist advises you to choose a brand name, strongly consider taking that advice.

Any pill is composed of two elements. The first is the amount of active ingredient by weight. This is always the same in both brand-name and generic drugs. The second and much larger portion is what's in the rest of the pill—the so-called excipients, which can include coloring agents, binders, and fillers. Excipients can make a slight difference in how much of the active ingredient your body will absorb. If you are sensitive to particular medicines, this difference can be significant. Generic forms of various drugs look different from the original versions, since the pills are a different color. Not all generic forms of a particular drug are exactly the same, although all contain the same amount of the active ingredient, which is why you purchase a particular drug in the first place.

If you switch from a brand name to a generic form of a drug, or vice versa, pay attention to the drug's effects on your body and let your doctor know if you experience a problem. The dose you take may need to be adjusted.

Insulin

Although insulin is an everyday necessity for people with Type 1 diabetes, supplemental insulin is used more sparingly in the treatment of Type 2 diabetes. Treatment with insulin often begins after hypoglycemic medications have lost their ability to control blood sugar. One indicator of when to add insulin to your therapy is a situation in which HbA1c levels stay above 8 on a program involving diet, regular exercise, and diabetes medications. For people whose insulin production is below normal, supplemental insulin may be recommended right away. According to the Centers for Disease Control and Prevention, approximately 12 percent of people with diabetes take both insulin and oral medications, and 19 percent of people with diabetes take insulin only.

While the idea of giving yourself shots may be frightening, understand that insulin will always help you control blood sugar. Better control can help prevent complications. When medical doctors are given the choice between good blood sugar control with supplemental insulin or poor control without it, the choice is always good control with insulin because the benefits far outweigh the risks to the patient's health.

It has been estimated that 20 to 50 percent of people with Type 2 diabetes may one day need insulin, because the production of insulin by the pancreas slowly decreases in all people as they age.

Fortunately, basic insulin can be one of the least expensive drugs on the market, as well as one of the most useful to people who require it. Insulin keeps people alive, and in some respects, it's as close as scientists have come to discovering a miracle drug for diabetes. Before the discovery of insulin, people with Type 2 diabetes who no longer produced adequate insulin could expect to live for several years but to function poorly and suffer many serious complications, such as blindness and gangrene. This is no longer the case.

The discovery of insulin in 1921 by Canadian researchers Frederick Banting and Charles Best was a major breakthrough in twentieth-century medicine. By injecting a primitive form of insulin into a dog whose pancreas had been removed, Banting and Best were able to keep the animal alive even though it produced no insulin of its own. This discovery extended many human lives.

The first insulin was made crudely, by grinding up the pancreases of pigs or cows; early users sometimes experienced side effects and autoimmune reactions caused by impurities. Today, human insulin is grown in huge lots, almost like biological farms. Commercial insulin derived from human insulin has been genetically engineered to clone itself on simple living organisms such as yeast or bacteria, resulting in a pure product. Although pork insulin is still manufactured, beef-pork insulin was phased out in 1999, despite protests from some users who felt this later-peaking insulin gave them superior control.

Two Strengths of Insulin. The two strengths of insulin are U-100 and U-500. U-100 means that there are 100 units of insulin per cubic centimeter, while U-500 indicates 500 units. Almost everyone uses U-100 insulin; U-500 is generally used for research purposes. In other countries, insulin is manufactured in various strengths, but most countries have begun to adopt U.S. insulin standards.

In addition to insulin, insulin analogs now on the market include lispro (Humalog), aspart (NovoLog), and glulisine (Apidra). These are all very fast-acting insulin analogs that work and dissipate quickly. Insulin glargine (Lantus) is a long-lasting analog without peak effects.

Insulin and insulin analogs are available in four types, all of which have different rates of absorption, different peaks, and different rates of time that they remain in the bloodstream. The four types are short-acting insulin, intermediate-acting insulin, long-acting insulin, and mixtures (see the table "Four Types of Insulin").

Since no type of insulin is ideal, premixed combinations of short-acting and intermediate-acting insulin are sold in the United States. These include 70/30 and 50/50 mixtures. Your physician may recommend that you take one of these combinations before meals, to provide fast insulin for the first-phase insulin response after eating (this response is often impaired in people with Type 2 diabetes) and to help with long-term control. Premixed insulins usually work best for people with stable insulin needs.

Different mixtures such as 60/40 and 90/10 are sold in Europe. If you are using a premixed combination of insulin and will be traveling overseas, find out beforehand from the manufacturer what's available in the countries that you will be visiting and take a supply of insulin with you.

Pramlintide (Symlin). In addition to insulin, the pancreas produces another hormone, amylin. A synthetic analog of amylin, a neuroendocrine hormone produced by the beta cells of the pancreas, was approved in 2005. This new drug, pramlintide (Symlin), lowers blood sugar and creates some weight loss for people using insulin. It is used in tandem with insulin, but in separate injections, for additional blood sugar lowering effects. Pramlintide is injected twice a day at meals. The initial recommended dose for people with Type 2 diabetes is 60 micrograms, increas-

Four Types of Insulin

	Onset	Peak	Duration
Short-Acting			
Lispro, aspart, glulisine	5 minutes	0.5–1 hour	3 hours
Regular	0.5 hour	2–5 hours	5–8 hours
Intermediate-Acting			
NPH	1–2 hours	6–10 hours	16–24 hours
Long-Acting			
Glargine	> 2 hours	None	> 24 hours
Detemir	1–2 hours	2–12 hours	16–24 hours
Mixtures			
70/30, 50/50, 75/25	0.5 hour	7–12 hours	16–24 hours

ing to 120 micrograms as tolerated. Some patients in clinical trials experienced nausea, which diminished with use. Low blood sugar reactions are the greatest potential danger; in such cases, insulin doses should be reduced immediately, and under a doctor's supervision, until stabilization is achieved. Also, rapid- or short-acting insulin doses before dinner should be cut by 50 percent when pramlintide is added to the regimen.

Your Insulin Dose. To a great extent, your exact dosage of insulin will be worked out as you go along. In the beginning, your physician will recommend a strategy for controlling your blood sugar by using insulin. Blood glucose testing will tell you and your doctor how your body is using the insulin that you are taking. Frequent tests will identify adjustments that should be made to compensate for changes in your blood sugar levels. Once a dosage and a schedule are established, use the same dose in the same amount, every day at the same time, unless your doctor makes another recommendation.

You should be in frequent contact with your health-care team when you begin taking insulin, because finding the right dose can involve some trial and error. For instance, you may need more insulin if you smoke. A study of smokers with diabetes, conducted at University Hospital in Copenhagen, found that they required 15 to 20 percent more insulin than did nonsmokers with diabetes.

A schedule of injections that follows the natural pattern of your blood sugar fluctuations can be established; when you adhere to this pattern, you will probably feel better immediately. With the exception of the fast-acting insulin analogs, insulin is typically taken thirty minutes before a meal, because it has a delayed reaction of thirty to forty-five minutes before it begins working.

Your insulin dose will be given at specified times of the day. Your life, especially your meal and snack times, will have to become more predictable when you take insulin. Watching the effects of insulin will allow you to space out your doses to accommodate your body's needs.

Remember that whether or not you use insulin, your eating schedule, exercise schedule, and stress level also affect your blood sugar. Insulin helps even out blood sugar fluctuations, but it can cause low blood sugar. Your blood sugar goals should be determined by you and your health-care team, based on your health history and age. Make sure that your doctor tells you what test results should prompt you to call.

Taking Insulin. At the present time, insulin must be introduced into the body through the skin. You may either inject insulin yourself or ask another person such as your spouse or a private nurse to do it. Most people find it convenient to do it themselves. Several devices on the market allow even people with a needle phobia to inject insulin. Pharmaceutical companies are also working to develop an insulin that can be taken in pill form, but their attempts have been unsuccessful so far because the acids in the stomach and intestines break down the insulin before it can move into the bloodstream, where it does its work.

Insulin may be injected with either a syringe, an automatic injection device called a syringe autoinjector, a type of air gun called a hydrospray injector, or a device called an insulin infusion pump. If you take insulin, you will need to learn how to measure a proper dose for yourself and how to inject it underneath your skin, into your fatty tissue. Sites to inject insulin include the abdomen (often a preferred site), the back of the arms, the upper buttocks, and the front of the legs. As a general rule, the higher up on the body that you inject insulin, the faster the insulin will peak. Recognizing these differences by tracking glucose levels when you begin is a better approach than random selection of sites. Work with your medical doctor or your diabetes educator when you begin site rotation to identify which sites give you best control at different times of the day. For some people, a good strategy is to inject the breakfast and lunch shots in the arms or abdomen so the insulin takes effect quickly, and to inject dinner and bedtime shots in the thighs and buttocks, where the usually slower absorption helps carry you through the night.

In the hospital, insulin may be administered intravenously (directly into the vein) through an IV, which is the fastest way to receive it. Insulin is sometimes injected by syringe into the muscle, where it acts more quickly than when it is injected subcutaneously.

Insulin needles are short and slender, and they cause little pain. Syringes cost about 20¢ apiece and are the least expensive way to administer insulin. For a cost of $30 to $40, injection devices can make it easier to get insulin into your system if you are squeamish about needles. Insulin "pens," sold under brand names like Accupen and NovoPen, use insulin cartridges. Autoinjection devices, with brand names such as Autojector, Inject-Ease, Injectomatic, and Monoject, are operated by pushing a plunger button to get the needle, or the needle and the insulin, under your skin.

Jet injectors cost between $600 and $1,400 and are sold under brand names such as Medi-Jector II, Tender Touch, Preci-Jet 50, and Vitaject II. These devices actually blow the insulin through the skin, with the depth of penetration adjustable by a nozzle, which must be kept scrupulously clean.

The newest and most sophisticated insulin-dispensing device is the insulin pump, which can provide better blood sugar control and allow more flexibility for planning meals, exercise sessions, and social events. You need a doctor's prescription to get a pump. Manufactured by companies such as Medtronic Mini-Med, Animas, and Smiths Medical, pumps currently cost around $5,000 to $6,000, and supplies cost about $100 per month. Pumps dispense insulin in short intervals, or pulses, throughout the day through a small needle or catheter placed under the skin into the subcutaneous tissue, more closely approximating the natural production of insulin by the pancreas. Insulin pumps are not automatic, because they cannot regulate the flow of insulin to compensate for changes in blood sugar; for now, this must be done manually based on blood sugar test results.

One company, Medtronic MiniMed, is marketing a continuous glucose-monitoring system approved by the FDA in 1999. This system utilizes a flexible sensor that, when inserted subcutaneously, acts as a continuous glucose monitor. At present, these devices are being used by physicians and consumers to monitor blood sugar fluctuations for a period of one to three days. In the near future, these devices will act in tandem with an insulin pump to regulate the flow of insulin based on blood sugar levels, providing a sort of artificial pancreas.

Pumps can often provide control of blood sugars that is equal to or better than that of insulin injections. A study published in the September 2003 issue of *Diabetes Care* found that people with Type 2 diabetes were more satisfied with the pump than with injections, because the pump was more convenient to use and allowed them greater flexibility. Pump users also typically use about 25 percent less insulin. A detailed explanation of insulin pumps can be found in the book *Pumping Insulin*, by John Walsh and Ruth Roberts, among other sources.

Insulin Injections. When you're using a syringe at home to inject insulin subcutaneously, as most people do, certain steps must be followed. These include properly measuring the amount of insulin and maintaining a clean, sanitary environment.

Syringes are disposable; the labels say to dispose of them immediately after use. However, some people reuse their own syringes as many as four times, because there is little danger of spreading disease when only one person uses the syringe. If this is done, the syringe should be cleaned and capped after use. When the needle has difficulty penetrating the skin, or when the injection begins to hurt, it's time for a new syringe.

People who have a fear of needles sometimes find that they can overcome their phobia by using something other than rubbing alcohol to rub down their skin, because the smell of alcohol frequently triggers the fear. Special equipment is available to help people who are blind or partially sighted get the right dose of insulin into the syringe and to help them read the syringe itself prior to injection. Classes on injecting insulin and self-care for people with a sight impairment are offered through organizations such as the Braille Institute and the National Federation of the Blind's Diabetes Action Network; contact information is listed in the Resources at the back of this book.

If you inject insulin, regularly rotate your injections among various parts of the body. A regular rotation of injection locations will prevent *hypertrophy*, a swollen or enlarged patch of skin that results when insulin is injected into the same location too many times, or *lipodystrophy*, a depression or dimpling of the skin. The doctor who treats your diabetes should also check for hypertrophy and lipodystrophy during examinations, even though this condition is becoming less common because of the purity of commercial insulin.

If you are using more than one type of insulin, diabetes educators Diana and Richard Guthrie suggest in *The Diabetes Sourcebook* that insulin bottles be color-coded or marked so that you can easily identify which one to inject at a particular time. Tape or rubber bands can also be used. Two U.S. insulin manufacturers are working with the FDA on a system of tactile identification of insulin vials, using bars or markings in braille. A standardized tactile marking system will benefit people who are blind or partially sighted and who must use more than one type of insulin.

Obtaining Insulin. You don't need a doctor's prescription to purchase insulin in the United States. Exceptions to this are the new insulin analogs, which all currently require a prescription. The original insulin regulations were written so that people with diabetes could get insulin in an emergency. Some states do regulate the purchase of syringes.

When you are traveling, always carry either your doctor's prescription or the name of your insulin written on a piece of

Injecting Insulin

Here are the ten basic steps for injecting insulin with a syringe:

1. Roll the insulin bottle between your palms, upside down and sideways.
2. Clean the top of the bottle with alcohol on a cotton swab or wipe (clean the tops of both bottles if you are mixing insulins).
3. Wash your hands.
4. Draw air into the syringe by pulling out the plunger.
5. Using the syringe, push air down the top of the bottle.
6. Turning the bottle upside down, pull insulin into the syringe, avoiding air bubbles, to your dose level.
7. Clean the injection site with an alcohol swab.
8. Pinch your skin with your fingers, and then insert the needle into the skin.
9. Inject the insulin.
10. Release the skin, and pull out the needle and lay it aside.

paper. Tearing off the top of your insulin box and putting it in your wallet or purse is another way to go.

Insulin bottles are marked with an expiration date, just like milk and other perishable items. Manufacturers won't guarantee their products' potency past this date. Insulin must be stored properly; it can be kept in the refrigerator but should not be frozen. If possible, keep an extra bottle on hand.

Bottles in current use may be kept at room temperature, but avoid temperature extremes. Don't store insulin in direct sunlight, near heaters, or near ice. Insulin stored at room temperature begins to lose its potency after about a month; if that happens, the insulin should be tossed out.

Disposal of insulin syringes is a nuisance. There are now exchange programs, such as the North American Syringe Exchange Program, which will dispose of your used needles and exchange them for new ones. Needle mail-back services are available. Needle destruction devices clip the ends off needles, making them safe to throw away. Some communities have special residential-waste pickup services or hazardous-waste drop-off collection sites. Used syringes should be placed in a sturdy container such as a coffee can with a lid taped securely shut. Add bleach to the container when it's full, and dispose of the container according to local regulations. Special disposal pouches are also sold. If you don't know what the regulations are regarding needle disposal in your area, ask your city sanitation department's public relations office. Don't just toss used needles into the trash—they can be picked up by curious children or by drug addicts. An improperly discarded syringe can spread disease.

Insulin is a wonder drug, one that can keep you alive and in better health when properly used. Remember that the basic idea is to coordinate the use of insulin with the rise and fall of glucose within your body. Striving for an insulin peak at about the same time as your blood sugars are expected to peak allows you maximum blood sugar control.

In addition to low blood sugar, side effects of insulin can include high blood pressure and headaches. Even if you're completely controlling your diabetes through diet and exercise, you still have diabetes; you may need lifesaving insulin for a while if you have a health problem and are hospitalized.

Coordinating Medications

Always tell the doctor who treats your diabetes what other medications you are taking, because those medications can interact with diabetes drugs. Most diabetes pills, and especially the sulfonylureas, should be cautiously taken with other drugs that affect blood sugar control, such as diuretics and beta-blockers, which are often prescribed for high blood pressure. Warfarin, an anticoagulant drug, and cimetidine, a heartburn medication, can interact with the sulfonylureas. Pain relievers such as the nonsteroidal anti-inflammatory drugs and many other highly protein-bound medications can lower blood sugar. If you are treated by a specialist for another medical problem, always tell that doctor which diabetes medications you take, since a specialist will not automatically receive this information. You can prepare a list of the medications that you take and hand it to any doctor. When you begin a new medication, many pharmacies now have computer programs that can automatically scan for drug interactions in prescription and over-the-counter medications.

In addition to the problem of drug interactions, drugstores occasionally make mistakes on prescriptions, and hospitals sometimes make mistakes in administering drugs. Errors can occur with dosages as well as with frequency in administering medications. Occasionally a pharmacist misreads a prescription—mistaking Humalog, a rapidly acting insulin, for Humulin, another type of insulin, or mistaking a prostate treatment drug such as Proscar for a diabetes treatment drug such as Precose. Check your medications when you pick them up. Do what you can to make sure you're taking the correct medicine in the correct amounts.

The doctor who treats your diabetes will help you assess the risks and benefits of medications in your treatment. If you experience a side effect that you don't understand, call your doctor and ask about it.

"Diabetes is a very complex thing because other conditions that you have can affect it," notes the owner of a construction company who has diabetes. "You can have certain symptoms and not be sure if they're coming from the diabetes or from other things. The trick is to sort all the symptoms out and to figure out

Drugs That Raise Blood Sugar

While insulin and hypoglycemic agents lower blood sugar, other medications can raise blood sugar levels, throwing off glycemic control. The following drugs can raise blood sugar and should be reported to the doctor who treats your diabetes:

- Birth control pills
- Decongestants
- Diuretics, or water pills, including thiazides
- Corticosteroids
- Phenothiazines
- Thyroid products
- Estrogen
- Phenytoin
- Nicotinic acid, or niacin
- Sympathomimetics
- Isoniazid

what it is that affects how you feel. You have to really educate yourself and find out about it to know for sure."

Oral hypoglycemic agents and insulin have an established place in the treatment of diabetes, but they are not substitutes for lifestyle changes that are proven to help control blood sugar. Combinations of diabetes pills, or pills and insulin, are sometimes useful in the treatment of diabetes. Always take medication as directed, and report any problems to your doctor. If you need insulin, work with your doctor to arrive at the optimum dose for you. And, of course, test your blood sugar levels as directed by your health-care team. Home glucose testing will help you, as will the medical tests explained in the next chapter.

10

Lab Tests

Laboratory Tests You May Receive and Why
They Are Important

THE DOCTOR WHO is treating your diabetes will give you certain tests, the results of which will be read in the office or in a laboratory. Knowing when to expect these tests and how to interpret the findings will improve your self-management. Also, understanding what each test actually measures may help you focus on the elements that are most meaningful and stop you from worrying about numbers that don't matter much. All of this knowledge and experience can further empower you.

From time to time, you'll visit the doctor who is treating your diabetes. The doctor will look at your eyes because they are the only openings in the human body in which a medical professional can actually see the condition of your blood vessels. In addition, the doctor will check your reflexes, look at your feet, and perform a general examination covering the relevant points listed in Chapter 3. The doctor should ask to see your own blood sugar test records and should arrange for you to receive pertinent laboratory tests to evaluate your physical condition.

Interpreting the results of laboratory tests is an important part of your doctor's job. The better you understand the meaning and implications of your test results, the better you can apply them. Testing provides information on how well you are controlling your blood sugar, your blood pressure, and the levels of fat in your blood. The tests you undergo help your physician assess the condition of vital parts of your body such as your vascular system and kidneys. You will probably receive several tests early on to establish a baseline against which subsequent test results can be measured.

The most common medical tests given to people with diabetes include blood pressure, HbA1c, a lipid profile that measures levels of fats in the blood, and procedures to detect protein in the urine. Specialized urine tests that can detect a loss of kidney function are useful in the treatment of kidney disease. All of these tests should be given regularly to people with diabetes, and the results should be carefully evaluated. Among other tests that may be administered are the oral glucose tolerance test and the fructosamine assay, typically given to pregnant women.

To your doctor, test results are merely pieces of information used to monitor and treat your disease. Consequently, your doctor may not share test results with you as a matter of course. If you're worried about the results of any test, or if you simply want to know the outcome, ask.

While most of the tests listed in this chapter are given in your doctor's office or a neighborhood laboratory, in some instances you may be required to do additional testing in your home. Some insurance plans reimburse for blood pressure monitors, for instance, which are used to check blood pressure at home. The most accurate home blood pressure monitor in current use is the mercury sphygmomanometer, which is typically seen in doctors' offices and is the most difficult to use at home. Aneroid monitors display results on a dial but need to be recalibrated once a year or so, a service that is usually inexpensive. In addition, home cholesterol tests are available, as are home tests for urinary tract infections. HbA1c and fructosamine tests for home use are also available; these are particularly valuable because they give longer-term reads on glucose control than those given by finger-stick tests.

You may choose to keep your own set of medical records, including copies of all of your test results. Keeping a personal file may have many practical benefits, especially if you must change doctors or health plans. In your logbook or file, write down all your test results, including the name of the doctor who performed the test and the date given. Or, if you wish, you may request computer printouts or photocopies of test results. A medical records file provides a central reference point for information on your physical health. Having all relevant data in one location, such as a loose-leaf notebook or a file in your computer, allows you to compare results from doctor visit to doctor visit or simply to cheer yourself on when the numbers improve. A few people even graph this information, so that they can chart their progress. Keeping your own medical file allows you to have information on hand if you need it in an emergency, or if you visit another specialist. You may wish to note any comments that your doctor makes to you in interpreting your test results or in prescribing medication.

As a medical consumer and as a patient who is attempting to form a partnership with a physician, you always have the right to know your test results. This is true whether tests are given in a doctor's office, a laboratory, or a hospital. Again, if you want to know the results of any tests, ask. Some doctors make it a practice to routinely share this information; others limit discussions about numbers and scientific tests because such information confuses some patients. Many people are bewildered or frightened by the medical system and have trouble remembering all the things that they are told.

If you believe your test results are higher than they should be, and your doctor doesn't mention it or make suggestions to bring the numbers down, ask for a concise explanation. Ask if there's something you can do to improve your results, or whether it's safe to ignore them. Remember, if you're a full partner in your treatment, you must spell out your concerns and take on some responsibility. In this partnership, it's your duty to point out items of concern that your doctor might not have noticed.

Blood Pressure

Your blood pressure should be checked every time you visit your doctor. A blood pressure test is a simple, noninvasive method of measuring the pressure inside your blood vessels, through which blood continually circulates, driven by the beating of your heart. High blood pressure may indicate that your blood vessels are constricted because of deposits of plaque, cholesterol, or other substances clinging to the vessel walls. High blood pressure is called *hypertension*. Normal blood pressure is 120/80 mmHG; numbers a few points different from these are of little concern. The number to the left of the slash, the systolic, shows the blood pressure of the heart muscle contracted. The number to the right, the diastolic, shows the blood pressure of the heart at rest. Readings are listed as millimeters of mercury, or mmHG.

You and your doctor should take steps to lower your blood pressure if tests show that it's too high. The United Kingdom Prospective Diabetes Study (UKPDS) found fewer heart-related complications and a lower death rate in participants with diabetes who tightly controlled blood pressure. Analysts of the UKPDS stated that controlling blood pressure was just as important as controlling blood sugar for people with diabetes who had both high blood sugar and high blood pressure. The Hyperten-

Checking Blood Pressure

120/80 mmHG	Normal
< 130/80 mmHG	Recommended
140/80 mmHG	High
200/140 mmHG	Extremely high

sion Optimal Treatment Study, completed in 1998, found that lowering the diastolic blood pressure to 83 mmHG from 90 could reduce the incidence of heart attacks by more than one-third in people with diabetes and that reducing this number to 80 could cut risks in half. However, these are admittedly difficult numbers to obtain.

The first stirrings of high blood pressure are systolic readings that are higher than 140 or diastolic readings that are higher than 80. Blood pressure above these numbers is dangerous and should be treated. Blood pressure in the range of 200/140 is considered extremely high. High blood pressure may be treated with medications, exercise, and changes in diet, including lowering your salt intake and increasing your intake of foods containing potassium.

Hemoglobin A1c Test

The hemoglobin A1c test, also called the HbA1c test, is the gold standard of all diabetes blood sugar testing. Your blood is drawn for this test. The American Diabetes Association (ADA) recommends at least two of these tests per year, and more if you are having problems controlling your blood sugar. At present, the medical profession is converting to standard measurements and results for this test, which measures the A1c portion of hemoglobin, although some practitioners still measure with an older glycosylated hemoglobin test whose numbers are slightly lower.

The hemoglobin A1c test is objective. The results will be accurate even if your blood sugar level is high or low on the day that you take it. This test yields a number that is useful to patient and doctor because it evaluates blood sugar control over a span of time.

Given in your doctor's office or a laboratory, a hemoglobin A1c test provides your doctor a precise reading of your average blood sugar levels over the past few months. It calculates your average blood sugar levels over the previous eight to twelve weeks, which is about the life of a red blood cell. Red blood cells are continually wearing out and being replaced in the human body. Hemoglobin is the red, iron-rich protein in red blood cells, which carry oxygen. Over time, hemoglobin attracts glucose in proportion to the amount of glucose present in the blood, and the test measures the percentage of damaged hemoglobin. This test shows you how successful you've been in your overall efforts to control blood sugar, because your own test results will be higher or lower than this average. The HbA1c test is sometimes used in combination with other tests to diagnose diabetes.

Many doctors set goals for their patients that are 1 percent higher than normal. Readings above 8 or 9 percent are now considered serious. A person whose diabetes is out of control may have HbA1c levels of 12 to 14 percent or more, which indicates that blood sugars have remained much too high over the past several months. The average reading for a person with diabetes in the United States is a 10, which is too high. The UKPDS established a 7.0 percent HbA1c as an ideal target for people with Type 2 diabetes. In that trial, the subject group with tight blood sugar control

Comparing Hemoglobin A1c and Blood Sugar

The following comparison between HbA1c and blood sugar levels gives you an idea of the relationship between this test and your blood sugar tests at home. In the following table, the normal range is 4 to 6 percent. The ADA recommends a target of below 7 percent for this test. Blood glucose correlations are from the National Glycohemoglobin Standardization Program, stated in plasma glucose, which is used now by most U.S. labs and most new blood glucose meters. Older meters often state results in whole-blood glucose values, which are also included here for comparison purposes.

HbA1c	Plasma Glucose	Whole Blood
6%	135 mg/dl	121 mg/dl (7.5 mmol/L)
7%	170 mg/dl	152 mg/dl (9.5 mmol/L)
8%	205 mg/dl	183 mg/dl (11.5 mmol/L)
9%	240 mg/dl	214 mg/dl (13.5 mmol/L)
10%	275 mg/dl	246 mg/dl (15.5 mmol/L)
11%	310 mg/dl	277 mg/dl (17.5 mmol/L)
12%	345 mg/dl	308 mg/dl (19.5 mmol/L)

whose HbA1c tests averaged 7.0 percent (versus 7.9 percent for the control group) achieved a 35 percent reduction in complications.

Note, however, that the hemoglobin A1c test is not a substitute for blood glucose testing at home. This is because results in the average range don't always mean that you've consistently kept your blood sugars in perfect control. Blood sugars may have bounced up and down, averaging out to a normal reading on the test even though control has actually been poor. Anemia can skew the results, as can other medical conditions such as sickle-cell disease. However, if you've made a serious effort to control your blood sugars, the results should be accurate and in line with those you recorded at home.

Ask what the equivalent blood sugar level is for your test results. If your own results don't jibe with the doctor's results, you may not be testing properly. Make an appointment with your doctor or a nurse educator to check your technique. Also check the accuracy of your blood glucose meter. A problem with your technique or your meter is more likely than a faulty reading of your test, although laboratory misinterpretation of test results occasionally happens.

Many doctors say that patients should know this test result number as well as they know their cholesterol level, because it is extremely important. One medical company is trying to develop a noninvasive form of this test that would not draw blood but would take measurements through a beam of light directed into the retina.

Lipid Profile

Another blood test, the lipid profile, measures the levels of such fats as cholesterol, triglycerides, and other lipoproteins. The American Diabetes Association recommends that you receive this test every year. Your lipid profile needs to be periodically evaluated by your doctor because these test results have a direct relationship with possible heart and vascular complications, such as hardening of the arteries.

A lipid profile will show abnormally high levels of fats, or lipids. If you have problems controlling fat levels, greater attention to blood sugar testing and control, plus redoubled efforts in the areas of diet and exercise, are often recommended. Lipid-lowering drugs may also be prescribed.

Cholesterol has received a lot of media attention in recent years, but cholesterol is not the only indicator of cardiovascular health. Cholesterol below 200 mg/dl, or 11.11 mmol/L, is considered acceptable, although the balance between "good" and "bad" cholesterol is more important. Recommendations for desirable levels of low-density lipoproteins (LDL), or "bad" cholesterol, have been lowered by the American Diabetes Association to < 100 mg/dl (2.6 mmol/L). Desirable levels of high-density lipoproteins (HDL), or "good" cholesterol, are > 40 mg/dl (1.1 mmol/L). LDL is called "bad" cholesterol because it builds up in the body, whereas HDL actually helps clear cholesterol out of the body. Having a good ratio of HDL to LDL is important. Hyperlipidemia, or diabetic lipemia, is associated with poor blood sugar control in Type 2 diabetes. This is reflected in high triglyceride

Lipid Levels

Low-Density Lipoprotein Levels

< 100 mg/dl (2.6 mmol/L)	Desirable
130–159 mg/dl (7.22–8.83 mmol/L)	Borderline
> 160 mg/dl (8.88 mmol/L)	High risk

High-Density Lipoprotein Levels

> 40 mg/dl (1.1 mmol/L)	Desirable

Triglyceride Levels

< 150 mg/dl (1.7 mmol/L)	Desirable

levels. Results vary from laboratory to laboratory, so if possible have the same laboratory perform all of your tests. Labs associated with academic medical centers and certified by the Lipid Research Clinics are the most reliable.

CRP Test

More frequently used is a test for C-reactive protein, or CRP. This test is used to assess heart disease risk, and several studies show that it apparently picks up potential heart problems that tests of cholesterol levels can't predict. Results are expressed in milligrams per liter, or mg/L. C-reactive protein, which is produced by your liver when you are sick, is a sign of inflammation. It may also predict the risk of developing diabetes.

CRP Test Results

< 1.0 mg/L	Low risk
1.0–3.0 mg/L	Average risk
3.0 mg/L	High risk

Urine Tests

Tests that check the level of protein in the urine help your doctor evaluate your kidney function. You should not have more than a trace of protein in your urine, because the kidneys normally recycle proteins. Excessive levels signal a loss of kidney

Microalbumin Test

< 30 mg	Normal
30–299 mg	Microalbuminuria
> 300 mg	Macroalbuminuria

function. A urine sample should be taken for analysis at every visit for the first five years of diabetes.

Concentrations of serum creatinine and blood urea nitrogen should be measured at least once a year. These are muscle breakdown products that are filtered through the kidneys. Levels of creatinine above 2.0 mg/dl or blood urea nitrogen higher than 30 mg/dl indicate a need for more frequent monitoring. Elevated levels of these substances indicate a decrease in kidney function.

A microalbumin test is now recommended as part of a comprehensive evaluation for all patients with diabetes. This test can find levels of excreted protein as small as 20 mg to 400 mg in the urine, a level of kidney damage that is still manageable—that is, the damage can be treated or reversed by medication.

An evaluation of kidney function includes a check of your blood pressure. High blood pressure hastens the progress of kidney problems and other complications of diabetes. If you have kidney problems and high blood pressure, they should be aggressively treated by your doctor.

In addition to urine tests, blood chemistry tests can measure levels of sodium, potassium, calcium, phosphate, and bicarbonate—chemicals that help a doctor assess the functioning of your kidneys, adrenal glands, and pituitary. Normal levels of each are as follows:

Blood Chemistry Test

Sodium	135–145 milliequivalents per liter of blood (mEq/L)
Potassium	3.5–5.0 mEq/L
Calcium	8.5–10.5 mg/dl
Phosphate	2.6–4.6 mg/dl
Bicarbonate	18–23 mEq/L

Oral Glucose Tolerance Test (OGTT)

Glucose tolerance tests involve drinking a solution containing glucose and then giving periodic urine and blood samples afterward. If the test reveals your blood sugar is significantly higher than normal, this confirms the presence of diabetes. Fasting is required prior to taking this test, which is typically given in the morning.

In people without diabetes who take a preliminary glucose challenge test, which involves the ingestion of 50 grams of glucose, blood sugar levels typically climb to about 140 mg/dl (7.8 mmol/L) in the first hour and then return to normal. If the results of this preliminary test are positive, a full oral glucose tolerance test should be given as soon as possible. Frequently, people with diabetes who undergo the OGTT experience symptoms of mild hypoglycemia, including weakness, sweating, or dizziness, during the second or third hour.

Oral glucose tolerance tests are not necessary for all people, but they are often used to diagnose gestational diabetes. The OGTT is recommended for only those pregnant women with positive preliminary screening tests and normal fasting plasma glucose levels. This test is not recommended for people who have been malnourished, have eaten fewer than 150 grams of carbo-

Indicative OGTT Readings

After an eight-hour overnight fast and then drinking 100 grams of glucose, called a "glucose load," pregnant women may be diagnosed with gestational diabetes if two plasma glucose readings equal or exceed the following levels:

Time Elapsed	Test Results
Fasting	90 mg/dl (5.3 mmol/L)
1 hour	180 mg/dl (10 mmol/L)
2 hours	155 mg/dl (8.6 mmol/L)
3 hours	140 mg/dl (7.8 mmol/L)

hydrates per day for more than three days, have been confined to bed for more than three days, or have been experiencing acute medical or surgical stress.

Fructosamine Assay

A relatively inexpensive test, the fructosamine assay checks the level of fructosamines, or sugars bound to certain proteins, over the pre-

Fructosamine Levels

1.4–2.7 mmol/L	Normal
2.0–3.9 mmol/L	Controlled diabetes
2.3–5.3 mmol/L	Sporadic control
2.8–5.0 mmol/L	Uncontrolled

vious seven days to three weeks. This test, like the HbA1c test, measures average sugar levels over a period of time, but the fructosamine assay is most frequently used to check blood sugar levels in pregnant women. Versions of this test have been approved for home use. One company is marketing a meter, similar to a glucose testing meter, that can be used approximately once a week to track changes in blood sugar control over the past two or three weeks.

Other Specialists, Other Tests

The monofilament test for sensation in the feet should be given at every doctor's visit. A foot specialist may also test you to determine if you have poor blood circulation in your extremities, which will show up as variations in your blood pressure. To find these problems, your podiatrist or orthopedist may use blood pressure cuffs, like those for testing blood pressure in your arm, but place them on your thigh, calf, ankle, and forefoot. These test results tell your podiatrist how effectively your blood is circulating to certain parts of your body, such as your feet and legs. In the special cases in which an artery may need to be reconstructed, a vascular surgeon may give you an arteriogram. This test involves injecting a special dye into an artery and taking x-rays, which can show where the arteries have become clogged.

Ophthalmologists, or eye doctors, perform most of their tests through visual examinations. A face-to-face examination by an ophthalmologist is considered better than a picture of the eye taken by a machine, which is being substituted for an eye exam by some health maintenance organizations. Testing for glaucoma, an easily controlled eye problem that affects many people over age forty, involves measuring eyeball pressure and cannot be done by a machine.

Frequency of Medical Tests

Here are some standard recommendations for the most important medical tests given by the doctor who is treating your diabetes:

Each visit
- Blood glucose (finger stick)
- Results of your blood glucose meter against lab test results
- Blood pressure
- Urine analysis (for protein)

At least every six months
- Hemoglobin A1c test

At least once a year
- Lipid profile, including cholesterols and triglycerides
- Blood counts and blood chemistry tests
- Blood and urine tests for electrolytes, blood urea nitrogen, and creatinine; urine testing for microalbuminuria, if complications involving the kidneys are suspected

Electrocardiograms and tests for thyroid-stimulating hormone are recommended for people with diabetes when certain clinical indications are present.

Medical tests are useful to you and your doctor in charting the progress of your health. Ask about your test results. If you wish, keep a medical file containing your own set of test results. Test results slightly above generally accepted guidelines may or may not be a cause for concern. Unacceptable results should prompt your doctor to recommend certain actions, including referrals to medical specialists. The next chapter examines the day-to-day prevention of minor problems, another aspect of self-management.

11

Vigilance

Good Daily Hygiene Prevents Many
Health Problems

SELF-MANAGEMENT SUCCEEDS one day at a time, but thinking ahead will help you ward off many of the problems associated with diabetes. This chapter offers recommendations on day-to-day hygiene and prevention. It introduces strategies to help you maintain a healthy heart as well as healthy feet, eyes, skin, kidneys, and teeth—areas of the body at particular risk. You'll also learn about precautions to take on sick days, when blood sugar almost always goes out of whack.

Good self-management essentially means taking good care of yourself. Assign yourself responsibility for educating yourself, coordinating your self-management efforts with the efforts of your medical team, adopting a healthier style of eating, and taking action to arrange for a less stressful, more physically active life. Connecting all of these diverse elements in a positive way helps you control your blood sugar, and this affects the way you feel.

In addition, taking good care of yourself demands spending a little time each day checking out your body, and taking sensible precautions with your health. A bit of daily vigilance may well prevent or minimize physical problems.

Things to Do Every Day

Every day, examine your body for a few minutes. Peruse your feet, skin, teeth, and eyes. These areas can be sites for complications. If you spot even minor problems developing, call the doctor who treats your diabetes and report your findings. Of course, diabetes doesn't immunize you against other health problems, so don't assume that every ache and pain you have is related to diabetes.

Think of the few minutes it takes you to make a daily self-examination as your personal early warning system. This is particularly applicable to the feet and skin, which you should scan every day for any unusual growth, swelling, redness, cuts, or bruises. Note any problems with your eyesight or with the general appearance of your eyes, as well as anything different in other parts of your body.

As you go about your life, take precautions that can prevent problems. For instance, always wear gloves or protective clothing for tasks such as working in the garden. Treat cuts, blisters, and other small medical problems promptly.

If you're not sure how to treat a problem, call the nurse at your doctor's office and ask. Write down what the nurse tells you, and follow these instructions. Be sure to find out what to look for over the next several days or as healing progresses. Also ask how soon you should call back to make an appointment if the problem doesn't go away. Unless you've been instructed otherwise, for minor problems, you should ask to speak with the nurse rather than the doctor. If the nurse can't handle the problem, or if it requires your doctor's attention, the nurse will ask the doctor to speak with you.

Regular Doctor Visits

Regular visits to a foot doctor, an eye doctor, and a dentist are effective preventive measures and a part of good diabetes care. If you aren't referred to a foot doctor or an eye doctor right away, you may have to assert yourself. Gently remind your doctor that you must be referred to medical specialists at certain times. When you bring this subject up, you may want to have a copy of the latest recommendations of the American Diabetes Association with you; you can obtain these guidelines by calling the organization's toll-free phone number, which is listed in the "Resources" section at the back of this book.

"My experience with managed care is that unless you educate yourself about what tests need to be done and when, you may not get those tests done," says an assertive woman who always sees the specialists she needs to see. "My doctor may be ready to refer me at one year, but if he doesn't, I'm there to remind him to do it."

Controlling your blood sugar is the best preventive measure of all because of the serious complications of diabetes that are linked to high blood sugar. Maintaining blood sugars within your normal range will accelerate the rate at which you heal, whereas out-of-control blood sugars will retard natural healing. Controlling your blood pressure through exercise and other means is also a top priority.

In much of the world, weather conditions change drastically throughout the year. Changes in weather mean changes of clothing and lifestyle for all people. As the seasons roll around, plan appropriately. Make sure that you have the items you may need, such as moisturizing cream and a hat in the winter, or a supply of sunscreen and sunglasses with UV protection in the summer and during ski season. Check the condition of your shoes from time to time, even if you live in the tropics, because shoes with proper support and cushioning help keep your feet in good shape.

Foot care, heart health, eye care, kidney function, skin care, and dental health are all areas in which you can take preventive action, in addition to controlling your blood sugar and blood pressure. What follows are some generally accepted recommendations and precautions to consider when formulating your personal program of preventive medicine.

Healthy Feet

Among the most common medical problems experienced by people with diabetes are problems related to the feet. The human foot was made to walk on uneven grass and dirt, notes Southern California podiatrist Arthur Fass, D.P.M., not on flat, hard surfaces such as concrete, which over time may break down the joints of the foot. Prevention through appropriate daily foot care is necessary. When you walk around in your daily work or when you exercise, do so in comfortable shoes. If you've received special instructions from your doctor or a foot specialist for treating your feet, follow those orders, and promptly report any symptoms as requested. Successful blood sugar control will help you sidestep many foot problems.

The human foot is a complex thing; though relatively small, it's strong enough to support the weight of the human body. Each foot is composed of twenty muscles and twenty-six bones. When you walk, each foot becomes slightly longer and wider when it touches the ground. Because your feet are vulnerable, you should select stable and well-cushioned shoes that match the shape of your feet as much as possible.

It's false economy to purchase cheap, uncomfortable shoes, or to wear shoes that are worn out. If you don't have a good pair of walking shoes or running shoes, go shopping. Most athletic shoe manufacturers sell suitable walking shoes, as does Rockport. These shoes may be worn every day. For certain types of exercise, hiking boots and athletic shoes come in various weights and styles. Buy high-quality shoes that fit comfortably the first time you slip them on. If you use orthotic devices, make sure that they fit into the shoes you're trying on. Orthotics, or shoe inserts, can relieve pressure in a problem area of the foot, perhaps one that has ulcerated and has been bandaged. If your foot has ulcerated, orthotics can help guard against further ulcerations, improve balance, and provide some control that may lessen pain. If you need special shoes, get them.

Rubber soles are often recommended over leather soles because rubber helps absorb shock. Proper shoes insulate the foot from shocks, rocks, and friction. Shoe inserts made by companies such as Spenco also can be helpful in absorbing friction from the foot, according to R. Diane Gilman, a doctor of podiatric medicine and an instructor at the University of Southern California. Some podiatrists recommend running shoes over walking shoes because they usually provide more support for the foot and more toe room. Whatever you select, always wear dry, comfortable socks—perhaps two pairs for longer walks. Treat problems when they appear. Foot pain, lower-back pain, blisters, bunions, and calluses can be signs of poorly fitting shoes.

Daily inspections are the key to heading off foot problems, which can include infections, ulcers, and deformities. Keep a watch for the following symptoms of poor circulation:

- Dry skin on the feet
- Loss of hair on the feet
- Cold feet
- No pulse in the feet
- Redness of the feet when they are hanging down (or a whitening of skin when feet are raised above the level of your heart)

Inspect both the top and bottom of your feet every day, using a mirror or magnifying glass if necessary. A thorough foot inspection will take less than a minute. If you cannot inspect your feet because your sight is impaired, or you have arthritis or are severely obese, enlist the help of another person, such as your spouse. In addition to the preceding indicators of poor circulation, be on the lookout for these other obvious signs of trouble:

- Redness
- Blisters
- Cuts
- Scratches
- Ingrown toenails
- Cracks between toes
- Discoloration of skin
- Any other observable changes

Wash and carefully dry your feet every day, using warm, soapy water. Do not use hot water, which can spread bacteria and can cause burns in people with reduced sensations in the feet. Many skin problems among people with diabetes are a product of the narrowing of small blood vessels near the skin, a condition called *microangiopathy*. This condition delays healing and increases the chances of an infection from the bacteria and fungi that live on the skin. Tissues can also dry, causing skin to crack and become infected. Good blood sugar control is the key to reducing the susceptibility to infection. Skin creams marketed to people with diabetes such as Alpha-Keri, Nivea, or Eucerin can do much to keep the skin moist. Most of these creams contain urea; a concentration of 10 to 25 percent urea is probably best, but some trial and error may be necessary. Apply the cream to the heel first and then work it toward the toes, but don't apply it between the toes, where excess moisture can be a problem. If your heels are very dry, try applying the cream before bed for two or three nights and wearing socks or a protective wrap during the night. To keep athlete's foot at bay, sprinkle antifungal foot powder between your toes, where sweat and moisture can accumulate.

File your toenails straight across so that they are even with the skin on the tops of the toes. Use only an emery board; you can take toenails down a bit at a time. Do not use razor blades, knives, or scissors to trim your toenails, because a slip of the blade will break the skin, possibly causing an infection. Avoid over-the-counter medicated corn or wart removers on your feet, because many contain an acid formula that can be harmful to skin (this is why the labels now contain warnings against their use by people with diabetes). Do not soak your feet, particularly if you have sores on them. Don't use a whirlpool. Also, it's better not to use nail polish, which can promote the growth of fungus under the nails. Rule number one for good foot care is this: if you see something wrong with your feet, such as redness or inflammation, get off your feet for a while.

If you notice a cut or scratch during your daily foot inspection, wash your feet and then apply a mild antiseptic such as Bactine. Cover the area with a dry sterile bandage, not cellophane tape or Band-Aids, which can irritate the skin. If a cut or scratch doesn't heal within a day or two, call your doctor. Try to stay off your feet until the site heals.

Use common sense when the weather turns very hot or cold, keeping in mind that you may not feel hot and cold sensations as well as other people do. Never walk barefoot, especially on hot sidewalks or in snow. Don't get your feet sunburned. Don't use hot water bottles or heating pads on your feet, which can burn the skin. Don't stick your feet into a hot bath without checking it first with your finger.

Numbness, shooting pains, and a pins-and-needles type of pain in the feet are signs of nerve damage, or *neuropathy*. If you have neuropathy, inspect your feet more than once a day. Changing shoes and socks several times a day will remind you to make more frequent visual inspections. All shoes basically allow the foot to slide after three to four hours of wear, so changing shoes and socks also minimizes your chances of getting blisters and infections. Don't cross your legs often or wear tight elastic hose. If you smoke, try to stop, especially if you have neuropathy.

If you suffer an ingrown toenail or other foot problem, see a podiatrist or an orthopedist; ingrown toenails can become infected and cause severe problems if left unattended. Follow your doctor's orders regarding foot care. For foot ulcers, which are difficult to heal, your doctor may ask you to try one of the new pharmaceutical products such as Apligraf, Dermagraft, Fibracol, or Regranex, which are available by prescription and in some cases must be applied by a health-care professional. There is more information on treatments for foot problems in Chapter 16.

The American Diabetes Association recommends that your doctor check for sensation in your feet at least once a year as a part of a comprehensive foot exam. Unfortunately, many doctors forget to do this test unless they are reminded to do it by patients. Simple home test kits have been developed at the Gillis W. Long Hansen's Disease Center, in Carville, Louisiana. While noting that home tests are usually accurate, researchers nevertheless recommend that any results obtained at home be confirmed by a health-care provider to guard against mistakes.

An estimated 15 percent of people with diabetes will develop a serious foot problem at some time in their lives. Some community-based studies found that foot ulcers occurred in 2 to 3 percent of people with diabetes over the course of one year. Part of the reason for this is that the feet are located at the farthest ends of the cardiovascular and nervous systems. As recommended by your doctor or exercise physiologist, a program of exercise may improve poor blood circulation, but your feet should be checked before and after any exercise sessions. Your doctor may prescribe drugs that help the red blood cells pass through clogged arteries. Not every person with diabetes has microvascular, or small blood vessel, disease in the feet, but this is a common site for it to appear.

A Healthy Heart

If you are more than 20 percent over your suggested weight, you can automatically lower your chances of having heart disease and high blood pressure by losing weight. Adopting a comprehensive program of self-management, including lifestyle changes, will help stave off heart problems. Exercise, stress reduction, and changes in eating all benefit your heart. These lifestyle changes are always preferable to more expensive medical interventions, which carry risks as well as benefits.

Out-of-control blood sugar is a major factor in vascular complications. When it comes to your ticker, high blood sugar should be considered toxic. High blood pressure is an additional hazard. Major risk factors for heart disease in all people are obesity, smoking, and high levels of cholesterol in the blood. Diabetes is another risk factor for heart attacks and strokes, which are the number one cause of death in Western countries.

The primary indicator of heart and vascular health is your blood pressure, which should be checked every time you visit a doctor. About 50 percent of people with diabetes develop high blood pressure. If your blood pressure is high, your doctor may ask you to lower the amount of sodium, or salt, in your diet; increase your potassium intake; and reduce your weight—all of which may help lower blood pressure and reduce the strain on the heart. Regular exercise can lower blood pressure as much as any other intervention.

In 1997, the American Diabetes Association recommended aspirin therapy for people with diabetes at high risk for cardiovascular disease, to prevent a first heart attack or stroke. It recommended aspirin at a rate of 81 mg to 325 mg per day (a baby aspirin contains 81 mg, an adult aspirin 325 mg). People who have had a heart attack, a stroke, or angina; people with a family history of heart disease; smokers; and people who are obese or have high blood pressure are among those considered high risk. However, people under age thirty as well as those who have active liver disease, a tendency to bleed, or certain other medical conditions are not candidates for aspirin therapy.

Lack of exercise is a major contributor to heart problems, as is cigarette smoking. Nicotine damages the linings of your blood vessels, makes your blood clot faster, and constricts your arteries—factors that can precipitate blockages in your blood vessels as well as strokes and heart attacks. Lowering your risk of heart problems is a compelling reason to stop smoking, something you and anyone else will eventually succeed in doing if you keep trying. Having a healthy heart is achievable if you maintain an optimum weight and a healthy lifestyle.

Healthy Eyes

Annual visits to an eye doctor will help you avert complications involving the eyes. See an ophthalmologist immediately after being diagnosed with diabetes, or when your doctor or optometrist recommends it. After the initial examination, you should see an ophthalmologist and receive an exam with your eyes dilated once a year, or more frequently if you have eye problems.

Good control of blood sugars slows the development of eye complications and often prevents the most severe problems. A research study published in the *Journal of the American Medical Association* in 1989 showed that people with diabetes who maintained good control—defined as blood sugar levels within 10 percent of normal—experienced no eye damage during the course of the study. In the same study, when blood sugars ran consistently higher than 50 percent of normal, 37 percent of the subjects experienced retinopathy or other eye complications.

Because both the common cold and the flu can be carried to the eyes by the hands, be sure to wash your hands before you touch the areas around your eyes if you are sick. Also, always wash your hands before putting in or taking out contact lenses.

Some ophthalmologists believe that eye exercises, such as looking into the distance periodically when doing close work, reduce eyestrain. Sunglasses that protect the eyes from ultraviolet rays are recommended when you're in bright sunlight, on the water, or in the snow.

If your eyesight is failing, or if your eye swells, call your doctor right away and ask for an appointment or a referral to an eye doctor. See an eye doctor immediately if you lose your vision or if you experience acute pain in your eye. Another symptom that needs immediate attention is the sensation that a curtain is being lowered in the eyes. In all of these cases, insist that your eye doctor see you right away.

Two studies published in the *Journal of the American Medical Association* found that age-related damage to a central part of the cornea, called the macula, is twice as common in smokers than in nonsmokers.

Healthy Kidneys

The kidneys are the janitors of the body, filtering out waste material from the blood and sending it through the bladder and urethra, to exit the body in the form of urine. The kidneys work by moving blood through a series of tiny tubes called nephrons, at the end of which are small, bunched blood vessels called glomeruli that actually do the filtering. The glomeruli eliminate harmful substances containing nitrogen and reclaim and recycle valuable proteins.

Every time you visit the doctor who's treating your diabetes, you should be tested for protein in the urine and for other signs of kidney damage. Even if you have lost some kidney function, you can rein in the deterioration of your kidneys by maintaining good blood sugar control—by eating healthy foods, exercising appropriately, and taking your medications. Work with your dietitian to develop a proper diet, which may be low in sodium or protein, a particularly important part of lowering blood pressure, which takes stress off your kidneys.

When pampering your kidneys, don't forget that old staple of dietary advice: drink plenty of water. Drinking a lot of clear, clean, calorie-free water every day will help keep you free from many kidney and urinary tract problems. As a bonus, drinking more water may make you a little more physically active in the form of frequently trotting to and from the bathroom, and you'll flush harmful bacteria and waste materials out of your system before they can cause serious problems.

Healthy Skin

Skin problems can be caused by high blood sugar damaging the tiny blood vessels that nourish the skin, restricting the availability of infection-fighting white blood cells. For people with diabetes, infections of the skin can be both more numerous and slower to heal.

To maintain healthy skin, avoid soaking your body in the tub for long periods of time, because this may cause dry, cracked skin. On the other hand, washing and carefully drying the skin every day will help prevent infections.

Severe sunburns are stressful to the body and can substantially raise blood sugar levels. Some exposure to light every day is healthy, but avoid excessive sunlight; if you must go out in the midday sun, protect your skin with a sunscreen of at least 15 SPF (sun protection factor). In the summer, check for skin rashes, particularly in the folds of your skin. Good skin care for all people means avoiding exposure to excessive wind and weather.

Extremely dry skin can be caused by dehydration, a result of inadequate consumption of fluids, illness, or poor blood sugar control. Achieving better control of blood sugars will minimize dryness. If your skin remains dry, try a moisturizing skin lotion containing lanolin. Always drink adequate water during the day, and drink more water than usual when you exercise.

Healthy Teeth and Gums

Brush your teeth at least twice a day with a soft-bristled toothbrush, and floss once each day, taking care to pull the floss a bit below the gum line. People with diabetes should see a dentist or periodontist at least every six months. Regular visits can help you avoid infections in the teeth and gums. Be sure to tell your dentist and the dental hygienist who cleans your teeth that you have diabetes, and specify what medications you take.

More frequent dental visits of at least one every six months are recommended for people with diabetes, particularly those who are older. This is because diabetes can retard the rate of healing from infections anywhere in the body, including the mouth. Excessively high levels of glucose in the blood nourish the sugar-eating bacteria that live in the mouth, allowing them to multiply more rapidly. In addition, the thickening effect that diabetes has on the blood inhibits the normal infection-fighting abilities of white blood cells.

Problems to watch for include gingivitis, or periodontal disease, which occurs around the teeth without pain in the gums. Periodontal disease results when bacteria grow between the teeth and gums over a long period. It is sometimes first identified when people notice blood on the toothbrush while brushing their teeth, or when a dentist notices that a patient's gums are discolored (a result of the infection). Bad breath can be another indicator of periodontal disease. Sometimes a dentist first suspects the presence of diabetes and recommends that the patient see a doctor.

Periodontal disease occurs more frequently in people who have diabetes, as well as in older people in general. About 80 percent of older adults have it. The worst cases are treated with oral surgery, followed by regular deep cleanings. If untreated, periodontal disease results in bone erosion and eventually loss of teeth. Periodontal disease should be taken care of for the simple reason that it makes dealing with diabetes more difficult. Infections in the mouth rile up your blood sugar, but having periodontal disease treated will help you control it. Brushing your teeth twice a day with fluoride toothpaste, flossing once a day, and eschewing sugary foods will help you control gum disease, as will good blood sugar control. When visiting a dentist or periodontist, try to have your blood sugar in goal range. If you are on insulin therapy, schedule your appointments at appropriate times for you to avoid low blood sugar.

A fungal infection called thrush is also more common in people with diabetes, particularly those who smoke or wear dentures, but thrush can be treated with medication.

Sick Days

Illness has pronounced effects on the body of someone who has diabetes. You'll have to handle yourself with special care on the days that you are sick. Sickness will make your blood sugar rise, sometimes to unusually high levels.

Call your doctor anytime you have an illness that lasts more than twenty-four hours, when your temperature exceeds 101 degrees Fahrenheit, or when you are vomiting and can't keep down liquids, foods, or medicine. If possible, be prepared to tell your doctor the time and results of your latest blood sugar tests, your temperature, and how much food and liquid you are taking.

Even a minor illness such as the common cold or the flu triggers the release of certain hormones that cause the liver to send additional glucose into the bloodstream. These hormones impede the action of insulin, raising levels of blood sugar.

Special Precautions

As a precaution, do not exercise when you are sick. Follow your meal plan and drink extra fluids, because your body will need plenty of nourishment to fight off disease.

If you take insulin, immediately report any illness to the doctor who treats your diabetes. You may require more insulin than usual when you are sick. If you take a diabetes medication, do not miss a dose; ask your doctor if you should increase the amount you take when you are sick.

When you are ill, try to monitor your blood sugar every three to four hours, or ask someone to do your blood testing for you. Ask your doctor what blood sugar test results should prompt you to call. A reading over 300 mg/dl (16.66 mmol/L) is probably a concern.

Drinking more liquids than normal is important to prevent dehydration when you are sick. Since your kidneys won't be able to handle all the excess glucose, it will spill out into your urine. You'll urinate more frequently, and this will pull additional fluids out of your body and dehydrate you. *The Joslin Guide to Diabetes* suggests that you guard against dehydration by drinking a cup (8 ounces) of fluid every half hour or so, alternating salty fluids such as broth or bouillon with low-salt liquids such as water. If you can eat, follow your meal plan but substitute sugar-free liquids such as water for other fluids. If you can't eat, the *Joslin Guide* suggests that you alternate foods containing sugar, such as fruit juices, Jell-O, and Popsicles, with sugar-free drinks.

Diabetic Coma

The most serious concern during illness is the diabetic coma, also called the *hyperglycemic-nonketotic coma*. It's brought on by a major physical stress to the body, such as surgery or infection, which causes a dangerous combination of high blood sugars, insulin deficiency, and excessive urination, resulting in serious dehydration. Undiagnosed diabetes combined with illness, as well as reactions to certain drugs, may also trigger the onset of this acute complication.

A diabetic coma comes on slowly, usually over a period of days or weeks. It's most common in older people; the average patient who experiences it is sixty years of age. Blood glucose readings average 1,000 mg/dl. This condition greatly upsets the

Seven Reasons to Stop Smoking

1. Smoking raises blood sugar.
2. Smoking raises blood pressure.
3. Smoking cuts the amount of oxygen reaching body tissues, leading to heart attack, stroke, stillbirth, and other dangers. For instance, the risk of dying of cardiovascular disease is three times higher among people with diabetes who smoke.
4. Smoking damages blood vessels and can lead to blood vessel disease and foot infections.
5. Smokers are more likely to get nerve damage or kidney disease.
6. Smoking makes limited joint mobility more likely.
7. Smoking can cause cancers of the mouth, throat, lung, and bladder.

normal balance of chemicals inside the body and, in the more severe cases, can lead to death. Medical treatment involves hospitalization and aggressive replacement of the fluids lost by the body, including potassium, which is typically depleted, and sometimes supplemental insulin.

Call your doctor immediately if you experience symptoms of this condition when you are sick—excessive urination, great thirst, hunger, drowsiness, nausea or vomiting, abdominal pain, mental disorientation, or shallow rapid breathing. Likewise, call your doctor immediately if your blood glucose levels test higher than 600 mg/dl, which is characteristic of this life-threatening complication. If you cannot reach your doctor, proceed to a hospital emergency room and explain your situation.

Taking a little time each day to practice preventive measures and good hygiene will help maximize good health. Vigilance in regularly checking and cleaning the feet, skin, teeth, and other parts of the body can prevent small problems from becoming big ones. Taking care of yourself on sick days is fundamental to dealing with the physical aspects of diabetes. And if you become pregnant, the topic of the following chapter, you'll have to take especially good care of yourself.

12

Pregnancy

Taking Good Care of Yourself
Prevents Most Problems

SEVERAL SPECIAL PRECAUTIONS are in order when women with diabetes become pregnant, or when pregnant women develop diabetes. The chances of a successful pregnancy are quite good when proper medical treatment is received.

When the twentieth century began, about 27 percent of women with diabetes who attempted to have children died giving birth. Most women with diabetes who were pregnant lost their babies. Today, due to medical advances, in the United States the survival rate for mothers with what is called gestational diabetes is the same as for all women: almost 100 percent. Infant survival rates now exceed 97 percent.

Although babies born to mothers with diabetes are at three times the risk for birth defects compared to babies born to mothers without diabetes, good medical care, built around a dietary and exercise regimen for the mother, helps produce normal, healthy babies.

Gestational Diabetes Mellitus

Gestational diabetes mellitus (GDM) is a form of Type 2 diabetes that develops during pregnancy and usually resolves itself after the baby is born. Pregnant women are at greater risk of developing gestational diabetes if they have diabetes in their families, if they weighed more than 9 pounds at birth, if they are obese, if they are over the age of thirty, if they experienced gestational diabetes in previous pregnancies, or if they have had a history of glucose intolerance. Other risk factors for gestational diabetes include frequent miscarriages, recurring urinary tract infections, a history of toxemia, and unexplained stillbirths. Gestational diabetes occurs in about 4 percent of pregnant women, although the incidence can be as high as 14 percent in some groups. Gestational diabetes may be controlled with adequate medical care and lifestyle changes.

This form of diabetes occurs because during pregnancy, the hormones produced by the placenta—including estrogen, progesterone, and human placental lactogen—cause insulin resistance, which is characteristic of Type 2 diabetes. Occasionally, routine blood sugar testing during pregnancy uncovers a case of Type 1 or Type 2 diabetes that has not been previously diagnosed.

An early indicator of diabetes in a pregnant woman is fasting blood sugar that tests above 100 mg/dl, which is considered impaired fasting glucose, or above 126 mg/dl, which is a provisional diagnosis of diabetes. True gestational diabetes is typically confirmed about six months into pregnancy through an oral glucose tolerance test. If a woman is considered high risk, a glucose tolerance test may be given immediately upon the discovery that she is pregnant and again at the usual time if the first test is negative.

Healthy Babies

Women who already have diabetes can conceive and deliver healthy babies. Ideally, they should develop and follow a plan to maintain good control of blood sugars before their pregnancies. Vitamin supplements—particularly folic acid, a B vitamin—have been shown to appreciably reduce the likelihood of birth defects. Iron and calcium supplements are also normally prescribed.

Some complications of diabetes, such as retinopathy, can worsen during pregnancy and then return to normal after the baby is born. This complication should always be evaluated by medical specialists. Women with Type 2 diabetes who take diabetes pills will be advised to stop taking them and to immediately begin taking insulin, which does not harm the fetus or cross the placental barrier. Insulin requirements often soar during the pregnancy, but they can drop during the final weeks.

Blood Sugar Control

A primary goal of pregnant women with diabetes should be maintenance of their blood sugar levels through diet, moderate exercise, and sometimes insulin. Gestational diabetes is not normally treated with diabetes pills, because their effects have not been studied very much or cleared by the U.S. Food and Drug Administration for use during pregnancy. It is generally believed that hypoglycemic medications could harm the fetus or result in poor blood sugar control during pregnancy. Good control of blood sugars is necessary for the proper development of the fetus, especially during the first trimester of pregnancy.

Under ideal circumstances, pregnant women with diabetes are cared for by a team composed of a nurse clinician, a dietitian, a counselor such as a social worker, an exercise specialist, and medical doctors, including a diabetologist or an endocrinologist. The ideal medical team also includes an obstetrician or a perinatologist (a doctor who specializes in high-risk pregnancies), and a pediatrician or neonatologist (a pediatrician who specializes in the care of newborn babies). Pregnant women with diabetes should visit their doctors more often than women who do not have diabetes.

The first line of therapy during pregnancy is a diet plan that involves eating six small, well-planned meals, including a bedtime snack, with some protein and fat in each meal to even out glucose response. Medical nutritional therapy is the only treatment necessary for perhaps 75 percent of women with gestational diabetes.

Moderate exercise is usually recommended for all pregnant women, but women with diabetes may have limits imposed on their activities. For instance, pregnant women with diabetes may be asked to limit their exercise to the same intensity and duration at the same time each day, to ensure maximum blood sugar control. If blood sugar or ketone levels are too high, insulin will be required, although a few doctors now offer sulfonylurea drugs as a second option.

Pregnant mothers are often asked to check their ketones before breakfast, and before taking insulin if that is part of their treat-

Blood Sugar During Pregnancy

Ideal blood sugar levels during pregnancy are as follows:

Fasting	< 95 mg/dl (5.33 mmol/L)
2 hours after a meal	< 120 mg/dl (6.7 mmol/L)

ment. If ketones are present in more than trace amounts for two days in a row, it's necessary to call the doctor. Ketones may indicate that starvation ketosis is present. Although it sounds serious, this condition is often remedied by a simple adjustment in eating schedule or by a change in the composition of the bedtime snack.

Pregnant women should also check their ketone levels when they are sick, even with a minor illness such as a cold or the flu. One problem is that some medications prescribed during pregnancy, such as Macrodantin and Pyridium, may cause false positive results in ketone tests. However, many doctors advise an immediate check of ketones if the blood sugar is above 200 mg/dl at any time during pregnancy. Blood glucose levels that are extremely high can result in harm to or the death of a fetus whose pancreas is working hard to produce extra insulin.

Among the noninvasive tests that pregnant women with diabetes frequently receive are an ultrasound test (including a biophysical profile), a fetal movement-counting test done by the mother at home, a fetal heart rate analysis, and an oxytocin challenge test. An amniocentesis is often done in women over age thirty-five. All of these tests monitor the condition of the fetus as it develops. Well-controlled blood sugar at the time of delivery minimizes the risk of complications in the newborn baby.

Breast feeding is usually recommended, with calcium and iron supplements for the mother. Breast feeding is delayed if the infant is placed in a newborn intensive care unit; in these cases, mothers can request breast pumps to stimulate their supply of milk.

An additional glucose tolerance test is often given from six to twelve weeks after delivery of the baby, to determine if the diabetes has disappeared or stabilized, or if glucose tolerance remains impaired.

If you have had gestational diabetes, even if it disappeared after your pregnancy, the scales tilt toward your experiencing it again the next time you become pregnant. If you return to an ideal body weight, controlling your weight through exercise and diet, your odds of developing Type 2 diabetes within five to ten years are less than one in four. If you were obese before pregnancy and remain so after pregnancy, you have a 60 percent chance of developing Type 2 diabetes within five to ten years. Family planning is requisite for all women who have experienced this form of diabetes and desire more children, since blood sugars should be under control before conception.

Gestational diabetes may usually be controlled through lifestyle changes and good medical treatment. But these days, even some children get Type 2 diabetes, as the next chapter explains.

13

Children with Type 2 Diabetes

Involve the Family in Lifestyle Changes

TYPE 2 DIABETES, once called maturity-onset diabetes because it almost never appeared in children, has been increasing rapidly in kids. The increase in children with diabetes parallels rising rates of childhood obesity and low rates of childhood exercise. Unfortunately, poor nutritional habits and exercise-free lifestyles are leading straight to metabolic problems for more and more children. If you are reading this book because you or a spouse has been diagnosed with diabetes, be aware that your children are also at risk for this disease.

Francine Kaufman, M.D., a Los Angeles pediatric endocrinologist and the author of *Diabesity*, emphasizes that ten years ago, a child with Type 2 diabetes would have been considered so rare that the case might have been written up in a medical journal. Today, her clinic at Children's Hospital is filled with children with Type 2 diabetes. These children are usually overweight, and this is often true of their parents.

"Diabetes is not a little bit of a problem. It's a huge problem for the people who have it," Dr. Kaufman states.

About one-third of the cases of diabetes found in juveniles are now Type 2 diabetes. The typical age for a child being diagnosed with Type 2 diabetes is thirteen and a half years, but the disease has been found in children as young as four. It has also been estimated that more than 4 percent of U.S. adolescents from twelve to nineteen years old have metabolic syndrome, which is associated with Type 2 diabetes.

Obesity is the greatest single risk factor for Type 2 diabetes in children, particularly obesity of the central type, creating an "apple shaped" figure, in which much fat accumulates around the belly and waist. More than 90 percent of children with Type 2 diabetes are overweight. Another risk factor is puberty, since insulin secretion increases and insulin sensitivity decreases by about 30 percent in adolescents. Kids with Type 2 diabetes frequently have a condition called *acanthosis nigricans*, which is characterized by dark or discolored folds of skin on the neck, armpits, or groin, but the condition improves with lifestyle changes.

It's no secret that American children are not any more physically active than American adults. Many children are spending large amounts of time watching TV, surfing the Internet, or playing video games, activities that require no exercise. Studies have shown that children who watch more TV undertake less physical activity and consume more sugary foods, which are advertised on children's TV programs at the rate of approximately twelve food advertisements per hour. In a study conducted at two California schools, reducing children's TV, video, and DVD watching from twelve to eight hours per week helped kids control their weight, compared with kids whose watching habits were not changed.

A Family Approach

The best approach to take is making the entire family's lifestyle healthier, rather than focusing a lot of negative attention on the child with diabetes. In many cases, some of the adults in the family also have diabetes, or are overweight, and toning up the entire family can help everyone concerned. With education and thoughtful changes, older family members, friends, and care-givers can be brought on board the healthy lifestyle caravan.

Although drug therapy can help, the real key to managing Type 2 diabetes in kids is increasing exercise and decreasing sweets or carbohydrate portions. Some families believe they need to keep cookies and chips in the house "for the kids." It's been established that one of the main culprits in obesity among young people is sugar-containing fluids, such as soft drinks and sweetened drinks of various sorts. Many soft drinks contain the equivalent of 6 to 8 teaspoons of sugar, often in the form of concentrated and highly fattening corn syrup. Switching to bev-erages such as water or tea at meals, minimizing the junk food and trips to fast-food restaurants, and keeping healthy drinks and snacks in the house is a good way to initiate a healthy fam-ily lifestyle.

A healthy diet for kids with diabetes consists of five to nine servings of vegetables and fruits daily, along with several serv-ings of whole grains, some low-fat dairy products, small portions of lean protein, and just a little fat or sugar-laden foods. This is a nutritious diet for all people.

Physical Activity

Physical activity is a must for kids with diabetes. Recent U.S. government guidelines recommend for children at least sixty minutes of physical activity on most, or preferably all, days of the week. For a child with diabetes who is overweight and inactive, exercise should begin gradually, but it should be done on a regular basis, increasing in occurrence and duration. If the child chooses to get more active by walking to school instead of riding when weather conditions permit, or participating in intramural or team sports, that is an excellent beginning.

Much more is possible, however. Diabetes is often a family problem, and there can be more of a family solution. Families can get more active as a group, rather than trying to force the family member with diabetes to exercise alone. Getting active does not necessarily mean joining a sports club, or even participating in organized classes, although this way of increasing exercise can work for some families.

Getting active can be as simple as having family walks after dinner, walking to a restaurant for breakfast on Saturday, taking family hikes, dancing, bicycling, roller-skating, golfing, or any other activity that family members enjoy. More pleasurable activity can have the effect of making the entire family a little bit healthier.

Drug Therapy

In addition to lifestyle changes, diabetes in young people is often first treated with an oral agent such as metformin, or with insulin, along with medications to lower blood pressure as needed.

Metformin is the first drug of choice because it has less risk of low blood sugar reactions and doesn't promote weight gain. If a combination of lifestyle changes and three to six months of metformin therapy doesn't bring blood sugar down adequately, another medication or insulin may be added. Treating first with insulin is the best option when the doctor is uncertain whether the patient has Type 1 or Type 2 diabetes, as sometimes occurs. Very small amounts of insulin are often effective.

Good diabetes care for children entails educational sessions on diabetes and nutrition by a diabetes educator, blood sugar monitoring at home, regular visits to the doctor, and checks of blood pressure and hemoglobin A1c levels every three months.

A Positive Approach

Adolescents with diabetes sometimes have no symptoms when the disease is diagnosed, but a positive approach emphasizing lifestyle changes is almost always best.

According to an analysis of diabetes in young people published in *Diabetes Care*, by Zachary T. Bloomgarden, M.D., an endocrinologist at the Diabetes Center in the Mount Sinai School of Medicine, in New York, therapeutic guidelines for asymptomatic children with Type 2 diabetes should focus first on improving the diet and increasing exercise. Changing your lifestyle is always easier said than done, Dr. Bloomgarden observes, but these changes are vitally important for young people with diabetes. Approaches that inspire self-confidence and a feeling of control, combined with weight maintenance and regular follow-ups, will probably work best with this age-group, he says.

Making children feel isolated and singled out with special exercise regimens and special diets, while constantly watching them, is not a happy solution for either the children or the parents. As behavioral experts have observed, many young people have a tendency to resist discipline and to take contrary action as a way of asserting their individuality.

Strong feelings may surface in the family as a result of your child's diagnosis of diabetes. If your child gets to the stage of noncompliance, or if you are feeling overwhelmed yourself, seek professional help right away.

Diabetes in children can be managed. If lifestyle changes are undertaken for the family, a healthier family can be the ultimate result. The emotional and social aspects of diabetes, which affect all people, are dealt with in the next chapter.

14

Mental Health

A Look at the Social and Psychological
Aspects of Diabetes

EMOTIONAL AND SOCIAL support is important to all people after a diagnosis of diabetes. However, you may face some new problems within your family or social circle—the people on whose support you rely. You may have to hone your communication skills to manage certain feelings and issues that arise. Along the way, psychological treatment or counseling may help. A diabetes support group may assist you in coping. Still, even with supportive family members and friends, you may occasionally face depression or some form of diabetes burnout. During these times, you need to uncover problems in your self-management routine, address them, and move on with your life.

Without thinking about it, most people form a network of people with whom they interact and who support them—a personal support system. Your family, your friends, your neighbors, your coworkers, the people in your religious life or community or social club—even individuals you see only occasionally, such as your barber or hairdresser—may regularly bolster you in ways that mean a lot to you. A diagnosis of diabetes, or your own attitudes about diabetes, may send emotional ripples throughout that support system and temporarily upset the balance of your life. Be prepared for this.

You may experience serious emotional distress at certain times, with intense feelings such as loneliness, anger, fear, and depression. Sometimes you may feel overwhelmed, fighting to cope with all the sensations and changes in your life as you adjust to the reality of having—and managing—diabetes. Frustration, despair, rage, even the fear of having forever lost control over life are common among people with a chronic illness. Since diabetes requires more of your own participation than almost any other disease, you may pressure yourself to stay on top of it twenty-four hours a day. The sheer volume of these demands may prime you for feelings of guilt and disappointment. Strong emotions intensify stress; constant stress can cause an emotional riot. Knocked off balance by powerful emotions, you may struggle to control your blood sugar and return stability to your life.

Connections with people who know you and care about you, in your family or your community, are fundamental in maintaining a healthy life. Research validates that people who interact with others live longer, healthier lives than those who exist in a lonely, isolated environment. Two lengthy research studies, one conducted near San Francisco and the other in eastern Finland, monitored the effects of social isolation on men and women over a period of five years or more. Both studies concluded that people who felt socially isolated were 200 to 300 percent more likely to die of various causes, compared with those who considered themselves part of a community. Even when the research subjects had a risky medical condition, such as high blood pressure, their membership in a church, synagogue, or social club provided substantial protection against dying from heart disease. Another study, centering on people aged sixty-five and older, conducted at Duke University Medical Center, in Durham, North

Carolina, found that people without social support were more than three times as likely to die during the course of the research, compared with people who had social support. No one lives forever, of course, but these and many other research studies indicate that it's healthy to participate in community life.

At all times, remember that you are more than a person who has a disease. You are not your diabetes. Many aspects of self-management of diabetes become routine after a while, requiring only a few minutes here and there. But to live a successful life, with or without diabetes, it's advantageous to have a positive self-image, an appreciation of what you have, an affirmative attitude, and the belief that you can help and empower yourself. In the drama of our lives, we all play many roles—child, sibling, parent, grandparent, friend, coworker. Having emotional and social support from the other players on the stage is a valuable asset, but such support is not always forthcoming.

Family Problems

According to Steve Degelsmith, a Los Angeles marriage and family therapist who facilitated support groups for people with diabetes for several years, family relationships can run awry in two main ways when a family member develops diabetes: through overinvolvement or through underinvolvement.

Overinvolvement

Family members may see the person with diabetes as someone who needs to be rescued, someone so fragile that the person can't care for him- or herself. This overinvolvement can create a powder keg of strong feelings and resentments on both sides. To the person with diabetes, family members may seem to be turning into parents. They may become the "diabetes police," monitoring your food and lifestyle choices to an extent that is humiliating to you. You may feel that you're being lectured everywhere you turn. If your family members become overinvolved in your self-management program, you may lash out at them with a burst of anger, or you may drift into a depression. Too much of this type of protection erodes intimacy and trust and creates a buildup of antagonism, guilt, anger, resentment, and other strong feelings that are not easily resolved.

Underinvolvement

On the other hand, family members may not be as involved with the person who has diabetes as that person would like. Certain family members may back off because they can't accept their own unresolved feelings about being abandoned, about supporting other people, or about disease. The faithful, caregiving family member may sometimes get tired of taking you to the doctor's office and hearing you complain. Underinvolvement may also spring directly from the person with diabetes, who projects an air of "I don't need help," causing other family members to withdraw because they believe that their help isn't wanted or needed.

Financial squabbles about who maintains the insurance or who pays which bills may become increasingly contentious and lead to feelings of resentment, isolation, or depression. Some people try to escape from these situations by throwing themselves into being good parents or grandparents, or becoming obsessed with a hobby or recreational activity. Some even become workaholics, which may serve to avert some conflicts for a while but doesn't resolve any emotional conflicts. There are variations on this scenario that can arise in many social situations as well as in the workplace.

Social Support

In almost every family, Degelsmith believes, better communication skills would soothe these wounds. Most people are only partially skilled in this area. When the feelings that accompany a chronic disease such as diabetes are added to the emotional mix, honest communication becomes both more important and more difficult. All family members need to develop the ability to tell other people how they feel and what they want, and to speak up when their feelings are hurt, all in an effective but nonjudgmental manner. Everyone can improve his or her ability to listen. The most productive actions and words tend to be those that express love, care, and concern. Effective support is respectful and sympathetic.

You may not always get all of the emotional or social support that you need. Family members who are emotionally upset themselves are often difficult to approach, and their responses can be unpredictable. They may be sitting on a different kind of emotional powder keg than the one you're on. Remember that anger frequently masks fear. Members of your family may be resentful or jealous of the attention that you receive (or of the attention they don't receive) because you have diabetes. The same feelings can occur outside the family. In the world of urban singles, for instance, where friends function much like extended families, a dispute with a friend may hurt you as deeply as a problem in your family.

Hold on to your hat. You may feel as if you've climbed onto an emotional roller coaster. Recognize that you may have emotional ups and downs, and give yourself permission to experience your own tempestuous emotions. All of the bad feelings will pass. Hold on to your sense of humor too. Give yourself permission to laugh at the stupid little things in your life that can seem so preposterously important at first. Be as patient and as kind with yourself as you are with other people.

Outside your inner circle, you'll have to decide whom to tell that you have diabetes. You aren't required to reveal your medical condition right off the bat to everyone you meet. You may choose to never tell certain people, particularly those who gossip about you or who may sabotage your efforts to keep your weight or blood sugar under control. Keeping your diabetes a secret from everyone you know probably isn't a wise strategy either, because this may make you feel isolated, dishonest, or guilty, as if you're hiding a terrible secret.

Be as honest and as open as possible. Keep in mind that the way in which you present your diabetes to other people helps shape how they view it.

Communication Skills

Diabetes may be accompanied by grieving, particularly when you are first diagnosed or when complications threaten. Give yourself leave to experience all of your strong feelings. Use stress-management techniques, such as those suggested in Chapter 5, to ratchet down the negative stress in your life. Talk about your feelings with family members or friends who can listen to you and align with you. You can sometimes defuse other people's frustrations by listening carefully to them and then responding candidly and tactfully to what they say. You may need to make a special effort to hear well-intended comments as support, rather than as criticism or unsolicited advice. Living with a chronic disease can also be stressful for your family members and friends, since they may become involved and feel some additional responsibility. This may bring some family members into contact with their own worst fears, such as the fear of being abandoned. If you're the person with diabetes, you will sometimes have to support other people rather than the other way around.

The trick is to assert yourself without getting aggressive or lapsing into passivity. An assertive communications style involves verbalizing things you think are important, asking for what you want directly, saying yes and no when you need to do so, and more or less "owning" what you say. This all takes some courage and tact, especially if important family members are involved, but assertiveness is a skill that can be learned. If the process seems intimidating, you can plan out what you want to say to a person beforehand, thinking of the best time and place to say it and then appropriately communicating your message.

Make an effort to communicate some of what you're going through. Listen when people who care about you speak. Try to make your verbal exchanges true conversations, containing genuine expressions of feelings, rather than lectures, evasions, contests, manipulations, or judgments. Begin sentences with "I feel" rather than "You should."

If you're the person with diabetes, don't forget to share even your small successes with family members or friends who will understand and be appreciative. Sharing good news will help them as well as you.

Honest, effective, two-way communication is a subtle art. It can be an inroad toward resolving emotional issues, or at least learning to live with them. Recognizing that you're not honestly or effectively communicating how you feel is a prerequisite. Identifying a particular problem or a pattern of miscommunication is another. Communicating your concerns in a nonjudgmental way can promote the healing process after the problems are identified. Remember that communication continues over the course of a relationship, rather than ending after one or two dismissive remarks.

Initiating a conversation about your medical condition will give other people permission to discuss it. Some individuals won't talk about it unless you break the ice. If you do begin this discussion, some family members or friends may feel that they're being put on the spot at first. You may have to introduce the subject more than once before they really feel that it's all right to talk about it. Others may surprise you by communicating or helping out more than you would expect.

If you ask for assistance from people, be specific. Your family or friends may be able to help by giving you magazine articles or books to read about diabetes, by offering you a ride or accompanying you to the doctor's office, by helping you shop for food, or by keeping you company while walking or in an exercise class. Children and grandchildren need to understand that they have not somehow caused your diabetes and that you don't expect them to be able to fix it. Classes on communication skills are presented in many communities and can be quite useful.

Depression

Depression is twice as common in people with diabetes, and the depression often is more severe and lasts longer than in people without diabetes. According to Sheldon Gottlieb, M.D., who directs the Diabetes–Heart Failure program at Johns Hopkins Healthcare, diabetes apparently doubles the risk of suffering from depression, although it is not clear whether the diabetes causes the depression, or vice versa. After you are diagnosed with diabetes, or have experienced a complication, depression can be part of the normal grieving process, but it should be treated if it persists. People who are depressed are more likely to engage in unhealthy behaviors such as overeating, not exercising, and not taking care of their diabetes. According to research at Washington University, in Saint Louis, people with diabetes respond well to psychological counseling, antidepressant medications, or a combination of both. Cognitive therapy is a simple form of therapy that teaches you to reframe destructive or self-defeating thoughts, and it has yielded good results at improving depression. Making a special effort to lower the level of stress in your life through exercise, meditation, or other means can also help. Controlling blood sugar can lead to improvements in depression, anxiety, and other conditions.

Professional Counseling

Your personal support system may not be enough to help you get through the first days and weeks of managing your diabetes, or deal with any complications. After all, you are simultaneously grieving the loss of your previous state of health and being forced to face your mortality. During difficult times, you may find it useful to visit a mental health professional or to join a diabetes support group.

Consider seeing a psychiatrist, psychologist, or social worker if you succumb to a depression that won't go away, or if you exhibit frequent and repeated self-destructive behavior, such as going on eating binges or forgetting to take your medicine. Also consider seeing a mental health professional if you have a constant sense of being overwhelmed or a sense of helplessness that blocks your ability to learn or to take action, or if you simply can't ask for help from anyone else. Another sign that you need to see a mental health professional is participation in negative social situations that hamper your self-management of diabetes. A 1999 study of people with diabetes who suffered from depression analyzed the results of medical care alone versus medical care and psychotherapy. Some 85 percent of the group receiving psychotherapy and medical care reported feeling less depression, versus 27 percent of the group receiving only medical care. In this study, people receiving psychotherapy also achieved lower HbA1c levels (9.5 percent, versus 10.9 percent).

Personal counseling may help things. Mental health professionals can be worthwhile additions to your health-care team because they can help you sort through the issues that you face and begin dealing with them. In addition, counseling with a minister, priest, rabbi, or other religious leader is often a source of comfort.

Support Groups

Joining a support group of people with diabetes can be beneficial in many ways. Support groups can extend and strengthen your emotional support system. They give people with diabetes, and sometimes their families, a safe place in which to confront the issues relating to diabetes. At their best, support groups provide a comfortable, secure place where unique feelings may be heard and understood.

Support groups should consist of compassionate, supportive men and women. They exist not only for people with diabetes but also for people dealing with other life and health issues, such as overeating or cancer. The format for support groups is similar to that employed in group therapy, where several people gather at a particular time to discuss issues of interest to them, under the eye of a trained facilitator. All of the discussions are confidential. In diabetes support groups, the common bond is diabetes.

Typically, support groups are not limited to the discussion of psychological problems. The best groups make sure to discuss personal successes with diabetes. Group members often underpin each other in a positive, caring way. Support groups provide a forum in which people can hear how others deal with problems, pick up practical tips, and receive encouragement in their own lives.

Contending with the daily ups and downs of diabetes can be a lonely and frightening process. Talking about it with people who are also tackling these situations can be profoundly helpful. There is comfort in people honestly discussing their problems and offering each other solace. Support groups give many men and women who participate in them an empowering lift.

"The support I've gotten from the people in this group is really important to me," one woman told her group.

"I got more information here than I ever got from any doctor," said another man.

Asked what she got out of the group, another woman sighed and replied simply, "Emotional support."

Diabetes support groups are open to everyone with diabetes. They're not ideal for everybody, but they can be a godsend. Each support group meeting is different and usually contains different people. Sometimes, discussion begins on a set topic. Most groups have members who attend every meeting and others who come only from time to time.

To locate a support group in your area, call your local American Diabetes Association (see the "Resources" section at the back of the book for contact information). Support groups are also sponsored as educational programs by hospitals, clinics, health-care organizations, and individual doctors. American Diabetes Association chapters can provide referrals to support groups or to one-on-one programs run by volunteers. Large cities often have several groups, making it easier to find one you like. If no support group exists in your area, you may want to start one; the American Diabetes Association can provide guidance.

How to Use a Support Group

Within a support group, you may be able to build your own smaller network of people to call or meet. Participating in a support group may enable you to better deal with some of your powerful feelings—and your tangible problems. Remember, however, that support groups are not composed of medical experts. They are not intended to be forums for medical advice or psychotherapy.

Ideally, support group facilitators are mental health professionals trained by the American Diabetes Association to understand the medical, psychological, and social issues relating to diabetes. Facilitators should know emergency procedures for any medical or psychological problems that arise. A facilitator should keep meetings on a supportive keel, stopping anyone who constantly complains or criticizes others. Avoiding medical misinformation is crucial; groups not led by a professional facilitator should have a medical resource person who can be called between meetings to clarify any medical questions that arise.

In the best support groups, people who have "been there" can warn you to avoid trying to do too much too fast. They can offer words of encouragement when you set or meet a goal and can make practical suggestions for managing some aspects of life with diabetes. A supportive group can help a member work through a crisis. People in support groups can even laugh about certain aspects of diabetes; this is a knowledgeable laughter that you may find nowhere else.

Most people in diabetes support groups have Type 2 diabetes. Groups typically meet in the evening or on weekends, when working people are better able to attend. Most are free. A group may be topic oriented or may provide speakers such as medical doctors who can answer questions. It's nice when members can suggest topics for future meetings.

You don't need a referral from your doctor to participate in a support group, although some doctors will happily refer you to one. Unfortunately, some doctors may discourage participation. If you think a support group might help you, make up your own mind. Attend three meetings or so before you decide whether the group is for you.

In places where support groups do not exist, educational meetings often take place from time to time. Such sessions can be handy places to meet other people who are dealing with diabetes. You may be lucky enough to meet somebody who can be your telephone buddy when you simply need someone to talk to. Be attuned to people with positive attitudes. Avoid negative types, who may hamper your efforts to learn and persevere.

Diabetes Burnout

It's not uncommon to occasionally feel "burned out" from the constant need to practice good self-management. You'll have days when you just don't want to test your blood sugar, don't want to go to your aerobics class, or don't want to pass up your family's favorite dessert. On such days, you not only don't want to have diabetes but also don't want to think about it at all.

Relief from burnout can sometimes be as simple as allowing yourself to take a holiday from your diabetes for a day or two. At other times, the reasons for your diabetes burnout may elude you. If that happens, step one is to identify problem areas in your diabetes management.

William H. Polonsky, Ph.D., the author of a book titled *Diabetes Burnout*, has developed a test to help people identify the areas in which they may be experiencing emotional distress with their diabetes. Polonsky has defined diabetes burnout as a feeling of being mentally overwhelmed by the disease, which can itself trigger poor self-management and subsequent physical and mental problems.

To identify the factors in your burnout, you may want to discuss your self-management program with a mental health professional or with a member of your health-care team. Here are some possible problem areas, according to Polonsky:

- Not having clear and concrete goals for your diabetes care
- Feeling discouraged about your diabetes regimen
- Feeling scared when you think about having and living with diabetes
- Uncomfortable discussions or confrontations about diabetes with family members, friends, and acquaintances who do not have diabetes
- Feelings of deprivation regarding food and meals
- Feeling depressed when thinking about having and living with diabetes
- Not knowing if the moods or feelings that you are experiencing are related to your blood sugar levels

- Feeling overwhelmed by your diabetes regimen
- Worrying about low blood sugar reactions
- Becoming angry when you think about having and living with diabetes
- Being constantly concerned about food and eating
- Worrying about the future and the possibility of serious complications
- Feelings of guilt or anxiety when you get off track with your diabetes management
- Not "accepting" your diabetes
- Feeling unsatisfied with your relationship with your diabetes physician
- Feeling that diabetes is taking up too much of your mental and physical energy every day
- Feeling alone with diabetes
- Feeling that your friends and family are not supportive of your efforts to manage your diabetes
- Coping with complications of diabetes
- Feeling "burned out" by the constant effort to manage diabetes

Distress and Burnout

Emotional distress related to diabetes is apparently quite common, according to Polonsky. Approximately 60 percent of the respondents in one of Polonsky's studies had a serious diabetes-related concern; no one in that study reported an absence of stress. Worrying about future complications and feeling guilty or anxious when getting off track with diabetes management were the most frequently cited complaints.

If you think that you're flunking some aspect of your self-management program, talk about your problem with an appropriate person on your health-care team, such as your medical doctor or diabetes educator. It may be that the weight-loss goals that you've set are too aggressive for you at this time. If so, make new goals that you can realistically achieve. Don't set your sights unrealistically high; that sets you up for disappointments. Try not to be too hard on yourself, because negative, self-defeating behavior can foster even more of the same.

If you're slipping into burnout, evaluate where you are. Whenever you think outside input might help, speak with a mental health professional or a religious counselor, or visit a support group. You may find other ways to help yourself. It may benefit you to keep up with medical advances in diabetes by attending lectures and educational programs covering the basics of good care, the latest medical discoveries, and new treatment techniques. This can freshen up your self-management program, since new ideas can be exciting. You may even want to participate in a clinical trial; several are usually under way at any one time.

Don't slip into the trap of self-pity. Looking at other people and imagining the stress-free, happy-go-lucky lives they have may sometimes throw you into a funk. Not everyone has diabetes, of course, but you stumble into an emotional trap by blithely assuming that everyone has a better life than you. All human beings have problems. Diabetes is merely a fact of your life. Recognize your own strong feelings about diabetes, accept them, and then move on.

The writer Robert Louis Stevenson lived an extremely productive life while afflicted by tuberculosis, an incurable disease in his time. "Life," the author of *Treasure Island* observed, "is not a matter of holding good cards, but of playing a bad hand well."

The psychological and social aspects of diabetes can affect your self-management in myriad ways. Problems can include either overinvolvement or underinvolvement of family and friends. Learning to communicate your feelings to the people you care about will help make your emotional ups and downs manageable. In some cases, psychological counseling or a support group may be the ticket to a better outlook. If you experience diabetes burnout or depression, identify the areas in which you are having problems, and look for help in the appropriate place. Among the changes you may experience are the effects of diabetes on your finances, the topic of the next chapter.

15

Money

How to Manage the
Financial Aspects of Diabetes

THIS CHAPTER LEADS you through some of the financial aspects of diabetes. While even perfectly controlled diabetes costs money, you can anticipate and manage many treatment costs to some extent. If you have health insurance, it will typically pay a major portion of many of the costs that you incur, although all costs are never covered. A summary of items to check for in your policy after you have been diagnosed with diabetes is included here, as are suggestions for interacting with insurance companies, health maintenance organizations, and Medicare. Getting new insurance, switching carriers, and other ways to pay the costs of diabetes are also discussed.

Diabetes is time intensive for both the people who have the disease and the doctors and other health-care providers who treat and educate patients. Dealing with diabetes for your entire life drives up treatment costs.

The American Diabetes Association estimates that the costs of treating diabetes, including lost productivity from missed days at work, totals about $132 billion per year in the United States. According to a consensus statement issued by the National Institutes of Health, the costs for dialysis as a result of kidney fail-

Estimated Costs of Diabetes

Ongoing Costs

	Estimated Cost per Year*
Medical Treatment	
Diabetes specialist,	
4 @ $150–$300 each	$600–$1,200
Eye doctor visit and exam,	
1 @ $100–$150	$100–$150
Foot specialist visit and exam,	
2 @ $85–$150 each	$170–$300
HbA1c test, 2 @ $40–$50 each	$80–$100
Lipid/cholesterol panel,	
1 @ $50–$60	$50-$60
Test Strips	
2 per day @ $0.50–$1 each	$365–$730
4 per day	$730–$1,460
Diabetes Pills	
No insurance (generic and	
brand name)	$600–$2,400
Insurance co-payments of	
$10–$45/month	$120–$540
Insulin	
1 bottle/month @ $30–$50 each	$360–$600
Syringes @ $17–$25/pack of 100	$50–$100

Occasional Costs

	Onetime Cost
Blood glucose meter	$0–$150
Food scale	$15–$70
6 glucose tablets	$1.50
Insulin and insulin supplies carrying case	$5–$30
100 insulin-disposal containers	$5

*Actual costs may vary from these estimates.

ure in people with diabetes totals more than $1 billion per year. Given that more people are being diagnosed, and at a younger age, the costs to society are expected to increase over the next several years.

Even perfectly controlled diabetes can cost a person $1,000 to $2,000 per year, not including reimbursements from health insurance. As shown in the accompanying sidebar, further costs are incurred when you factor in the frequency of doctor visits, medications for diabetes, and supplies. Four visits to the doctor who treats your diabetes, one visit to the eye doctor, and two visits to a foot specialist each year are recommended by the American Diabetes Association, as are two HbA1c tests and at least one lipid profile. The services of a diabetes educator, a dietitian, an exercise physiologist, a mental health professional, and other medical specialists may be partially covered by health insurance or Medicare.

Some of the costs of diabetes treatment are covered by most health insurance policies. Most routine medical costs, such as doctor visits, medicines, and laboratory tests, should also be covered by insurance. A portion of the costs of a home glucose testing meter and supplies may be covered. Complications inflate total medical expenses, but coverage by Medicare, Medicaid, health insurance, or government programs may soften this financial blow.

As with any purchase, shopping around will save you money on items that you must purchase out of your own pocket, since costs vary from pharmacy to pharmacy, and some items are available online. Rebates are offered on many glucose testing meters, and a few meters are practically given away. If you are a regular customer who buys many medications, you can sometimes negotiate discounts with pharmacies on medications and supplies, particularly if you do some price shopping, present merchants with evidence of the lowest prices you can find, and ask them if they'll match these prices. Some insurance companies have special discount arrangements with certain pharmacies. Also, some mail-order houses specialize in diabetes supplies.

Several of the diabetes pills are available in generic form, which can be 70 to 90 percent less expensive than brand-name medications. Insulin syringes and lancets may be bought in bulk and be reused to cut costs, although sensible sanitary precautions must be taken to keep the needle points protected and clean.

Lifestyle Costs

When you are referred by your doctor, the services of a diabetes educator may be covered by insurance. The services of a registered dietitian are covered by many insurance plans on a case-by-case basis. The services of an exercise physiologist are usually not covered, although a few plans do pay for them. The services of a mental health professional may be covered within certain limits.

The doctor who treats your diabetes may work with a particular diabetes nurse educator or refer you to an educational program. Although diabetes education is cost-efficient and necessary, the costs of such programs conducted outside your doctor's office may not be reimbursable by your health insurance, Medicare, or Medicaid. Take advantage of any educational programs available to you through your health-care provider. If you have not been through an outpatient program that teaches how to manage the day-to-day aspects of diabetes, consider paying for such a program out of your own pocket. Most are inexpensive and a wise investment in your health. You can locate a local diabetes educator or an educational program by calling the toll-free number for the American Association of Diabetes Educators, listed in the "Resources" section at the back of the book. Watch for lectures and panel discussions on diabetes treatment offered through clinics, hospitals, universities, health-care organizations, or your local chapter of the American Diabetes Association.

Except for the services of a nutritional consultant or a registered dietitian, out-of-pocket meal costs should actually decline if your whole family adopts a healthier eating style. Avoid the more expensive processed foods by incorporating home cooking and unprocessed whole grains, fresh fruits, and vegetables in your meals to replace those TV dinners. A food scale, some measuring cups, and a few good cookbooks are all modest, onetime expenses.

Out-of-pocket expenses for adopting a more physically active lifestyle can be as modest as $50 or $60 for a good pair of walking shoes, or a few dollars for an exercise class at the local YMCA. The cost can rise to thousands of dollars per year if you decide to invest in a sports club membership, regular sessions with a personal trainer, special vacations such as cross-country skiing trips, or home exercise equipment.

If you need to see a psychologist, psychiatrist, or social worker, insurance may pay a portion of these fees, particularly if the therapy is short term. Many communities have mental health clinics where counselors will see you at low cost; fees are generally based on a sliding scale according to the client's income level. In most cities, low-cost psychological counseling can be obtained at clinics run by colleges and universities. Some private therapists will accept less than their normal hourly rates if you explain that you do not have insurance coverage. Also, many ministers, rabbis, and other religious leaders counsel their members. Support groups affiliated with the American Diabetes Association do not charge a fee, but bear in mind that support groups are not a substitute for therapy.

Miscellaneous costs that are not covered by health insurance include new—and smaller—clothes that you must have if you lose weight, travel to and from the doctor's office, parking fees, and subscriptions to magazines or newsletters specializing in diabetes.

Managed Care

In an effort to contain rising medical costs, the insurance industry is moving toward managed care. Health insurance was once almost exclusively a fee-for-service model, in which the patient paid a portion of the bill and the insurance company paid the rest, often an 80-to-20 split, with the insurance company paying 80 percent. A deductible of perhaps $1,000 per year, the amount you paid out of your own pocket, was imposed, with services beyond that covered according to the policy. Under these plans, you could usually see any doctor you wanted to or any specialist to whom you were referred. By 2004, however, more than half the population was being covered by some form of managed care. All together, 177 million Americans were in some form of managed care—109 million in preferred provider organizations (PPOs) and almost 69 million in health maintenance organizations (HMOs).

PPOs are networks of doctors, hospitals, and other providers who render services as patients are received. Claims for PPO visits are submitted after the visit and are reimbursed minus the co-payment. In the health maintenance organizations, the patient pays a premium in advance and then makes a small co-payment of perhaps $5 to $10 for each doctor's visit, test, or procedure. In both PPOs and HMOs, the primary care physician acts as gatekeeper for all medical services, referring the patient to specialists such as endocrinologists, ophthalmologists, and podiatrists. This arrangement can sometimes relegate the diabetologist or endocrinologist to the role of consultant, with your primary care physician handling many of your regular visits and tests. This works fine if your primary care physician is experienced in treating diabetes and understands what is involved in proper treatment. However, the HMO or PPO structure becomes a problem when you think you need to see a specialist but your primary care physician won't refer you. In such a case, you may have to assert yourself to get the referrals. So far, only a few HMOs have "point of service" options that allow you to see a specialist on your own, even if your primary care physician doesn't think it's necessary to refer you.

There are several types of HMOs, and many are operated by insurance companies. Some involve groups of physicians. Some, like Kaiser Permanente, are large nonprofit organizations. A few that were nonprofit, such as Blue Cross, are developing HMOs and for-profit divisions. Moreover, some health-care companies and hospitals are merging. Even government programs such as Medicare are shifting toward the HMO arrangement. The gist is that not every expense will be covered under any insurance policy. Check what your policy covers, and be prepared to explain your coverage to your doctor if necessary.

You could be fortunate enough to get one of the really good doctors in a particular HMO. This doctor should understand diabetes care and make all of the referrals suggested by the American Diabetes Association's Patient's Bill of Rights at the appropriate time. If this is not the case, and you are not happy with your care, ask to see another doctor. If you don't wish to exercise that privilege, perhaps you could help educate your doctor about diabetes. The American Diabetes Association's 2005 Clinical Practice Recommendations are a good place to begin. These guidelines are easily available by calling the toll-free number listed in the "Resources" section. Respect your doctor's training and expertise, but respect yourself, too.

Know the standards for good diabetes care, and insist on them from your physician. If your doctor says that you need a test or a referral to a specialist, and your health plan won't cover it, you can usually prevail if you are tenacious and assertive. Put your case in writing, and send copies to the appropriate people. Get an appeal started right away, meet all the stated deadlines, and ask for another hearing if you're turned down. If the issue is important, be prepared to carry your case as high as it will go. If you can't seem to get what you need from the health insurance company's bureaucracy, ask your doctor to support you. If the dispute drags on for too long, and your medical doctor says you need the treatment promptly, consider getting the treatment and paying for it yourself under protest, or putting it in financial limbo by withholding payment until the issue is resolved.

Costs Covered by Insurance

If you have just been diagnosed with diabetes, you may want to find out which costs your insurance plan will cover. This knowledge will help you plan a budget, since costs not covered by insurance are your responsibility. Each insurance plan is different.

When checking your policy or shopping for a new one, consider your needs to see particular doctors, your out-of-pocket payments for medications and supplies, and coverage for hospitalization and ancillary services. Many PPOs cover blood testing supplies, including a meter and strips. HMOs often cover some supplies. Many health insurance providers offer a pharmacy plan that involves co-payments of $5 to $10 for a thirty-day supply of any prescribed drug. Always ask about deductibles and co-payments, which are your responsibility. The following sections highlight points to weigh when looking over or comparing health insurance plans.

Doctors' Visits

Can you keep your present doctor and continue to visit the specialists you've already seen? Can you see a doctor or specialist when you need to see one, or are limits imposed?

Diabetes Supplies

Are needed supplies such as a glucose testing meter, strips, and syringes completely covered? If not, what are the limits of the insurance plan? Does your coverage limit your reimbursement to a specified number of strips per month or per year? Are syringes, meters, and strips covered as durable medical equipment—equipment that can be used repeatedly? Are all types and brands of meters and strips covered, or only a few? Do you need a doctor's referral in order for your supplies to be covered? Will these items be covered under the pharmacy benefits section of the plan, in which a prescription will be needed and limits may apply? Are specific medical requirements necessary in order for your doctor to approve the purchase of any of these items?

Diabetes Medications

Can you get all of the medications and prescriptions that you need this year? What are your out-of-pocket costs? Is there a limit, or a ceiling, on your prescriptions? Are only brand-name or only generic medications covered? Is your choice of a pharmacy limited, and if so, how convenient is the available pharmacy? What co-payment is required?

Hospital Coverage

If you need hospitalization, are you required to go to a particular hospital? Which doctor will take care of you in that hospital? If you're not sure what type of care you will receive, call the hospital's public affairs office and request a copy of the mission statement, which will help you understand the emphasis at that hospital. Or walk into the hospital lobby and get the "feel" of the place firsthand.

Ancillary Services

Are services such as a diabetes educator, a dietitian, physical therapy, dialysis, social services, and psychiatry covered by the insurance plan? Are there dollar limits or provider limits to these services? Is your use of these services restricted to a certain number of visits per year?

Insurance Coverage

The first thing you should do when reviewing your health insurance policy is to make sure that your premium payments are current. Ask for the most recent plan booklet from your carrier, and be certain that you understand what benefits are available, so that you can receive all the coverage to which you are entitled. This is not the insurance company's responsibility. If you don't submit a claim in a timely manner for something covered by your policy when necessary, some insurance companies won't pay the claim.

If you know ahead of time what procedures you'll need, you may file for preauthorization before receiving medical services. Your request should specify the proper preauthorization code numbers, as well as a description of any treatment you expect to have. The insurance company can then tell you in writing how much it will authorize for a particular treatment.

If you have a question about what your policy covers, call the insurance company's toll-free claims department hotline, and ask for a supervisor. Many experts say that it's best to politely ask for help, rather than to shout or rave at insurance company employees. Even so, at times, you may need to bravely and politely assert yourself. Whenever you speak with someone at your insurance company over the telephone, write down that person's name, the date of your conversation, and what you were told. Always ask the person to whom you speak to put what he or she tells you in writing. If a written document or fax is not forthcoming, write a letter to that person spelling out exactly what you understood the person to have said and asking for written clarification if you've misunderstood or misinterpreted anything from that conversation.

You may want to collect all your insurance and medical information in a medical records file. It can be useful to have a central location for all the paperwork related to your medical treatment. You can keep medical records you receive anywhere, such as in a portable filing cabinet or even in an old shoebox. You may find this file helpful when working out a dispute with your insurance company or when you need to locate copies of documents or letters to establish a point. Organized materials can further help you in evaluating your overall financial costs and help you at tax time, since some out-of-pocket costs not covered by health insurance, such as travel to and from the doctor's office, may be tax deductible.

If your plan requires you to file specific forms for reimbursement, request a supply of blank forms to keep on hand. Make copies of all the forms that you submit, along with all correspondence with the insurance company. Carefully review your medical bills for accuracy, and report any errors.

Insurance reimbursements and payments can be aggravatingly slow. Don't give up if your insurance company won't pay a claim that you believe is legitimate. The staff at your doctor's office can sometimes be helpful in getting resolution. For instance, they can check to see if your claim contained the correct procedure code and diagnosis when it was submitted.

If your insurance problem is difficult to resolve, get on the telephone and speak with your insurance broker or an insurance company representative. If the first person to whom you speak doesn't want to help you, or doesn't seem to understand what you are saying, ask to be transferred to that person's immediate supervisor. Continue this procedure until you get someone who will respond to your complaints. Insurance companies all have procedures to review claims; the company will review your claim if you follow its procedures. If a hearing doesn't allow your claim, small claims court can be an option for relatively small (often under $3,000) claims. If you strike out with the insurance company, you can also call the state department of insurance, since insurance companies are certified by the states. Write to your member of Congress. Speak with a lawyer. As a last resort, hold a press conference. In most cases, legitimate insurance claims are eventually paid, although it can take a lot of patience and time.

To resolve a dispute with your doctor in an HMO, call a care manager or benefits supervisor at your HMO. When you call, explain your rationale; HMO staff members can frequently negotiate with your primary care physician. If the dispute intensifies, however, it may be in your best interest to switch doctors.

Medicare's PPO and HMO members also have the right to appeal decisions about what medical services their HMOs will cover. However, appeals may take six months or longer to be resolved. In 1995, according to Medicare statistics, appeals with Medicare HMOs regarding payment for nursing home care, hospital bills, ambulance bills, and care by a nonplan doctor were settled in the member's favor 25 to 39 percent of the time.

New Insurance

Some forty-six states now require insurance plans regulated by the state to cover basic diabetes care. With the exception of a few federal laws, such as the Consolidated Omnibus Budget Reconciliation Act of 1985 (COBRA), most health insurance laws are passed by individual states. The American Diabetes Association's website has information on each state's regulated health insurance programs for diabetes, along with insurance options available in particular states.

Laws can vary considerably from one state to the next. One Western state has passed a law that insurance companies can't turn down anyone who applies for insurance. A state in the East passed a law that all medical supplies required by people with diabetes be covered by insurance policies.

Insurance companies look at certain criteria when writing policies for people with diabetes. These criteria minimize the financial risk to the companies. In California and some other states, for a person with diabetes to even have a chance of being insured, insurance companies require that the person be within 15 percent of normal body weight; have a history of good blood sugar control, with an HbA1c test of under 8; and have had no complications. According to an insurance broker who writes many policies for people with diabetes, some insurance companies also like to see a history of regular visits to your doctor (every six months or so) before they will write a policy.

It may not be easy to find new health insurance if you have diabetes. Insurance companies consider diabetes to be "high risk." Most consider diabetes a preexisting condition and will insure you only if they can find a way to minimize their financial risk. If an insurance company considers you to be high risk, you may be offered insurance at the normal rate without coverage for diabetes. Or you may be offered coverage for diabetes at an additional charge.

A few insurance brokers specialize in finding insurance policies for people who are high risk—your local American Diabetes Association chapter may be able to recommend a broker who can help you. High-risk policies are always more expensive than standard insurance.

In some states, high-risk health insurance pools will insure anyone, regardless of health. However, many states limit the number of people that they will insure in this manner and also limit the amount of coverage. HMOs sometimes have "open enrollment" periods when they will accept anyone, regardless of previous medical conditions.

If you are laid off from a job that provided you with insurance coverage, and your former employer has more than twenty employees, your former employer's insurance company is obligated to offer you COBRA coverage. This continuing insurance coverage, mandated by the federal government, lasts for eighteen months, but you must pay the premium yourself. Coverage will be more expensive than what you paid for the same policy before.

If you are covered by a COBRA policy, insurance advisers recommend that you not wait until the month before it runs out to shop for more insurance. This is because some insurance policies have a ninety-day waiting period before you can be treated for a preexisting condition such as diabetes.

In the past, the difficulty of securing new health insurance almost forced some people with diabetes or their spouses to work for companies longer than they cared to, simply to retain insurance coverage. The Health Coverage Availability and Affordability Act of 1996, known as the Kennedy-Kassebaum Bill, makes it easier for people to retain health insurance coverage when changing jobs or leaving jobs to start new businesses, since insurers are now required to renew the policies of people whose coverage might have been dropped in the past. Government jobs often provide health insurance without exclusions for preexisting conditions.

Health savings accounts are not a good idea for most people with diabetes. These accounts allow you to contribute an amount up to the deductible on your family's insurance policy and to deduct it from your gross income on federal taxes, but they also require copious record keeping, and the tax savings are almost meaningless for people in lower tax brackets. They do not cover people who are over age sixty-five or on Medicare.

Financial Help

According to Maureen Harris, director of the National Diabetes Data Group, government-funded programs such as Medicare, Medicaid, and veterans' hospitals cover 57 percent of American adults with diabetes, including 96 percent of men and women with diabetes who are over the age of sixty-five.

The primary health-care program for older people in the United States is Medicare. Medicare is a two-part program that will pay some of the expenses associated with diabetes. Medicare Part A provides certain coverage for all qualified recipients. Medicare Part B is optional and pays for more health-related expenses. Medicare expenses are billed according to CPT diagnosis codes or procedure code numbers. Reimbursements to health-care providers vary based on the insurance carrier, whether services are received as an inpatient or outpatient, the procedure code under which the expense is billed, and the amount of other medical expenses billed to Medicare during a particular period.

Beginning in 2005, Medicare Part B covered self-management training and also covered medical nutrition therapy for people with diabetes who have a doctor's prescription for these services. Up to ten hours in an educational program with a diabetes educator is allowed. In addition, Medicare now covers three hours of medical nutrition therapy with a certified diabetes educator the first year and two hours of annual follow-up nutritional therapy. Blood sugar testing equipment, test strips, and lancets also are now covered by Medicare, as are HbA1c tests, dilated eye exams, glaucoma screening tests, and flu and pneumonia shots. A free booklet explaining benefits, "Medicare Coverage of Diabetes Supplies and Services," is available through the Centers for Medicare & Medicaid Services, listed in the Resources section of this book.

If your doctor requires you to take insulin, Medicare will pay for a blood glucose testing meter, as well as for strips and syringes, but won't pay for the insulin. Neither insulin nor diabetes medications are covered under Medicare Part A or Part B. At the present time, insulin or diabetes pills are covered only under "Medigap"-type policies. Medicare covers 100 percent of approved hospital costs and 80 percent of medical expenses (including dialysis) for most patients with permanent kidney failure. See the "Resources" section for other sources of assistance.

The special provisions and exceptions in Medicare's coverage of diabetes-related expenses are spelled out in the U.S. Health Care Financing Administration's HCFA Publication 6, available at www.medicare.gov. Doctors and hospital billing personnel don't always know exactly which diabetes-related expenses will be covered by Medicare, since many factors affect a Medicare reimbursement, and government regulations are subject to change.

The much ballyhooed federal Medicare prescription drug benefit passed in 2004 is voluntary for Medicare recipients. At the time of this edition, the plan was basically a catastrophic drug plan that covered a good portion of prescription drug costs up to a $2,250 threshold, nothing more until a total of $5,100 is spent, and then most of the costs after that. Among its defects, the new law does not allow Medicare itself to negotiate lower drug prices, forcing taxpayers to pay top dollar for prescription drugs. Since a person who takes insulin can spend more than $3,000 a year on insulin and supplies, many people with diabetes will obviously have to pay more to cover the Medicare "hole" between $2,250 and $5,100 as the law is currently written.

Some insurance plans cover only up to the level that Medicare will cover. To receive full coverage of your diabetes-related expenses, a secondary "Medigap" policy such as those sold by the American Association of Retired Persons, or AARP, must be purchased. Although benefits are the same in these plans, such as Plans H, I, and J, which apply to drugs, prices for premiums can vary widely, and these can be compared from plan to plan.

Medicare recipients with diabetes may see a podiatrist, or foot specialist, every sixty days for routine foot care, but if pain is experienced, recipients may be seen on an emergency basis. Orthopedic shoes are sometimes covered, depending on how the expenses are billed.

In addition to Medicare, low-income people may have other expenses covered under Medicaid. In many states, Medicaid can help with some expenses for people with diabetes who qualify.

Veterans' hospitals treat male and female military veterans at no expense to the patient and provide drugs at a low cost. Native Americans and merchant marine veterans may be treated free of charge at public health service hospitals.

Teaching hospitals that conduct research on diabetes often bill for patient services using a sliding scale. Participants in clinical trials that test new diabetes medications or strategies of treatment are sometimes not charged for the medical care they receive during the trial.

Most drug companies have programs that may provide free drugs to people without health insurance, although your doctor must contact the program and enroll you in it. Many of these programs will provide at least a three-month supply of medication to qualified people, which can sometimes be renewed. Some states also have programs that offer discounted prescription drugs for low-income people. See this book's "Resources" section for further information on these programs.

A few private doctors will treat people with diabetes who have no health insurance for lower fees. If you are eligible for Medicare, ask your doctor if he or she will accept the Medicare assignment, which is the amount Medicare will actually pay for the expenses or treatment in question. Many doctors will accept this amount as their full payment if you ask them.

Sometimes, to save money, supplies such as insulin, lancets, or strips can be bought in bulk, in frequent-buyer programs that are less expensive, or from suppliers who offer "buy ten bottles of insulin, get one free." Pharmacies sometimes offer specials on diabetes supplies, which can be attractive buying opportunities. You can do some price shopping before making your purchase, utilizing not only pharmacies but also mail-order and Internet suppliers, although medications that are for short-term use are best purchased locally. There are some deals on the Internet too. Websites licensed as a Verified Internet Pharmacy Practice Site are the safest bet online. Always make sure you can use the products within the expiration dates, if applicable.

Consumer Reports recommends that you do an annual "brown-bag" review of your medications. Put all your drugs and supplements in a bag, and ask your pharmacist and your doctor to review them and suggest any less expensive options. Your pharmacist or doctor may be able to recommend an older or over-the-counter drug that is cheaper but has the same effects as the one you are using. Some pills can be bought for the same price at a double dose, and you can split the pills, to save money. Your pharmacist can check for possible drug interactions. Likewise, drugs that are no longer needed can be dropped.

Other Types of Insurance

Life insurance is usually available for people with Type 2 diabetes who have fairly normal weight and reasonable HbA1c levels, although the premiums can be hefty. Protein in the urine, indicating kidney problems, or a recent history of severe complications such as heart problems may completely disqualify you from purchasing life insurance.

Disability insurance is difficult to acquire. If it is available, the premiums are often extremely high because of the "high risk" factor. Disability insurance also imposes a long waiting period before the policy becomes effective.

In addition, auto insurance premiums can be a little more expensive. A few insurance companies will not write insurance on people with health problems such as diabetes.

Discrimination

Discrimination against people with diabetes occurs in day care centers, schools, penal institutions, and workplaces. The American Diabetes Association has become active in legal advocacy and is pushing for regulatory, legislative, and litigation changes. The association has set standards of care for schools, day care centers, diabetes camps, and the management of diabetes in correctional institutions. To get an information packet on discrimination, call (800) DIABETES (342-2383-7). You can discuss a specific discrimination problem with one of the association's legal advocates.

More than two thousand people have filed complaints with the U.S. Equal Employment Opportunity Commission alleging mistreatment at work because of their diabetes. People with diabetes are protected by disability discrimination law. The Americans with Disabilities Act offers legal recourse for all people who are discriminated against in companies with fifteen or more workers.

The financial aspects of diabetes can be frustrating if you are obliged to wrestle with an insurance company to resolve a claim, or if you must take on a bureaucracy to receive all the medical services you need. After you are diagnosed with diabetes, check your policy to see what is covered in the way of doctors' bills, medicines, supplies, and other expenses. Keep records of your correspondence with insurance companies, and assert yourself as needed. Some financial help is available to people with diabetes, but even if you have excellent health insurance, you will bear out-of-pocket costs. Medicare and other programs may ease the burden. Among the most costly aspects of diabetes to insurance companies are the long-term medical complications that can arise, the subject of the next chapter.

16

Complications

*Understanding and Treating the
Long-Term Effects of Diabetes*

THIS CHAPTER LOOKS at the complications of diabetes and explains related medical treatments. Complications that spring from diabetes are almost always traceable to excessive levels of glucose in the blood for many years. High blood sugar over a long period slowly weakens certain parts of the body, such as the eyes, kidneys, and skin. High blood sugar gradually damages the blood vessels and the nervous system, affecting parts of the body such as the feet, and even affects sexual function. Since the need for self-management of diabetes doesn't suddenly stop when your health takes a turn for the worse, and since a healthy and physically active lifestyle benefits everyone, exercises appropriate for people with various complications accompany the discussions. A few things to consider during a hospital stay conclude the chapter.

Heredity

Some people with diabetes can sail through their entire lives without suffering any complications, even if they don't take perfect care of themselves. At the same time, a few "good diabetics" suffer complications despite doing almost everything by the book. Most people fall between these two extremes. This is because the genes that you have inherited affect your health.

Some people seem genetically predisposed to have certain complications, while others seem predisposed not to. The genes you were born with are not within your control, but you can lower the risk of complications by practicing good self-management and taking good care of yourself. Keep in mind that when you were diagnosed with diabetes, you might already have had the disease for years without realizing it. One prominent Southern California doctor estimates that the average person with Type 2 diabetes had the disease for eight to ten years before the incidence of diabetes was discovered. This means you could have sustained some damage from high blood sugar before you were even diagnosed.

Good control of blood sugar is the overriding factor in preventing the appearance of complications and in mitigating some of their worst effects. You can considerably reduce your chances of complications through a program of good self-management. Think of your efforts at good hygiene and the other preventive measures that you take as something akin to careful driving. If you drive within the speed limits, there will be less chance of your having an accident than if you always drive too fast.

It's never too late to help yourself by controlling your blood sugars, losing a few pounds, or stopping smoking. Obesity has a correlation with many diseases. Smokers with diabetes are eight times as likely to have complications as are nonsmokers. Many times in your life, you can undertake a new and better program of self-management that includes blood sugar testing, stress reduction, lifestyle changes, and medications prescribed by your doctor. Practicing good self-management will help you now and in the future.

Len's Story

A man we shall call Len, forty-one years old, has come through several complications of diabetes with an affirmative attitude.

"I know I'm not going to die from diabetes, and I know that good blood sugar control can stop or minimize the chances of complications," says Len, who works for a major hospital's diabetes education program, which serves people with Type 2 diabetes. "With diabetes, there are a lot of physical battles and a lot of psychological battles. Sometimes you find you're fighting yourself."

Len was twenty years old and ready to try to pitch his way into major-league baseball when he was diagnosed with Type 1 diabetes. The doctor who diagnosed him was quite insensitive, brusquely informing Len that he had diabetes and then hurriedly offering to show him how to inject insulin. Len almost fainted.

"The second doctor I saw was better," he says. "He told me I had to get my blood sugars under control. I remember his telling me that if I didn't, ten years down the line, I'd have problems. I realize now that my blood sugar control after that was not what it could have been."

Len confides that he felt embarrassed after he was diagnosed. None of his friends knew that he had a medical condition or that he was required to eat differently and take insulin to stay alive. He remembers feeling deprived because he couldn't eat the same things that his friends ate.

According to Len, for the first ten years that he had diabetes, he didn't do a responsible job of keeping his blood sugar under control. It didn't seem to matter, he says with chagrin. He had a gift for business; he had started one successful company after another. His life was going well, and he had a nice house and a nice car.

But four years ago, Len's life became a nightmare. First, he was diagnosed with diabetic retinopathy. His eyesight failed; he went completely blind. Then his kidneys failed. He found himself the youngest person in a convalescent hospital, undergoing kidney dialysis three times a week. As his business, house, and cars slipped away, he himself slipped into a depression.

"Many mornings, I'd wake up and be disappointed that I didn't die in my sleep," he recalls.

About this time, he also broke his leg, a Charcot break, which occurred because his bones had been weakened from the dialysis.

After four long months of believing that he might be blind for the rest of his life, Len was blessed with partial restoration of his sight, owing to the efforts of a superior eye doctor who persisted with treatments and did not write Len off as others had done. Len's broken leg healed. After he received a kidney transplant, his health came back.

Len soon began work as a volunteer at a diabetes education center, where he is employed today. He wears an insulin pump on his belt and says that he feels better than he has felt in years, because he has better blood sugar control than he ever had before. When he was younger, he acknowledges, he would have worried that someone might notice the pump on his belt and reject him. Now, he says, it doesn't bother him one way or the other: he has come through a difficult time with a new appreciation for life.

"My work is very rewarding," he states. "Sometimes I can relate to our patients on a personal level, because I know what it feels like when your blood sugars are running high. I know what it feels like to go to a birthday party and be the only one there who doesn't get to eat cake. My health is pretty good now, although I have physical limitations. At the end of the workday, I'm pretty tired. But I can't feel sorry for myself, because there are a lot of people worse off than I am."

If you have been diagnosed with any of the complications of diabetes, you may be weighed down with additional stress and worry. You may have to grieve all over again, with the attendant emotional ups and downs. As outlined in Chapter 5, reducing the level of negative stress in your life can put you in better shape to assess and control the situation. Eating healthy foods and remaining physically active will also help. Remain in contact with the people you care about—and who care about you—family, friends, and members of your support system. Don't hesitate to pursue psychological counseling if you feel completely over-whelmed. Learning more about your medical condition may give you a firmer feeling of control.

Many improvements in medical treatment have occurred in the past several years, and more advances are on the way. If you experience complications, the doctor who treats your diabetes will probably refer you to a specialist. You may undergo additional tests and even spend some time in the hospital. All the medicines you take should be prescribed by a doctor who is knowledgeable about your medical condition. Keep a written list of what you take and when you take it, and give a copy of the list to any new doctor you see.

Possible Long-Term Complications

Possible complications of diabetes cited in this chapter include damage to blood vessels (vascular problems) and problems with the feet, eyes, nerves, and skin, as well as kidney, urinary, and sexual functions. This information is background material, not medical advice. The ultimate authority on your medical care is always your own doctor.

Vascular Complications

Diabetes affects the small (micro) and large (macro) blood vessels. Driven by the rapid beating of your heart, your cardiovascular system includes many miles of veins, arteries, and smaller blood vessels, called capillaries. If your heart stops beating, or if major blood vessels clog, you could die.

Heart attacks are a prime cause of death in middle-aged people with Type 2 diabetes, who have fatality rates two to four times higher than those of middle-aged people without diabetes. A recent study showed that between 35 and 50 percent of heart attack victims had abnormal blood sugar levels at the time of the attack. People with high blood pressure are also at higher risk.

The cardiovascular system is compromised by high levels of glucose and fats in the blood, much as plumbing pipes are slowly encrusted by the mineral deposits in tap water. Fortunately, the lifestyle changes you make to control diabetes, such as good diet and regular exercise, are the same lifestyle changes recommended to reduce heart disease.

Large blood vessel, or macrovascular, complications can affect the brain, heart, legs, and feet in people with diabetes, as well as in older people in general. Small-blood-vessel, or microvascular, disease can lead to problems with the eyes, skin, kidneys, and nerves and can retard healing.

Vascular problems are almost all related to atherosclerosis, a hardening or stiffening of the arteries that results from a buildup of deposits along blood vessel walls. This situation can trigger a heart attack, which doctors call a *myocardial infarction*. A sharp chest pain known as *angina* can occur if the arteries supplying oxygen to your heart muscle are blocked, whereas a stroke results when a blockage of blood vessels occurs in your brain. A blood clot built up in the brain is called *thrombosis*. A blood clot in the body that breaks off and travels to the brain is called an *embolus*. Blood vessels also may hemorrhage, or bleed into surrounding tissues.

The condition of high fat levels in the blood is known as *hyperlipidemia*. Atherosclerotic heart disease results from fat-clogged blood vessels. The combination of insulin resistance, high blood sugar, high blood pressure, and high levels of fats such as HDL cholesterol in the blood is called *metabolic syndrome*, also sometimes called *syndrome X*. The U.S. Centers for Disease Control and Prevention estimates that 22 percent of all Americans have metabolic syndrome, which increases the risks of atherosclerotic heart disease. High levels of homocystine, an amino acid, are also increasingly believed to factor into incidences of heart disease.

A prime indicator of heart health is your blood pressure, which should be checked every time you visit a doctor. Between 60 and 65 percent of people with diabetes have high blood pressure. Glucose and fats cause the blood vessels to constrict. Smoking is also hazardous because nicotine causes your blood vessels to constrict, including those leading to the heart, brain, hands, feet, and skin.

Very high blood pressure is dangerous for people with diabetes and should be treated. The American Diabetes Association (ADA) recommends that doctors treat blood pressure to reduce it to a level of 130/80 mmHG or less. To accomplish this, your doctor or a heart specialist, called a cardiologist, may ask you to lower the amount of sodium, or salt, in your diet; increase your intake of foods high in potassium; refrain from smoking;

exercise more; and reduce your weight, all of which can lower blood pressure. The Dietary Approaches to Stop Hypertension (DASH)—a diet stressing whole grains, vegetables, fruits, and legumes—are often recommended. Regular exercise can lower blood pressure as much as hypertensive drugs can.

An annual check of lipid levels is also advised. To lower lipid levels, lifestyle modifications such as reducing saturated fat intake, losing weight, and regular exercise are typically the first recommendations.

As needed, medications may be prescribed by your physician. For many people with diabetes, medicines that control blood pressure such as calcium channel blockers, angiotensin converting enzyme (ACE) inhibitors, and alpha-blockers are preferred to the diuretics and beta-blockers, which are frequently prescribed to control blood pressure in people without diabetes. Diuretics and beta-blockers actually *decrease* insulin sensitivity in people with diabetes and can contribute to impotence in men. Aspirin therapy, in the form of a baby aspirin a day, is recommended for people with diabetes to lower the incidence of heart problems. Heart and blood pressure medicines may be discontinued if the problems are brought under control through such methods as weight loss or exercise—another reason why it's an excellent idea to get your blood pressure checked every three months if you have experienced any cardiovascular complications.

Heart-Healthy Exercise. Most older people have some level of atherosclerosis, whether or not they have diabetes. Aerobic exercise may contribute to controlling high blood pressure. For a healthy heart and circulatory system, exercise such as walking, bicycling, or swimming is recommended because these activities utilize the large muscle groups. Isometric exercises, in which the muscles push against themselves and don't move, are not recommended if you have high blood pressure or heart problems. Also not advised for people with high blood pressure are weight-lifting exercises that use only the arms. Recommendations made by Dr. Claudia Graham and her coauthors in *The Diabetes Sports and Exercise Book* are the basis of many of the exercise suggestions in this chapter. However, you should always check with your doctor before beginning any new program of exercise, particularly when any complications from diabetes occur.

Foot Complications

People with diabetes spend more days in the hospital with foot infections than with any other complication. At some point in their lives, approximately 15 percent of people with diabetes will develop a foot ulcer. Untreated foot infections are dangerous because they can turn into gangrene, a putrefaction of soft tissue that can necessitate the amputation of a toe, foot, or leg. People with diabetes are much more likely to have a complication involving gangrene, compared with the general population. An estimated 54,000 lower-extremity amputations are performed each year in the United States because of diabetes. The probability that a person with diabetes will experience an amputation during his or her lifetime is less than 1 percent, but the risk is higher in people who smoke. Authorities estimate that the number of amputations could be decreased by half through proper professional care.

In addition to peripheral neuropathy, other risk factors for amputations include insufficient blood flow to the extremities, foot deformities, stiff joints, calluses on the feet, and a history of ulcers on the feet or a previous amputation. Good blood sugar control lessens the chances of any complication.

326 THE TYPE 2 DIABETES SOURCEBOOK

New techniques, such as grafting blood vessels onto clogged blood vessels that carry blood to the feet can prevent amputations that once were unavoidable. Hyperbaric oxygen therapy can sometimes help stubborn foot ulcers heal, by exposing bacteria to pressurized oxygen. A European study published in 2003 of people with reduced blood flow to their feet found that after thirty hyperbaric oxygen treatments, lingering foot ulcers completely healed in five of eight people, versus no healings in the control group. However, another 2003 study found no improvement with oxygen treatments two weeks after the study ended. Among other new techniques, research published in 2003 in *Diabetes Care* found that sterile maggots were very effective in debriding nonhealing foot and leg ulcers in a study of male veterans with diabetes.

Foot problems occur primarily because of poor blood circulation to the feet. Poor circulation is a result of arteries in the legs and feet becoming clogged with plaque (atherosclerosis). Arteries in people with diabetes also become somewhat less flexible, partially as a result of high blood pressure and excess weight, which increases triglyceride levels. *Claudication* is another effect of reduced blood circulation and it develops in the calf or another part of the leg when muscles don't get enough blood, creating pain or cramps when the person walks or a deep ache when the foot is at rest. Many people with diabetes have a diminished ability to feel sensations in the foot. This nerve-deadening complication, called *neuropathy*, can decrease the sensation of pain. This is why you must remember to examine your feet on a daily basis, even if they don't hurt, as explained in Chapter 11.

Your feet should be checked at every visit by your doctor. The American Diabetes Association recommends that your feet be examined once a year by your doctor to identify any high-risk foot conditions, and more frequently if you have neuropathy or other serious problems. A good foot exam assesses sensation in your feet and looks at foot structure, biomechanics, and the condition of your blood vessels and skin. If you have a problem with your feet, such as ingrown toenails or a fungal infection, your doctor should immediately refer you to a foot specialist, preferably one experienced in treating people with diabetes.

Foot problems require immediate attention because many people with diabetes have a lowered resistance to infections. People with diabetes often take four to six weeks to heal after foot surgery, much longer than normal. For that reason, foot problems that should be treated promptly include ingrown or fungus toenails, athlete's foot, dry and cracked skin, calluses, ulcers, warts, deformities such as bunions and hammertoes, night cramps, and pain.

Charcot's foot occurs in approximately one in seven hundred people with diabetes. It appears most frequently in people who are overweight and who already have some loss of feeling, or neuropathy, in their feet. A Charcot break may occur in any bone in the foot or ankle. It occurs because the bones in the arch become soft; the arch can collapse, changing the weight-bearing dynamics of the foot. This can result in skin breakdowns or infections. If your foot inexplicably swells, with no break in the skin, and feels unusually warm, you may have a Charcot break. Charcot's foot is primarily treated by staying off your feet for several months or by placing the foot in a cast.

When you have foot problems, you should be referred to a foot doctor, either a podiatrist or an orthopedist who specializes in the foot and ankle. If your family doctor or primary care physician cannot refer you to a foot doctor, your local chapter of the American Medical Association, your local American Diabetes Association chapter, or a professional group such as the American College of Foot and Ankle Surgeons can help you.

Surgery can correct many foot deformities, such as hammertoes and bunions. Foot surgery is more commonly done on people with diabetes now than in the past, because a 1978 research study refuted the notion that blood vessels of people with diabetes collapse in the face of an infection, triggering gangrene. Vascular bypass surgery from the knee to the foot can be performed when an ulcer on the foot isn't healing and a greater blood supply is needed.

Exercises for People with Foot Problems. Any exercise program should minimize the stress on your feet. Exercises to help with peripheral neuropathy should lower blood sugar and increase strength, flexibility, and blood circulation. These include water aerobics, water sports, and swimming. Wear special water socks made of neoprene to protect the soles, because skin can be easily scratched on the bottom of a swimming pool. Never go barefoot. Some exercises may be done in a sitting position, as on a rowing machine. Bicycling, rowing, armchair exercises, and such floor exercises as leg lifts may be alternatives. Since muscles and joints might have lost flexibility, pain may be experienced. Take care that you don't overdo stretching exercises, since with neuropathy, you've lost some feeling, so you may sometimes lose warning signals of pain from the ligament areas. Don't put too much pressure on the joints through exercises such as deep knee bends. Check your feet before and after each exercise session as a matter of course.

Eye Complications

While blindness was once a common complication of diabetes, regular visits to eye specialists and good medical treatment have made it much less common, now affecting fewer than 2 percent of people with diabetes. Among older people with Type 2 diabetes, between 10 and 20 percent have some problem with their eyes, which weaken with age in all people. The eye does not require the presence of insulin to utilize glucose; many eye problems spring from the damage done by excess glucose to the tiny blood vessels in the eye. Approximately 90 percent of people with diabetes will have some blood vessel changes in their eyes after having diabetes for twenty-five years.

Most eye complications are treatable. Laser treatment by ophthalmologists, doctors specializing in the care of the eye, controls many eye problems by cauterizing the small blood vessels, but this must be coupled with effective blood sugar control to be successful. If eye complications are caught early enough, damage that has already occurred can sometimes be reversed.

The most serious eye complications are forms of *retinopathy*, the enlargement, breakage, or leaking of tiny blood vessels in the eye, which can spill blood into the eyeball and threaten vision.

Background retinopathy is a common complication of diabetes, involving tiny "bulges" that resemble miniature water balloons along the small eye vessels. Background retinopathy may be harmless. *Macular edema* is more serious; this occurs in the early stages of retinopathy, when retinopathy is concentrated on the small but crucial central part of the retina, called the macula, which controls daytime vision and color sensitivity. *Proliferative retinopathy* is a more advanced condition, in which the bulges created during background retinopathy break and bleed onto the retina. This bleeding blocks vision and interferes with sight. Occasionally, the bleeding stops on its own, and the eye tissues merely absorb the blood. Proliferative retinopathy can be treated using the safe blue-green argon and green-only argon lasers, which are beams of light that cauterize broken blood vessels in the eye. This procedure can restore or improve sight, but it can also affect other aspects of sight such as peripheral vision and night vision.

A *vitreous hemorrhage* is a leaking of blood from vessels near the retina into the fluid inside the eyeball, which clouds the vision. A delicate surgical procedure called a vitrectomy, done in a hospital, can clear up this condition by removing the blood from inside the eye and replacing it with a clear fluid. This procedure can restore sight to people who have gone blind.

Cataracts cloud the lens of the eye, preventing light from entering. Cataracts are normally related more to aging than to diabetes, but poor blood sugar control can accelerate their development. If finances permit, artificial lenses may be implanted in the eye to replace lenses clouded over by cataracts.

Glaucoma, an eye disease in which pressure builds inside the eye, occurs in older people but is not directly related to diabetes. All people over age forty should be tested for glaucoma. Eyedrops can be prescribed to control it.

The American Diabetes Association recommends an annual eye examination by an opthalmologist or optometrist knowledgeable about diabetic retinopathy, and more frequent exams if retinopathy is progressing, based on the opinion of the eye care professional. See an eye doctor immediately if you experience a sudden loss of vision or change in vision, or if you have acute pain in your eye. Another symptom that needs immediate attention is the sensation of having a curtain lowered in the eyes. In these cases, insist that the eye doctor see you right away.

If your vision is impaired, both the National Federation of the Blind and the Braille Institute, whose telephone numbers are listed in the "Resources" section of this book, offer excellent programs to help people who are blind or partially sighted manage their day-to-day tasks. The National Federation of the Blind's

Diabetes Action Network produces a well-regarded free newspaper for people with diabetes, available in several forms including audiotape.

Exercises for People with Eye Problems. Cycling, swimming, and walking may be good aerobic exercises for people with retinopathy. Low-intensity exercises such as using rowing machines, stationary bicycles, and treadmills also work well; in addition, you may want to try some other exercise machines, tandem bicycling, and dancing. Exercises that jar the body or increase blood pressure, such as boxing, trampoline jumping, or weight lifting, should be avoided. Also, don't do exercises in which your head is lower than most of your body, such as handstands, diving, or yoga postures like "the plow." Finally, don't scuba dive or climb mountains, since the higher atmospheric or undersea air pressure poses additional risks to the eyes.

The Nerves (Neuropathy)

Numbness in hands and feet, or cold, tingling, burning feelings can be symptoms of neuropathy—a common complication of the nerves or nervous system. Neuropathy typically begins with the so-called stocking and glove effect, which is a slight numbness that starts at the tips of the toes or fingers and then moves back. This is a problem because when you can't feel normal sensations such as pressure or pain, you can't compensate by shifting positions as you would otherwise. Poor blood circulation is two to three times more likely to occur in people with diabetes, and neuropathy affects 60 to 70 percent of people with diabetes in mild to severe form. The pains associated with neuropathy frequently worsen at night and during very hot or cold weather, and they can be intensified by the touch of sheets or bedclothes. These feelings can last for months and then subside. They can also turn into numbness in the same areas, caused by a blunted ability to feel sensations. Such numbness is a reason to inspect the feet and skin every day, and to always wear shoes when walking. It's best to not ignore these problems, because people with diabetes are twenty times as likely to experience nerve-related leg problems, such as gangrene and blockages, as the general population.

Some types of neuropathy are manageable; the effects may sometimes be reversed by a combination of lowered blood sugar and medical treatment.

It is not fully understood why nerves are affected by diabetes. Nerves are somewhat like electric cords, with a protective outer layer of cells. One theory is that excess glucose in the blood may cause the outer Schwann cells that surround nerve bundles to swell, irritating and finally choking off the more functional inner nerve cells.

Sensory neuropathy is the form of neuropathy most closely associated with diabetes. One aspect of this condition, *peripheral neuropathy*, affects the areas of the body farthest from the heart, such as the legs, feet, arms, or hands, and sometimes the skeletal muscles. Numbness, coldness, or the feeling of walking on pins and needles can be a symptom. One effect of neuropathy is the common human experience of "foot drop," which occurs after you wake up, and your foot feels as if it's flapping when you walk. Neuropathy can manifest itself as a tight feeling in the chest, called *truncal neuropathy*, which is sometimes mistaken for a heart attack. Charcot's joint and a muscle-wasting condition called *amyotrophy* can result from sensory neuropathy. *Mononeuropathy* and *radiculopathy* are diseases of the spinal nerves or cranial nerves and can sometimes be reversed.

Autonomic neuropathy involves the nerves whose functions are more or less automatic—those that control the stomach, sweat glands, digestive tract, intestinal system, bladder, penis, and circulatory system. *Gastroparesis*, a neuropathy-related digestive problem, can include symptoms of nausea, diarrhea, or constipation. Medications can give relief for most symptoms of gastroparesis, as can such simple changes in eating habits as eating smaller meals more frequently and adjusting the amount of fiber in the diet.

Good blood sugar control is the most effective single way to improve the symptoms of neuropathy, which may disappear over time. New drugs recently approved for the treatment of neuropathic pain include duloxetine hydrochloride (Cymbalta), an antidepressant that can relieve neuropathic pain, and pregabalin (Lyrica), a pain reliever that binds to nerve cells to decrease pain but does not affect the underlying neuropathy. In one trial funded by the manufacturer, Lyrica relieved about 50 percent of the pain in 48 percent of research subjects. Mild pain relievers, such as aspirin or Tylenol, or nonsteroidal anti-inflammatory drugs may also be prescribed for pain. Antidepressant medications such as promazine or amitriptyline are sometimes prescribed in small amounts to help people with neuropathy. Drugs used to treat other disorders, such as the epilepsy drug gabapentin, sometimes bring relief. Local anesthetics and muscle relaxants also sometimes help. Narcotics such as codeine and morphine are almost never prescribed for neuropathy, because they aren't particularly effective and can lead to drug dependence.

Folk remedies such as 2 teaspoons of apple cider vinegar with lunch can sometimes help assuage night cramps, another manifestation of neuropathy. Cayenne pepper oil, applied topically while wearing gloves, sometimes relieves the "pins and needles" pain. The active ingredient in cayenne peppers, capsaicin, is the basis of over-the-counter medications such as Zostrix and Arthi-Care, which are approved by the U.S. Food and Drug Administration (FDA) for treating chronic pain, although they don't work for every person. Some people try Fosfree, a remedy available at health food stores. A quarter of a tablet of quinine sulfate is sometimes prescribed by doctors.

A study utilizing electrotherapy with patients with Type 2 diabetes, reported in the spring 1999 issue of *Diabetes Technologies and Therapeutics*, showed that 83 percent of the patients whose lower extremities were treated for thirty minutes a day for a month reported relief. In a smaller substudy, two dozen patients found some additional pain relief by utilizing both electrotherapy and the antidepressant medication amitriptyline, 50 mg at bedtime. Transcutaneous electrical nerve stimulation units—called TENS units—relieve pain with mild jolts of electricity and may be operated at home, although they require a doctor's prescription.

A small study at New York Medical College completed in 1998 found that 75 percent of people with diabetic neuropathy who wore magnetic insoles in their shoes for four months experienced a reversal or reduction of their symptoms. Another noninvasive new therapy called anodyne therapy uses infrared energy, and it showed decreased pain, restoration of sensation, and better balance after treatment in many subjects, according to a double-blind study published in the January 2004 issue of *Diabetes Care*.

Self-help techniques applicable to foot neuropathy include soaking the feet for a few minutes in lukewarm water before bed, walking around a bit before retiring, and using a foot cradle to keep bedsheets from touching the feet. Stretching exercises may be helpful for muscle aches and pains.

In the realm of diet, some studies have also shown that supplements of minerals and vitamins such as magnesium, calcium, and vitamin B_6 (at a rate of 200 mg per day) can have a positive effect on neuropathy. A couple of studies have found that supplements of alpha-lipoic acid can improve the symptoms of neuropathy.

Stress-relieving techniques such as those listed in Chapter 5 may help reduce some of the symptoms of neuropathy. Biofeedback, hypnosis, acupuncture, and massage may aid in reducing stress or managing pain. One randomized study conducted at the University of Wisconsin found that biofeedback used daily over three months healed chronic foot ulcers in fourteen out of sixteen participants, while only about half of controls were completely healed. A WarmFeet kit developed by diabetes educator Birgitta Rice utilizes these techniques, and is being sold for home use to improve peripheral blood flow to the feet, which can reduce neuropathic pain and promote wound healing.

Exercises for People with Peripheral Neuropathy. If you have peripheral neuropathy, which affects balance and can numb the feet, avoid exercises that use the feet, such as jogging or running. Using a treadmill machine so that you can stabilize yourself is preferable. Swimming, water polo, aqua-aerobics, and exercises that can be done while seated are best. Bicycling, rowing, canoeing, floor exercises, and armchair exercises are options. To mitigate pain, stretch before doing exercise or yoga, but be careful to avoid overstretching the ligaments and muscles, since you may not be able to feel certain pains. Check your feet for cuts or blisters before and after exercising, and wear properly fitting shoes and good-quality, clean socks.

Exercises for People with Autonomic Neuropathy. Since the autonomic nervous system controls sweating and other automatic functions, the ADA recommends that people with autonomic neuropathy avoid exercises that cause rapid changes in body position or that cause a sudden change in heart rate or blood pressure. Daily exercise is best, with slow and careful increases under a doctor's guidance. Adequate water should be consumed, and exercise in very hot or cold environments should be avoided.

Kidney and Urinary Tract Complications

The most serious complication of diabetes involving the urinary tract is *nephropathy*, which involves the kidneys. Nephropathy usually occurs in people who have had diabetes for a long time. It develops because the nephrons, small arteries within the kidney, gradually harden. Nephropathy sometimes is a product of a urinary tract infection that has spread to the kidneys. According to one estimate, 20 to 30 percent of people with Type 2 diabetes may develop moderate to advanced kidney disease. Controlling your blood glucose levels and blood pressure will help prevent kidney disease, as will controlling cholesterol levels, stopping smoking, and perhaps consulting a dietitian to help you plan meals. If your doctor recommends it, blood pressure medications such as ACE (angiotensin-converting enzyme) inhibitors can have a protective function for the kidneys.

Symptoms of nephropathy include swelling of the ankles, hands, face, or other body parts; loss of appetite, perhaps accompanied by a metallic taste in the mouth; skin irritations; difficulty thinking clearly; fatigue; and extreme difficulty managing blood sugar. Report any of these symptoms to the doctor who treats your diabetes.

The first stage of malfunctioning kidneys is hyperfiltration, in which larger amounts of blood than normal move through the kidneys to compensate for damaged nephrons. This does not necessarily foreshadow more serious kidney problems, particularly if blood sugar and blood pressure are well managed. In the early stages of kidney disease, called *microalbuminuria* and *protein-uria*, the kidneys release small quantities of protein into the blood. This problem can be detected by a microalbumin test, which the American Diabetes Association now recommends for people with diabetes every year, since at this stage the kidney disease is still fairly treatable. Some doctors are also now recommending an annual glomerular filtration rate (GFR) test for people with Type 2 diabetes; this test sometimes catches a problem in its early stages even when microalbuminuria is not present. More severe problems result when the body retains waste products that are normally excreted. At the later stages of kidney disease, a swelling called edema can occur because excess fluid is retained in the body. Kidney and urinary tract complications may be treated by a kidney specialist, called a nephrologist, or by a urologist, who specializes in the care of the urinary tract.

Advanced kidney disease causes rising levels of the muscle waste product creatinine. End-stage renal disease occurs in approximately one-fourth of 1 percent of people with diabetes. It can be treated with dialysis, a process that periodically filters impurities from the blood. Hemodialysis takes blood out of the arm and runs it through a machine for three to five hours to filter out waste materials and then returns it to the body, a procedure done an average of three times a week. Peritoneal dialysis involves inserting a waste-absorbing fluid into the body through a tube inserted just below the navel; this can be done at home, several times a day. Peritoneal dialysis can also be performed overnight, using a machine.

Kidney transplants are another possible method of treating kidney failure. Transplanting one of the kidneys of a close relative, versus an unrelated donor, is generally preferred. Medical risks are inherent in this operation, since the immune system must be suppressed to allow the transplanted kidney to "take." Blood sugar control after the transplant is a priority.

According to Richard David, M.D., a Los Angeles urologist, 15 to 20 percent of people with diabetes who are over age sixty-five have some problem involving the urinary tract, kidneys, or bladder. Of these, up to 40 percent either have trouble urinating or have some bladder dysfunction. One reason for this is that excessive glucose in the bloodstream draws water out of the tissues, creating excessive urination; neuropathy is another reason. Urological complications can often be prevented by good blood sugar control; likewise, if they develop, their progress can be stopped with good blood sugar control.

Symptoms of urinary tract infections include painful urination, frequent urination, and cloudy or bloody urine. In their earliest stages, urinary tract infections may have no symptoms at all but show up on a urine test given by your doctor.

As a general rule, bladder infections occur more frequently in people with diabetes. Infections of the urological tract, more common in women than in men, can begin in the bladder or ureters and can spread to the kidneys, where they create additional problems. Kidney stones, for instance, can cause infections. Bladder infections may also be caused by incomplete emptying of the bladder; the infection often develops without painful symptoms, but it sometimes causes a bit of leakage. A nonfunctioning bladder may develop because of nerve damage in the bladder area associated with diabetes. When the bladder doesn't empty normally, urine is held longer, and bacteria may grow. When blood sugars are elevated, sugar can be found in the urine. Bacteria multiply rapidly in a high blood sugar environment. Drinking plenty of water every day will help prevent a nonfunctioning bladder by flushing bacteria out of the system before they can multiply. Be aware that medications that you take can affect urination.

Most bladder infections can be treated with bacteria-killing antibiotics. Before prescribing an antibiotic, your doctor may order a culture to determine which type of bacteria is causing your infection, since certain antibiotics are most effective on certain types of bacteria. If you are prescribed antibiotics, make sure that you take all the medicine, even if the symptoms subside while you still have some left. If you don't take all the medicine you were prescribed, you may miss killing a few of the stronger bacteria, and they will come back again, more resistant to antibiotics than before. This is true for all antibiotics.

Yeast infections in women flourish when blood sugar is high, another reason why blood sugars should be controlled.

Neuropathy can also complicate bladder problems, since the blunted nerves don't always feel the bladder getting full. Neuropathy can cause you to lose the ability to squeeze the muscles that empty your bladder, resulting in incontinence, which strikes approximately 60 percent of people over sixty years of age whether or not they have diabetes. Incontinence may also be caused by weak abdominal muscles, muscle spasms in the bladder, or a blockage or other problem that impedes urination. Certain medications, irritating foods including alcohol and caffeine, impaired movement from arthritis or an injury, and poor blood sugar control can bring on incidents of incontinence. Muscle-strengthening exercises, biofeedback, and drug and other medical treatments can help.

Even if you have begun to lose some kidney or urinary tract function, you can appreciably slow this process by maintaining good blood sugar control and by modifying your diet, exercising, and taking medications as prescribed. Lowering your blood pressure slows kidney disease; you may be asked to take your blood pressure at home and report any changes to your doctor. Working with a registered dietitian or nutritionist to develop a proper diet, which may be low in sodium or protein, is particularly important in lowering blood pressure. The DASH diet cited earlier, emphasizing fruits, vegetables, and whole grains, is often recommended. Eliminating all protein from animal sources is sometimes recommended. Medications can lower blood pressure and lighten the workload for the kidneys. Stress-reducing activities and exercise also help control blood sugar, as does participation in the joyful events of your life.

Exercises for People with Kidney Problems. Don't exercise if you have excessive levels of protein in the urine, or proteinuria. Don't do any marathon running or long-distance bicycling in the heat, which dehydrates the body and may cause more protein to accumulate in the urine. Also avoid activities that will increase blood pressure, such as weight lifting. Cycling, water exercises, archery, golf, and bowling should be fine. Moderate armchair-type exercises can be done almost anytime and have the effect of improving both the person's frame of mind and ability to get around.

Issues Specific to Men

Impotence is a common complaint of men with diabetes. Between one-third and two-thirds of men with diabetes have trouble getting an erection. Impotence manifests itself as lessening rigidity of the penis and the eventual inability to achieve an erection. It is sometimes caused by nerve and small blood vessel damage, which is related to blood sugar control. Another sexual problem linked to diabetes is retrograde ejaculation, in which ejaculation goes backward into the bladder, a condition that feels unusual but is not harmful. Retrograde ejaculation affects an estimated 2 percent of men who have diabetes.

Men with diabetes have from two to five times the normal incidence of impotence, a condition that increases with age in the general population. Some men with diabetes may experience these problems ten to fifteen years earlier than normal. If blood sugars are out of control, either too high or too low, it's necessary to bring them under control.

Impotence typically comes on gradually. If a man is impotent with a sexual partner but continues to get erections in his sleep, the problem may be emotional or psychological. One method of determining this is to paste a strip of postage stamps around the penis before going to sleep. If the strip is broken in the morning, it's likely that a nocturnal erection occurred. According to Harley Wishner, M.D., a Los Angeles urologist, if a doctor treating the condition needs more precise information, the patient can perform nocturnal tumescence monitoring by hooking himself up to a machine for a night and letting the device record the number and intensity of nighttime erections.

Impotence is not always caused by diabetes. The source may be medications prescribed for other medical problems, such as high blood pressure, in which case discontinuing or changing medications may have a positive effect. The use of drugs such as tranquilizers, alcohol, or marijuana can also cause impotence. In addition, negative emotional stress affects the libido. Impotence frequently has psychological roots, even in men with diabetes, since even small decreases in potency can sometimes create an anxiety that further depresses sexual performance. Even your diet can make a difference in sexual performance. One new measure of blood circulation in the arteries is endothelial dysfunction, which is associated with erectile dysfunction. In one study, subjects' endothelial function became abnormal within an hour after their eating a standard McDonald's breakfast of an Egg McMuffin, sausages, and hash browns, containing 50 grams of fat, and did not return to normal for five hours.

Men with diabetes who smoke run a greater risk of impotence. Since nicotine causes the blood vessels to constrict, smoking can reduce the supply of blood to the penis. A study of men conducted at Boston University School of Medicine found a decrease in blood flow to the penis in direct proportion to the number of cigarettes smoked. In Washington, D.C., a study of twenty impotent male smokers showed that seven of the twenty achieved nocturnal erections six weeks after they quit smoking.

If you are beginning to experience impotence, discuss this problem with your doctor. If possible, ask your spouse or significant other to accompany you to the doctor's office and participate in some of the discussions. Your doctor may refer you to a urologist who specializes in the treatment of impotence or to a mental health professional. If your impotence has a psychological or emotional basis, you may benefit from talking with a licensed therapist or a family therapist or from working with a sex counselor. You can locate a clinician trained in sex counseling through a professional organization such as the American Association of Sex Educators, Counselors, and Therapists, which is listed in the "Resources" section of this book.

In situations in which the primary care doctor or urologist determines that impotence has physical causes that cannot be corrected, several methods allow men to resume sexual activity, which is often connected to feelings of self-worth and self-esteem.

One strategy involves the use of medicines called external vasodilators, which are ointments applied to the penis to stimulate blood flow. Although their effectiveness has not been scientifically proved, minoxidil and nitroglycerin ointment may be useful when the problem is insufficient blood flow through the arteries into the penis. Nitroglycerin ointment should be used with a condom, to prevent the subsequent onset of headaches in a sexual partner, a side effect of nitroglycerin. Yohimbe, an herbal remedy made from the bark of the yohimbe tree, may be useful in a few cases. Supplemental testosterone, a male steroid hormone, may be administered by a doctor, but it increases potency only if testosterone levels are abnormally low prior to treatment, and it has some risks. For overweight men, losing weight and keeping it off is a risk-free way to increase testosterone.

Among the drug treatments, sildenafil (Viagra) and similar drugs like vardenafil (Levitra) and tadalafil (Cialis) can help some men with diabetes. However, these drugs have side effects that should be discussed with your doctor. Sildenafil, for instance, can interact with drugs that expand the blood vessels, such as nitroglycerin, so it is recommended that men stop taking those drugs for at least twenty-four hours prior to using sildenafil. One study of men with diabetes found that subjects taking Viagra were successful in achieving suitable erections about half the time, versus about one-eighth of the time with a placebo. In research tests, this drug was most successful among men with milder impotence problems—that is, men who could achieve a partial but inadequate erection.

An FDA-approved drug sold under the brand name Caverject has a success rate of about 80 percent. This drug is injected into the base of the penis, causing an erection that lasts for a sufficient period. Drugs of this type are available with a doctor's prescription and should be tested in the doctor's office prior to home use. These drugs have few side effects beyond the occasional scarring of the penis by the syringe, although some men experience pain where the drug is injected. An alternate method of administering a potency drug involves dispensing the medication directly into the urethra.

A commercial product sold under the brand name Rejoyn is a support sleeve that holds the flaccid penis in a rigid position to permit intercourse. Another commercial product is a vacuum cylinder device, which sells for about $200. These devices, which look a bit like bicycle tire pumps, create a vacuum that draws blood up into the penis to create an erection; a tension ring similar to a rubber band is placed at the base of the penis to hold the erection. The tension ring should be removed after half an hour to prevent bruising the penis.

The most expensive—and invasive—treatment involves prosthetic devices implanted in the penis. These devices have more than a 90 percent success rate and can be put to use almost immediately after the patient has healed from the surgery.

Keeping yourself healthy and controlling your blood sugar through stress-reduction techniques, a balanced diet, and regular exercise is the best bet. And don't forget the other legitimate and pleasurable expressions of love. Beyond sexual intercourse, there are hundreds of ways for you and your sexual partner to experience mutual pleasure, including hugging, kissing, dancing, and sensual massage.

Issues Specific to Women

A study published in the *Journal of the American Medical Association* in 1999 found that 43 percent of women and 31 percent of men had a "sexual dysfunction," a term that includes not only impotence but also any trouble getting sexually aroused, loss of interest in sex, problems with orgasms, and other reactions such as pain.

Women with diabetes can have difficulty achieving sexual climax. This is because women with diabetes can experience a loss of sensation in the genital region, which can inhibit sexual gratification. They are also susceptible to yeast infections, which can make sexual intercourse painful. The normal volume of lubricating fluids produced in the vagina may diminish due to the effects of neuropathy, which may also be a cause of pain. Good blood sugar control is the only real cure for this condition, although your doctor may prescribe a salve to give some relief. The use of a safe, water-soluble vaginal lubricant such as K-Y Jelly, applied before intercourse, may help make intercourse more pleasurable for both partners.

Emotions such as fear, anxiety, resentment, and depression may inhibit sexual performance in women, as they can in men. If the roots of the problem are emotional, then psychological or family counseling may help.

Women with Type 2 diabetes are fertile before menopause and can become pregnant. Therefore, birth control methods should be used until the pregnancy is wanted and can be planned. Women with diabetes should get their blood sugars under control before attempting to become pregnant, since poor blood sugar control is associated with birth defects, spontaneous abortions, and other complications. The subject of gestational diabetes, or diabetes that develops during pregnancy, is dealt with in Chapter 12.

Women with diabetes and poor blood sugar control can suffer greater levels of bone loss than normal, and they are 1.7 times more likely to develop hip fractures, according to the Iowa Women's Health Study. Controlling blood glucose, coupled with weight-bearing exercise and calcium supplements, may reduce the bone loss of osteoporosis. Hormone replacement therapy does not affect blood sugar or blood pressure, and it is not recommended solely to prevent bone loss.

In general, women smokers are three times more likely to be infertile than are women nonsmokers, and they reach menopause two years earlier. Women who smoke are also more likely to have problems with pregnancy and to have infants with birth defects.

Skin Problems

Problems with the skin are among the least serious complications of diabetes, but they can be troublesome and distressing because the skin figures so prominently in people's self-image and self-esteem. The most visible skin problems are associated with poor control of blood sugars.

Xanthomas are orange fatty plaques that can appear around the eyes or on the elbows, shins, or ankles. They are sometimes related to fat levels in the body, particularly levels of cholesterol or triglycerides. Lowering the percentage of fat in your diet and achieving better blood sugar control can help make them go away. Doctors can prescribe medications to lower fat levels in the blood.

A physically disfiguring but medically harmless condition called *necrobiosis lipoidica diabeticorum*, or NLD, sometimes accompanies diabetes. NLD often appears as a pink or red discoloration of the skin, which tightens and becomes shiny, not unlike the skin of a red apple. NLD is believed to develop when the skin gets thinner because of an inflammation, causing the loss of a normal layer of fat. NLD may first appear or intensify during times of poor blood sugar control. For some reason, NLD occurs more frequently in women than in men. Fortunately, it is completely harmless and will eventually go away. No reliable treatment for NLD exists, although a few cases have responded to cortisone. Some clinical trials involving antiplatelet medications are under way to treat this condition by slowing its normal progress.

So-called shin spots sometimes appear on the front of the legs, but they too are harmless.

A yeast infection, or candidiasis, can appear in the mouth, under the arms, or in the genital area in the form of a rash. It may be treated with prescription medicines. If you develop many infections, boils, carbuncles, or other skin eruptions, your doctor may wish to take a culture and prescribe a medication to help clear them up. Additional insulin is sometimes prescribed.

Since many skin problems are triggered or intensified by stress, using the stress-reduction techniques described in Chapter 5 may help with control.

Thyroid Disease

Thyroid disease is more common in people with Type 1 diabetes, but it sometimes develops in people with Type 2 diabetes. The thyroid is a small gland located in front of the windpipe that plays a role in metabolism.

People with diabetes have a 10 to 15 percent greater incidence of *hyperthyroidism*, in which an overactive thyroid gland secretes high levels of hormones, usually causing weight loss. Women over age forty, with or without diabetes, are at increased risk. Both hyperthyroidism and *hypothyroidism*, in which an underactive gland causes weight gain, develop over time and disturb efforts to control blood sugar.

Hashimoto's thyroiditis, an inflammation of the thyroid gland caused by an autoimmune attack, is the most common cause of thyroid disease.

Symptoms of thyroid disease include excessive nervousness, fatigue, and sleep problems. Thyroid problems should be treated by an endocrinologist, a doctor who specializes in the endocrine system, which includes the pancreas and the thyroid gland. A blood test called a thyroid panel is given when diabetes is diagnosed or when thyroid problems are suspected.

Hospitalization

If you experience serious complications, or if you have other health problems not related to diabetes, you may be admitted to a hospital for treatment. If you do land in the hospital, make sure that all your doctors and nurses understand that you have diabetes. Take all the precautions that you can.

If the hospital encourages it, and you have time to prepare for your stay, take along your glucose meter and strips. Some hospitals are eager for you to self-test, while others require the use of their blood testing equipment. Take your health insurance information with you as well. Also take your meal plan, the book in which you record your blood sugar levels, and any special equipment, vitamins, or clothes that you may need. Since the doctors who examine you in the hospital may need to know what medications you take, make a list of all of your medications, including insulin, and indicate when you take each one. If you have time, you can make several copies of this list in advance and give one to each person who asks for the information.

You may feel more in control of the situation if you keep your own set of medical records while in the hospital, including a record of your test results.

If you don't understand the logic behind a treatment recommendation, buttonhole the appropriate doctor and ask questions. Have your spouse or a friend sit in on conferences with your doctors, if possible. You can also tape-record hospital discussions and listen to them later, when they might make more sense.

In most hospitals, you will probably have some help planning your meals. In California, for instance, people with diabetes are legally required to have their nutritional needs assessed by a dietitian within seventy-two hours of entering a hospital.

Many hospitals provide a menu that allows you food choices. Some hospitals have a dietitian on staff with whom you may be able to discuss food-related concerns.

If you feel up to it, ask your doctors for exercises to do during your stay. You may be able to remain physically active by doing armchair-type exercises in your bed. If you're going to be in the hospital for several days, ask about the availability of physical therapy. Stress-relieving techniques such as deep breathing or visualization may be helpful. Many people are comforted by talking to a religious counselor, and most hospitals have chaplains who will speak with you on request. Some hospitals have a chapel on the premises.

The American Hospital Association's Patient's Bill of Rights states that anytime you are hospitalized, you have the right to receive complete information about your diagnosis, treatment, and expected outcome. You have the right to review your medical records and the right to refuse any test or treatment. You have the right to keep the details of your treatment confidential from anyone not directly involved in your care; if you don't want a particular person to know the details of your medical condition, inform your caregivers of your wishes.

Last but not least, don't forget the importance of keeping your blood sugar under control when you're hospitalized. If you are undergoing a physical stress such as surgery, your blood sugar levels will go up. Even if you don't normally take insulin, you may be given some to help you maintain control while being hospitalized.

Many of the medical complications of diabetes can be treated. You can take the sting out of the worst aspects of some complications by redoubling your efforts to control your blood sugars and by adopting a program of good self-management based on a well-balanced diet, exercise, and tests and treatments recommended by your medical team. Continue to learn, because new treatment methods can be surprisingly effective. You can read more about what medical discoveries the future may hold in the final chapter.

17

New Horizons

Searching for the Cure for Diabetes

DIABETES IS A chronic disease that must be managed for the rest of your life. Although good self-management will help you rein in diabetes right now, medical breakthroughs could occur over the next few years to change how medical science treats and thinks about this disease.

Receptionists at some chapters of the American Diabetes Association answer the telephone with the greeting, "Until there's a cure." No one knows when that cure for diabetes may come, if it ever does. More than likely, progress in eradicating diabetes will be incremental, coming in thousands of small, painstaking steps rather than in one dramatic breakthrough such as the discovery of the first polio vaccine by Dr. Jonas Salk.

But every day, research proceeds, and it is realistic to expect that medical treatments will continue to improve. Ongoing research into the effects of lifestyle changes, including the interaction of the mind with the body, as well as refinements in nutrition, pharmacology, and equipment technology may improve the lives of millions of people. For now, good self-management can hold diabetes at bay for a long while.

In the United States alone, about $12 billion a year is being spent on diabetes research. The National Institutes of Health, the American Diabetes Association, and the Juvenile Diabetes Foundation are the major sources of funding for this research. On the pharmacological front, promising new drugs being tested for the prevention or treatment of diabetic neuropathy include advanced glycosylation end-product inhibitors, neuroprotective drugs, antioxidant drugs, aldose reductase inhibitors, and nerve growth factor. Alpha reductase inhibitors may prevent cataracts, and lipoic acid is being tested to see if it can prevent macular degeneration. Leptin, discovered with great hoopla in 1995 as a hormone linked to weight gain, is among the substances being tested as a weight-loss drug in humans.

All over the world, researchers are scrutinizing every conceivable aspect of diabetes treatment. An implantable insulin pump, developed by Medical Research Group LLC and already approved in the European community, is currently in the investigational stage at the U.S. Food and Drug Administration (FDA). Scientists are looking at particular combinations of stress-reduction techniques, nutritional strategies, and exercises. Transplants of real and artificial body parts are under way. Much research is going on at the cellular and molecular levels, quantifying the way in which various chemicals interact in the bodies of people with diabetes. According to an article in the May 7, 1999, *Los Angeles Times*, researchers have isolated a molecule from a fungus that controls blood glucose levels in diabetic mice. This molecule may be taken by mouth, raising the possibility of its having a similar effect in human beings, acting as a possible "insulin equivalent" that could replace injected insulin. The potential benefits of current research can only be imagined, since the results are as yet unknown.

Preventing Diabetes

A great deal of current research focuses on identifying people with Type 2 diabetes at an earlier stage of their disease, or even before diabetes develops. Scientists may one day conclude that diabetes is easier to prevent than to treat.

Impaired glucose tolerance has been established as an early indicator of Type 2 diabetes, high blood pressure, and heart problems. In 2001, the National Institute of Diabetes and Digestive and Kidney Diseases completed a long-term study called the Diabetes Prevention Program to determine whether four thousand overweight people over the age of twenty-five with impaired glucose tolerance (IGT) could prevent the onset of diabetes through dietary changes and exercise, or through preventive doses of diabetes drugs. The news was good. People who lost a little weight and exercised reduced their risk of being diagnosed with Type 2 diabetes by 58 percent. Specifically, these participants lost 5 to 7 percent of their body weight and exercised about half an hour a day. Participants who took the diabetes medication metformin reduced their risk by about 30 percent, an encouraging number but only about half as much improvement as was shown by lifestyle changes. All together, five impressive studies to date have shown that early interventions can reduce the risk of diabetes or significantly delay its onset.

An estimated 20 million people in the United States have IGT, which is also called prediabetes, chemical diabetes, or borderline diabetes, among other names. The American Diabetes Association recommends screening for IGT in high-risk groups, such as overweight adults over the age of forty-five. Clinical practice guidelines released in 2005 call for counseling on weight loss and increased physical activity and follow-up counseling for people with IGT.

Prevention and healthy lifestyles among parents may be the best strategy for limiting the rate of Type 2 diabetes among children, too. Studies of Native Americans have shown lower rates of diabetes among children when infants are breast-fed. Even the amount of sleep we get at night could turn out to be a factor. Recent research at Boston University School of Medicine showed a link between people who sleep too much or too little and impaired glucose tolerance.

At the University of Calgary, in Alberta, a vaccine that prevents Type 1 diabetes with only one injection is currently being tested. An oral form of insulin is now being used in trials to see if it can prevent Type 1 diabetes. Scientists are examining the possibility that the presence of adequate levels of a simple B vitamin, niacin or nicotinamide, in residual cells helps prevent diabetes.

Genetic scientists are working to find the genes that identify a person likely to have Type 2 diabetes. The genetic connection has been established, in that a history of first-degree relatives with Type 2 diabetes makes a diagnosis more likely within the family. Efforts are being made to identify the inherited gene and the chromosome that carry Type 2 diabetes. When this gene or set of genes is identified, it may be possible for all people to be routinely tested for diabetes. If the testing is done on a large scale and followed by preventive measures, diabetes could be kept from developing in people who are predisposed to have it. It is theoretically possible to identify a gene that protects against diabetes and insert that gene into a living person such as a newborn baby. It is also theoretically possible, with the aid of genetic modifications, to produce insulin in other areas of the body. Better testing may one day help identify people at risk for particular complications and then create preventive treatments that mitigate the worst effects.

Science and Technology

On the surgical front, transplants of the pancreas, the pancreas and kidneys, and the islet of Langerhans have met with some success for the past two decades. Several thousand of these transplants have been done, almost all on people with Type 1 diabetes, but only in a research setting. About one in four of these transplants fails.

Transplanting a body part from one person to another is extremely difficult. The recipient's immune system must be suppressed to counteract the body's natural tendency to reject something that is not of itself, even an organ such as a kidney that is needed for survival. Infection is also a major problem, since the immune system has already been compromised by diabetes. But progress is being made. At the University of Alberta, in Edmonton, a protocol for transplanting islet cells has allowed more than 80 percent of patients to remain insulin free after one year, much higher than rates of 10 percent previously reported.

As equipment becomes more sophisticated, it becomes smaller and lighter. Engineers are envisioning an artificial pancreas, somewhat like a pacemaker for the heart, that might be similar to timed-release birth control pills and other medications that allow several months' supply to be implanted in the body. Insulin pumps may be the first step toward the development of a working artificial pancreas. A glucose sensor that operates in tandem with the pump, which has already been approved for limited use, could be a second step. An artificial pancreas would mimic the normal functioning of the human pancreas, continuously monitoring blood glucose levels and releasing insulin as needed to keep blood sugar at a desirable level. A large machine called a Biostator can accomplish this already.

A surgically implanted gastric electrical stimulation device called Enterra Therapy was recently approved by the FDA and shows promise for people with gastroparesis, a form of nerve damage that affects an estimated 20 to 50 percent of people with diabetes. The device uses painless electric shocks to stimulate the vagus nerve, which is damaged by high levels of glucose. Early studies have shown some improvement in symptoms and greater glucose control after one year in many research subjects.

Infrared light beams, lasers, radio frequencies, and skin patches are now being used to develop the first noninvasive home blood testing equipment. Two companies are working on devices that measure glucose in the interstitial fluid by shining light onto the skin. One company is developing a tattoo of fluorescent molecules that glow brightly when blood sugars are low and fade when blood sugars are too high. Another company is developing an implant that can be placed in a contact lens or in the lower eyelid and that changes color when it meets the glucose in human tears.

Rapid advances in other areas may come from computer technology, which can make rapid, complex, and precise mathematical calculations and present the results in easily understood graphic form. Available computer software programs already contain glucose plotters, diet analyzers, and insulin therapy analyzers. When computer technology meets more sophisticated measuring and testing equipment, who knows what might become possible?

The Best Response

We already know that the effects of Type 2 diabetes can be slowed considerably through the use of many of the lifestyle changes recommended in this book. Since diabetes runs in families, you can definitely help your children and grandchildren by setting a good example and living a healthy lifestyle. You may want to share what you know and explain how to reduce stress, enjoy healthy physical activity, and eat a healthy diet that helps control weight.

Until there's a cure, good self-management is the best response to diabetes. Find—and work with—good doctors and a good health-care team. These people are your first line of defense. Educate yourself. Test your glucose as recommended. Take steps to relieve your stress. Eat regular, well-balanced meals that are appropriate for you. Remain physically active. Take the medications that your doctors prescribe. Don't ever stop educating yourself about ways to improve your health. If you continue to learn, you will continue to improve your self-management.

You will have difficult moments in your life whether or not you have diabetes. You will also have moments of pleasure and success. Participate in activities that you enjoy and that make your life worthwhile to you. Speak up for yourself when necessary. Communicate your feelings and thoughts to family and friends. Work to help other people as you can, and work to keep up your spirits by maintaining a healthy social life.

Self-management is extremely important. Practicing good self-management one day after another will slowly but surely empower you.

Glossary

ACANTHOSIS NIGRICANS A skin condition characterized by discolored patches around the armpits, neck, or groin, which can be an early sign of Type 2 diabetes, especially in young people.

ACIDOSIS A medical condition that can occur in people who do not produce insulin in their bodies or who do not receive adequate insulin, causing the body to become acidic.

ADULT-ONSET DIABETES A term once commonly used for non-insulin-dependent diabetes mellitus, or Type 2 diabetes.

ATHEROSCLEROSIS A disease in which fat accumulates in blood vessels, which can slow or stop blood flow.

BETA CELLS Cells located in the pancreas that produce insulin.

BLOOD GLUCOSE LEVEL The concentration of glucose—a form of digested sugar, commonly known as blood sugar—in the bloodstream at a particular time. In the United States, the blood glucose level is measured in milligrams per deciliter, or mg/dl. Some countries use millimoles per liter, or mmol/L.

BLOOD SUGAR TEST A simple medical test in which a person with diabetes uses a blood glucose meter to check the level of glucose or sugar in his or her blood.

CALORIE A measure of food energy. Technically, a calorie is the amount of energy needed to raise the temperature of a thousand grams of water 1 degree centigrade.

CARBOHYDRATE A primary and necessary category of nutrients for the body, composed mainly of starches and sugars.

CARDIOVASCULAR DISEASE A disease of the heart and large blood vessels that can occur more frequently in people with diabetes.

CERTIFIED DIABETES EDUCATOR A diabetes educator who has passed a comprehensive test on the management of diabetes given by the National Certification Board for Diabetes Educators.

CHARCOT'S BREAK A degeneration of the stress-bearing action of joints, such as the ankles, that is chronic and progressive.

CHOLESTEROL A fatlike substance, necessary for good health, that is manufactured in the body and that also can be eaten in foods. High levels of cholesterol can increase the risk for heart disease.

COMBINATION THERAPY Treatment utilizing more than one medication.

COMPLICATIONS OF DIABETES Diabetes-related conditions that can involve the feet, eyes, nerves, teeth, cardiovascular system, skin, thyroid gland, kidneys, and urinary tract.

DAWN PHENOMENON The normal rise in blood sugar levels in the early morning.

DIABETOLOGIST A medical doctor specializing in the treatment of diabetes.

DIETITIAN A person who helps plan meals for people with special health needs. A registered dietitian is one who has been certified as a specialist in this area by the American Dietetic Association.

EMPOWERMENT The process by which an individual gains a measure of power and control over his or her life.

ENDOCRINOLOGIST A medical doctor who treats problems relating to the endocrine system, including the hormone-producing glands of the body, such as the pancreas and thyroid glands.

EXERCISE PHYSIOLOGIST A medical specialist who focuses on how physical activity affects the cells, tissues, and organs of the human body.

FAT A nutrient needed to sustain life, as in saturated and unsaturated fats.

GESTATIONAL DIABETES Diabetes that appears for the first time during pregnancy, and which should be treated. Can be a precursor of Type 2 diabetes.

GLUCAGON A hormone manufactured in the pancreas that raises the level of sugar in the blood, complementing the action of another hormone, insulin, which lowers blood sugar.

GLUCOSE A medical term for a form of sugar found in the blood that is used by the body's tissues for energy.

GLUCOSE TOLERANCE TEST A medical test, sometimes called oral glucose tolerance test, or OGTT, in which the patient drinks a particular amount of glucose and then has blood glucose levels measured for a few hours after ingestion. Used to diagnose gestational diabetes.

GLYCEMIC CONTROL A medical term for controlling blood sugar levels. Also called blood glucose control.

GLYCOGEN The form in which glucose is stored in the liver, after conversion by a natural process called glycogenesis. Glycogen can be released back into the bloodstream as glucose during a fast or during an insulin reaction.

GRAM A tiny metric unit of weight, used in calculating how much of which foods to eat during dieting. There are 453 grams in 1 pound.

HBA1C TEST A blood test that shows the average blood sugar level during the past few months. Used by a doctor to get a quick read on how a particular patient is managing his or her blood sugar levels.

HDL CHOLESTEROL The "good," high-density lipoprotein cholesterol—this is the form in which cholesterol is swept from the body.

HEMOGLOBIN A1C Protein substances in the red blood cells that carry oxygen to body tissues. Measurement of the level of blood sugar attached to these proteins is done in an HbA1c test.

HIGH BLOOD SUGAR Excessive blood glucose levels. Also called hyperglycemia.

HORMONE A chemical produced in a gland or tissue of the body that stimulates an effect in other tissues or organs after being carried there in the bloodstream. Insulin and adrenalin are hormones.

HYPERGLYCEMIA A medical term for high blood sugar.

HYPERTENSION A medical term for high blood pressure.

HYPERTROPHY A medical term for thick, puffy skin over the site where insulin is injected, which may slow down the rate of absorption of insulin in people who inject it.

HYPOGLYCEMIA A medical term for low blood sugar.

HYPOGLYCEMIC AGENT A drug that can lower blood sugar levels.

IMPAIRED GLUCOSE TOLERANCE (IGT) Blood sugar levels higher than normal but not adequate to diagnose diabetes. Also called prediabetes or impaired fasting glucose.

INJECTION AREAS Areas on the body into which insulin can be injected, such as the abdomen, the outer area of the upper arm, the upper area of the buttocks, and the outer front of the middle of the thigh. The location of each injection given is called an injection site.

INSULIN A chemical hormone manufactured in the pancreas and released into the bloodstream that lowers the sugar level in the blood by helping the body tissues utilize digested food.

INSULIN REACTION Symptoms experienced by people with very low blood sugar, including weakness, shakiness, nervousness, sweatiness, and confusion.

INSULIN RESISTANCE The tendency of cells in the body to resist the normal effects of insulin, causing insulin levels to rise, a characteristic of Type 2 diabetes.

ISLET OF LANGERHANS The part of the pancreas gland that produces insulin and glucagon.

KETOACIDOSIS A serious medical condition combining ketosis and acidosis. When inadequate insulin exists in the body, large amounts of sugar and ketones accumulate in the blood and urine. Affects people with Type 1 diabetes, not Type 2.

KETONES Chemicals produced when the body burns fat for energy, rather than sugar.

KETOSIS A potentially serious medical situation in which ketones are present in the urine due to excessive breakdown of fats.

KIMMELSTIEL-WILSON SYNDROME A medical term, first described by two doctors, for lesions on the kidneys that are caused by a degeneration of the blood vessels as a result of diabetes that is poorly controlled.

LDL CHOLESTEROL Low-density lipoprotein, or "bad," cholesterol—the form of cholesterol that remains in the blood. High levels of LDL cholesterol increase the risk of heart disease.

LIPID A scientific name for fats in the body.

LOW BLOOD SUGAR Blood glucose levels that are excessively low. Also called hypoglycemia.

MAINTENANCE DOSE The dose of a particular drug that achieves stability for a set period.

MEAL PLAN A strategy for eating carefully, in which particular foods are chosen to be eaten at particular times and in particular amounts.

MEDICAL NUTRITION THERAPY (MNT) Diet therapy by a health-care professional for a person with diabetes.

MENTAL HEALTH PROFESSIONAL A person who specializes in mental health and who may counsel individuals during times of great emotional need. Can be a psychiatrist, who is a medical doctor specializing in mental health and who can prescribe medications; may also be a psychologist or social worker. May work with either individuals or groups with particular needs.

METABOLIC SYNDROME Also called syndrome X or insulin resistance syndrome, a combination of factors including central obesity plus any two of the following: increased triglyceride levels, reduced HDL cholesterol, high blood pressure, high fasting blood sugar, or Type 2 diabetes. Increases the risk of heart problems and diabetes, if diabetes is not already present.

METABOLISM A medical term for the ongoing chemical processes inside the body, such as those that convert food into energy, that collectively keep the body alive.

MG/DL Milligrams per deciliter. Used to measure blood sugar and levels of some other chemicals in the body.

MICROALBUMINURIA An early sign of kidney disease in which small amounts of protein are detected in the urine.

MICROANEURYSMS Small opened-out areas in the very small blood vessels called capillaries, such as those found on the retina of the eye, that can burst or bleed.

MONOTHERAPY Treating a disease with one drug rather than several.

NEPHROPATHY A medical term for kidney damage occurring in the filtering portions, or nephrons, of the kidneys, which may be a long-term effect of diabetes.

NEUROPATHY Nerve tissue damage that may occur as a long-term complication of diabetes.

NON-INSULIN-DEPENDENT DIABETES MELLITUS (NIDDM) Another name for Type 2, or adult-onset, diabetes.

NUTRITIONIST A person who provides advice on nutrition.

OPHTHALMOLOGIST A medical doctor specializing in the care of the eyes.

ORAL HYPOGLYCEMIC AGENT A pill that lowers blood sugar.

ORTHOPEDIST A medical doctor who deals with the loco-motor structures of the body, such as the bones, joints, and muscles. Can specialize in particular areas, such as the feet and ankles.

PANCREAS An organ just behind the stomach that produces insulin, glucagon, and digestive enzymes.

PANCREAS (ARTIFICIAL) A small implanted device under development that withdraws blood and reinserts it into the body, mimicking the functions of the beta cells. It can be set to inject insulin or glucose to maintain normal levels in the blood.

PODIATRIST A doctor specializing in the care of feet.

POLYDIPSIA A medical term for extreme thirst that comes with increased drinking of water.

POLYPHAGIA A medical term for excessive hunger resulting in more eating.

POLYURIA A medical term for excessive output of urine.

PREDIABETES Blood sugar levels higher than normal but below a diagnosis of diabetes. Also called impaired glucose tolerance.

PREMIXED INSULIN An insulin containing a mixture of short- and intermediate-acting insulins, such as 70/30.

PROTEIN A nutrient required to sustain life, used to build and repair body tissues.

RECOMBINANT DNA TECHNOLOGY The chemical process of making biosynthetic human insulin.

RENAL A medical term for something having to do with the human kidneys.

RENAL THRESHOLD The so-called spill point, a bit different in every person, at which glucose is drawn out of the bloodstream and begins to spill from the kidneys into the urine.

RETINOPATHY A medical term for damage to the eye, specifically the blood vessels of the retina at the back of the eye, which can be a long-term complication of diabetes. Includes background retinopathy and the more advanced proliferative retinopathy, which cause blurred vision and other symptoms.

SATURATED FAT A type of fat, usually derived from animal sources, that is solid at room temperature. Lard and butter are examples of foods that contain saturated fats.

SELF-MANAGEMENT All your efforts to control diabetes, which may include stress reduction, blood glucose testing, dietary changes, exercise, and the use of medications.

SELF-MONITORING Your own testing and recording of test results, such as blood glucose or sugar levels.

SULFONYLUREA A class of drugs that stimulate the pancreas to produce additional insulin.

SUPPORT GROUP A group of people, and sometimes family members, who share a common disease or concern and who meet regularly to discuss life issues, often with a trained group leader.

TYPE 1 DIABETES Once known as juvenile-onset diabetes, a type of diabetes in which the body does not manufacture insulin. Also known as insulin-dependent diabetes mellitus (IDDM).

TYPE 2 DIABETES Once known as adult-onset diabetes, a type of diabetes most commonly found in older adults. The most common type of diabetes, Type 2 diabetes is a condition in which insulin is available to the body but cannot be properly utilized. Also called non-insulin-dependent diabetes mellitus (NIDDM), non-ketosis-prone diabetes, adult diabetes, or maturity-onset diabetes in the young (MODY).

UNSATURATED FATS Fats that are typically liquid at room temperature, such as vegetable oils. Monounsaturated fats, such as those in olive oil, do not lower HDL cholesterol. Polyunsaturated fats, such as those in corn oil, are more chemically complex forms of unsaturated fats.

Resources

Many excellent resources are available when you're ready to learn more about diabetes. This newly revised section provides telephone and Internet contact information for government and nonprofit health organizations, educational organizations, professional groups, and some pharmaceutical companies and manufacturers. It also lists publications of interest, including magazines and newsletters, books, and many websites and Internet addresses.

Government, Educational, and Nonprofit Organizations

Diabetes Information

American Association of Diabetes Educators
100 W. Monroe Street
Chicago, IL 60603

(800) 338-3633

www.aadenet.org

This organization can provide a list of certified diabetes educators in your area.

American Diabetes Association

1701 N. Beauregard Street

Alexandria, VA 22331

(800) 342-2383

www.diabetes.org

The largest diabetes organization in the world, encompassing consumers and professionals who treat people with diabetes. Makes recommendations on diabetes care and publishes magazines, educational materials, and books such as the free 32-page booklet "Choose to Live: Your Diabetes Survival Guide." Provides information on clinical trials, local medical specialists, and support groups. English- or Spanish-speaking operators can refer you to state, provincial, or local associations that are good sources of information on local doctors, educational meetings, and other services.

American Dietetic Association

120 S. Riverside Plaza, Suite 2000

Chicago, IL 60606-6995

(800) 877-1600; consumer nutrition line: (800) 366-1655

www.eatright.org

Canadian Diabetes Association

National Life Building, 1400-522 University Avenue

Toronto, ON M5G2R5

(800) 226-8464

www.diabetes.ca

Indian Health Service National Diabetes Program
5300 Homestead Road NE
Albuquerque, NM 87110
(505) 248-4182
www.ihs.gov/medicalprograms/diabetes

International Diabetes Center
3800 Park Nicollet Boulevard
Minneapolis, MN 55416
(888) 825-6315 or (952) 993-3393
www.idcdiabetes.org

Joslin Diabetes Center
1 Joslin Place
Boston, MA 02215
(800) 567-5461 or (617) 732-2415
www.joslin.org
   A well-known diabetes care center, with several affiliates around the United States.

National Diabetes Education Program of the
National Institutes of Health and the
Centers for Disease Control and Prevention
1 Diabetes Way
Bethesda, MD 20814-9692
(800) 438-5383 or (301) 496-3583
www.ndep.nih.gov
   This program offers two free educational kits for people with diabetes, "Feet Can Last a Lifetime" and "Do Your Level Best."

National Diabetes Information Clearinghouse
1 Information Way
Bethesda, MD 20892-3560

(800) 654-3327

www.diabetes.niddk.nih.gov

The National Institutes of Health's information clearinghouse on diabetes is a prime source of information.

National Kidney and Urologic Diseases Information Clearinghouse
3 Information Way
Bethesda, MD 20892-3580
(800) 654-4415
www.kidney.niddk.nih.gov

Medical Information

American Board of Medical Specialties
(800) ASK-ABMS (275-2627)
www.abms.org

This organization will verify a doctor's credentials as a specialist or refer you to a board-certified specialist in your area.

American Board of Podiatric Surgery
(415) 553-7800
www.abps.org

This organization can provide a list of local board-certified podiatrists.

American College of Foot and Ankle Surgeons
(800) 421-2237, (773) 693-9300, or
(888) THE-FEET (843-3338)
www.acfas.org

Joint Commission on Accreditation of Healthcare
Organizations
(603) 792-5000
www.jcaho.org
This organization checks and accredits hospitals in the United
States.

National Osteoporosis Foundation
(202) 223-2226
www.nof.org

Neuropathy Association, Inc.
(212) 692-0662
www.neuropathy.org

Visiting Nurse Association of America
99 Summer Street, No. 1700
Boston, MA 02110
(617) 737-3200
www.vna.org

Athletics and Fitness

American College of Sports Medicine
PO Box 1440
Indianapolis, IN 46206
(317) 637-9200
www.acsm.org

American Council on Exercise
4851 Paramount Drive
San Diego, CA 92123

(800) 825-3636
www.acefitness.org

American Volks-Sports Association
1001 Pat Boorer Road
Universal City, TX 78148
(800) 830-9255
www.ava.org

Aquatic Exercise Association
PO Box 1609
Nokomis, FL 34274
(888) AEA-WAVE (232-9283)
www.aeawave.com

Armchairfitness.Com
7755 Sixteenth Street NW
Washington, DC 20012
(800) 453-6280
www.armchairfitness.com

Diabetes Exercise and Sports Association
8001 Montcastle Drive
Nashville, TN 37221
(800) 898-4322
www.diabetes-exercise.org

National Organization of Mall Walkers
PO Box 256
Hermann, MO 65041
(573) 486-3945

Sierra Club
85 Second Street, Second Floor
San Francisco, CA 94105
(415) 977-5500
www.sierraclub.org

United States Association of Blind Athletes
33 N. Institute Street
Colorado Springs, CO 80903
(719) 630-0422
www.usaba.org

YMCA of the USA
(800) 872-9622
www.ymca.net

Acupuncture

American Academy of Medical Acupuncture
4929 Wilshire Boulevard, No. 428
Los Angeles, CA 90010
(323) 937-5514
www.medicalacupuncture.org

Biofeedback

Association for Applied Psychophysiology and Biofeedback
10200 W. Forty-Fourth Avenue, No. 304
Wheat Ridge, CO 80033
(303) 422-8436
www.aapb.org

Diet

American Dietetic Association
120 S. Riverside Plaza, Suite 2000
Chicago, IL 60606-6995
(800) 877-1600
www.eatright.org

Overeaters Anonymous
PO Box 44020
Rio Rancho, NM 87174-4020
(505) 891-2664
www.oa.org/index.htm

Weight Watchers
(800) 651-6000
www.weightwatchers.com

Financial and Insurance Information

American Association of Retired Persons (AARP)
(888) 687-2277
www.aarp.org

Centers for Medicare & Medicaid Services
(800) 633-4227
www.medicare.gov
    Can provide a free copy of the booklet "Medicare Coverage of Diabetes Supplies and Services."

For financial help with some ancillary costs not covered by Medicare for dialysis and kidney transplants, some assistance may be available through:

American Kidney Fund
6110 Executive Boulevard, Suite 1010
Rockville, MD 20852
(800) 638-8299; Spanish: 866-300-2900
www.akfinc.org

National Kidney Foundation
30 E. Thirty-Third Street
New York, NY 10016
(800) 622-9010
www.kidney.org

Medicare Information Line
(800) 638-6833
    Provides information about Medicare, Medicare supplemental insurance, HMOs, and special programs for low-income people.

Office of Disability Employment Policy
c/o U.S. Department of Labor
Frances Perkins Building
200 Constitution Avenue NW
Washington, DC 20210
(866) 633-7365
www.dol.gov/odep

Pharmaceutical Research and Manufacturers of America
1100 Fifteenth Street NW
Washington, DC 20005
(800) 762-4636 or (202) 835-3400
Novo-Nordisk only: (800) 727-6500
www.helpingpatients.org
Spanish language: www.espanol.helpingpatients.org

This group will provide a brochure listing the programs offered by drug companies to help people without insurance secure necessary medicines.

Together Rx Access
(800) 444-4106
www.togetherrxaccess.com
Several pharmaceutical companies offer discounts of 20 percent to 40 percent on prescription drugs for uninsured low-income people under age sixty-five.

U.S. Equal Employment Opportunity Commission
(800) 669-4000
www.eeoc.gov

State Pharmaceutical Assistance Programs
www.ncsl.org/programs/health/drugaid.htm
Website offering a list of states with drug assistance programs to help low-income elderly or disabled people who don't qualify for Medicaid.

Sight Impairment

American Council of the Blind
1155 Fifteenth Street NW
Washington, DC 20005
(800) 424-8666
www.acb.org

Braille Institute
741 N. Vermont Avenue
Los Angeles, CA 90029

(800) 272-4553 or (323) 295-4050

www.brailleinstitute.org

Maintains a library of braille and talking books and offers classes in California locations on survival skills, including using insulin.

Guide Dogs for the Blind

(800) 295-4050

www.guidedogs.com

National Federation of the Blind

1800 Johnson Street

Baltimore, MD 21230

(410) 659-9314

www.nfb.org

The National Federation of the Blind's diabetes division, the Diabetes Action Network, produces an excellent free newsletter, *Voice of the Diabetic*, available in print or on audiocassette. The federation offers classes and educational programs, some several months long, that focus on living skills and coping with blindness.

National Library Service for the Blind and Physically Handicapped

(800) 424-8567

Free library of recorded books and magazines.

Stop Smoking

American Heart Association

(800) 242-8721

www.americanheart.org

Offers a free stop-smoking kit, "Calling It Quits."

American Lung Association
(800) LUNG-USA (586-4872)
www.lungusa.org
   Offers stop-smoking information.

Support Groups

American Diabetes Association
(800) 232-3472
   Will refer you to a local support group.

Friends Health Connection
PO Box 114
New Brunswick, NJ 08903
(800) 483-7436
www.48friend.com
   This organization connects people to others with similar
health problems.

National Family Caregivers Association
10400 Connecticut Avenue, No. 500
Kensington, MD 20895-2504
(800) 896-3650
www.nfcacares.org
   Networking services for caregivers of all types.

Therapy

American Association for Marriage and Family Therapy
(703) 838-9808
www.aamft.org

American Association of Sex Educators, Counselors,
and Therapists
(800) 752-0026
www.aasect.org

National Campaign on Anxiety and Depression Awareness
(888) 442-2022
www.freedomfromfear.org

National Institute of Mental Health
(800) 421-4211
www.nimh.nih.gov
   Offers depression publications.

Travel

International Association of Medical Assistance for Travelers
(716) 754-4883; in Canada: (519) 836-0102
www.iamat.org
   Sells a directory of English-speaking doctors around the
world.

International Diabetes Federation
www.idf.org
   This Belgium-based federation can provide a list of doctors
who specialize in treating diabetes for foreign travelers.

Yoga

International Association of Yoga Therapists
PO Box 2513
Prescott, AZ 8602
(928) 541-0004
www.iayt.org

Pharmaceutical and Equipment Companies

Glucose Meter Manufacturers

Abbott Diabetes Care
(888) 522-5226
www.abbottdiabetescare.com

Bayer, Diagnostics Division
(800) 348-8100
www.bayercarediabetes.com

LifeScan, a Johnson & Johnson company
(800) 227-8862
www.lifescan.com

Roche Diagnostics Corporation
(800) 858-8072
www.roche-diagnostics.us

Insulin Pumps

Animas Corporation
(877) 937-7867
www.animascorp.com

Medtronic MiniMed
(800) 826-2099; outside U.S.: (818) 576-5555
www.minimed.com

Smiths Medical
(800) 826-9703
www.cozmore.com

Insulin Manufacturers

Sanofi-Aventis
(800) 981-2491
www.sanofi-aventis.us

Eli Lilly Company
(800) 545-5979
www.lillydiabetes.com

Novo-Nordisk Pharmaceuticals, Inc.
(800) 727-6500
www.novonordisk-us.com

Medical Supplies

Diabetic.com
(800) 993-4223
www.diabetic.com

Maxi-Aids
(800) 522-6294
www.maxiaids.com
    Products for people with visual and physical impairments.

Medic Alert Foundation International
(888) 633-4298; outside U.S.: (209) 668-3333
www.medicalert.org

Reading

Magazines and Newsletters of Interest

Diabetes Forecast
(800) 232-3472
www.diabetes.org
    Published by the American Diabetes Association.

Diabetes Health
(800) 488-8468
www.diabeteshealth.com

Diabetes Self-Management
(800) 234-0923
www.diabetes-self-mgmt.com

Diabetes Wellness News
(877) 633-3976
www.diabeteswellness.net

Voice of the Diabetic
(410) 659-9314
www.nfb.org/voice.htm

Books

Anderson, James. *Diabetes: A Practical New Guide to Healthy Living.* New York: Warner Books, 1991.

Beaser, Richard S., and Joan V. C. Hill. *The Joslin Guide to Diabetes: A Program for Managing Your Treatment.* New York: Simon & Schuster, 1995.

Bernstein, Richard K. *Diabetes Type II: Including Dramatic New Approaches to the Treatment of Type I Diabetes.* Englewood Cliffs, New Jersey: Prentice-Hall Press, 1990.

Cousins, Norman. *The Healing Heart.* New York: W. W. Norton, 1983.

Drum, David. *Alternative Therapies for Managing Diabetes.* New York: McGraw-Hill, 2002.

Edelwich, Jerry, and Archie Brodsky. *Diabetes: Caring for Your Emotions.* New York: Addison-Wesley, 1986.

Ezrin, Calvin, and Robert E. Kowalski. *The Type 2 Diabetes Diet Book.* Los Angeles: Lowell House, 1995.

Gordon, Neil F. *Diabetes: Your Complete Exercise Guide.* Champaign, Illinois: Human Kinetics, 1993.

Graham, Claudia, June Biermann, and Barbara Toohey. *The Diabetes Sports and Exercise Book.* Los Angeles: Lowell House, 1995.

Hansen, Barbara Caleen, and Shauna S. Roberts. *The Commonsense Guide to Weight Loss for People with Diabetes.* Alexandria, Virginia: American Diabetes Association, 1998.

Jovanovic-Peterson, Lois, Charles M. Peterson, and Morton B. Stone. *A Touch of Diabetes: A Straightforward Guide for People Who Have Type 2, Non-Insulin-Dependent Diabetes.* Minneapolis: Chronimed Publishing, 1995.

Monk, Arlene, et al. *Managing Type 2 Diabetes.* Wayzata, Minnesota: DO Publishing, 1988.

Polonsky, William H. *Diabetes Burnout: What to Do When You Can't Take It Anymore.* Alexandria, Virginia: American Diabetes Association, 1999.

Walsh, John, and Ruth Roberts. *Pumping Insulin: Everything in a Book for Successful Use of an Insulin Pump.* San Diego: Torrey Pines Press, 1994.

Cookbooks

Brody, Jane. *Jane Brody's Good Food Book.* New York: Bantam, 1987.

Exchange Lists and Meal Planning. Rev. 1995. American Diabetes Association and American Dietetic Association. Available in braille and on audiocassette from American Diabetes Association, 1701 N. Beauregard Street, Alexandria, VA 22331.

Family Cookbooks. Vols. 1–4. American Diabetes Association and American Dietetic Association, 1701 N. Beauregard Street, Alexandria, VA 22331.

Finsand, Mary Jane. *The Complete Diabetic Cookbook.* New York: Sterling Publishing, 1987.

Gillard, Judy, and Joy Kirkpatrick. *The Guiltless Gourmet.* Rancho Mirage, California: Nutrition Wise Partnership, 1990.

Nissenberg, Sandra K., Margaret L. Bogle, and Audrey Wright. *Quick Meals for Healthy Kids and Busy Parents.* Minneapolis: Chronimed Publishing, 1995.

Polin, Bonnie, Fran Giedt, and Joslin Nutrition Services Department. *The Joslin Diabetes Gourmet Cookbook.* New York: Bantam Books, 1994.

Soneral, Lois. *The Type 2 Diabetes Cookbook*. Los Angeles: Lowell House, 1997.

Warshaw, Hope S. *The Restaurant Companion*. Chicago: Surrey Books, 1990.

Wedman, Betty. *American Diabetes Association Holiday Cookbook*. Englewood Cliffs, New Jersey: Prentice-Hall, 1986.

Electronic Information

Here are a few additional websites of possible interest.

www.brighamandwomens.org/healtheweightforwomen
Boston women's hospital site—shopping tips and menu ideas.

www.caloriecontrol.org
Calorie Control Council site—lets you calculate BMI, or body mass index, and calories expended with exercise.

www.calorieking.com
Food information, featuring a searchable database on foods, including fast-food fare.

www.cdc.gov
Federal Centers for Disease Control and Prevention.

www.centerwatch.com
Clinical trials listings.

www.cookinglight.com

Cooking Light magazine website—recipes and nutritional information.

www.crbestbuydrugs.org

Consumer Reports public education website—compares prescription drugs based on price, safety, and effectiveness.

www.diabetictraveler.com

Newsletter for people with diabetes who travel.

www.drugdigest.org

Drug Digest includes consumer information on prescription drugs, over-the-counter drugs, and vitamins and supplements; offers a "Drug Library" to check drugs by name and a "Check Interactions" feature that allows you to check interactions between drugs you specify.

www.fda.gov/medwatch

The U.S. Food and Drug Administration's website on drug and medical device safety.

www.gourmetconnection.com

Diabetes Gourmet magazine site offers great recipes and information.

www.intelihealth.com

Johns Hopkins Hospital Health Information site offers extensive information plus a drug search capability.

www.mayoclinic.com

Weight-loss information under Diseases and Conditions (click letter *W*), including reviews of diet books and a weight-loss quiz.

www.nal.usda.gov/fnic/foodcomp/search

A database listing nutritional information for 6,500 fresh and packaged food items compiled by the U.S. Department of Agriculture.

www.ndei.org

National Diabetes Education Initiative (Type 2).

http://hin.nhlbi.nih.gov/portion

National Heart, Lung, and Blood Institute. Offers a portion-distortion quiz.

Index

Renaissance Popes

Martin V (Colonna), 1417-31
Eugenius IV (Condulmer), 1431-47
Nicholas V (Parentucelli), 1447-55
Calixtus III (Borgia), 1455-58
Pius II (Piccolomini), 1458-64
Paul II (Barbo), 1464-71
Sixtus IV (Della Rovere), 1471-84
Innocent VIII (Cibo), 1484-92
Alexander VI (Borgia), 1492-1503
Pius III (Piccolomini), 1503
Julius II (Della Rovere), 1503-13

Leo X (Medici), 1513-21
Adrian VI (Dedel), 1522-23
Clement VII (Medici), 1523-34
Paul III (Farnese), 1534-49
Julius III (Ciocchi del Monte), 1550-55
Marcello II (Cervini), 1555
Paul IV (Carafa), 1555-59
Pius IV (Medici), 1560-65
Pius V (Ghislieri), 1566-72
Gregory XIII (Boncompagni), 1572-85
Sixtus V (Peretti), 1585-90

Bibliography

ACKERMAN, J. S., "The Belvedere as a Classical Villa," *Journal of the Warburg and Courtauld Institutes*, 14 (1951), 70-91
— *The Cortile del Belvedere*, Studi e documenti per la storia del Palazzo Apostolico Vaticano, 3 (Vatican, 1954)
— *The Architecture of Michelangelo* (Harmondsworth: Penguin, 1971)
— "The Planning of Renaissance Rome, 1450-1580," in *Rome in the Renaissance: The City and The Myth*, ed. P.A. Ramsey, Medieval and Renaissance Texts and Studies, 18 (Center for Medieval and Early Renaissance Studies,Binghamton, N.Y., 1982), 3-18
AIKIN, R., "Christian Soldiers in the Sala dei Capitani," *Sixteenth Century Journal*, 16 (1985), 206-27
ANTONOVICS, A.V., "Counter-Reformation Cardinals: 1534-90," *European Studies Review*, 2 (1972), 301-27
ALBERTI, L.B., *On the Art of Building in Ten Books*, trans. J. Rykwert et al (Cambridge, Mass.: MIT Press, 1988)

BAROLSKY, P., *Daniele da Volterra: A Catalogue Raisonné* (New York and London: Garland, 1979)
BAUMGARTEN, P. M., *Von den Kardinälen des sechszehnten Jahrhunderts* (Krumbach: F. Aker, 1926)
BENEDETTI, S. et al, *L'Arte in Roma nel Secolo XVI*, 2 vols, Istituto Nazionale di Studi Romani (Bologna: Cappelli, 1990-92)
BENTIVOGLIO, E., and S. VALTIERI, *Santa Maria del Popolo a Roma* (Rome: Bardi Editore, 1976)
BOBER, P. P., and R.O. RUBINSTEIN, *Renaissance Artists and Antique Sculpture: A Handbook of Sources* (Harvey Miller and Oxford University Press: London and New York, 1986)
BOSEL, R., *Jesuitarchitektur in Italien, 1540-1773. Die Baudenkmäler der Römischen und Neapolitanischen Ordensprovinz*, 2 vols (Vienna, 1985)

BOSSY, J., *Christianity in the West, 1400-1700* (Oxford: Oxford University Press, 1985)
BRADY, T.A., H.A. OBERMAN, and J.D. TRACY (eds), *Handbook of European History 1400-1600. Late Middle Ages, Renaissance and Reformation*, 2 vols (Leiden and New York: E.J. Brill, 1994)
BRODRICK, J., *The Origin of the Jesuits* (New York: Longmans Green, 1940)
BRUMMER, H.H., *The Statue Court in the Vatican Belvedere*, Stockholm Studies in the History of Art, 20 (Stockholm: Almquist and Wiksell, 1970)
BRUSCHI, A., *Bramante architetto* (Bari: Laterza, 1969); shorter, revised English edn. *Bramante* (London: Thames and Hudson, 1977)
BUDDENSIEG, T., "Zum Statuenprogramm im Kapitolsplan Pauls III," *Zeitschrift für Kunstgeschichte* 32 (1969), 177-228
BURROUGHS, C., "Below the Angel: An Urbanistic Project in the Rome of Pope Nicholas V," *Journal of the Warburg and Courtauld Institutes* 45 (1982), 94-124
— *From Signs to Design. Environmental Process and Reform in Early Renaissance Rome* (Cambridge, Mass., and London: MIT Press, 1990)

CEEN, A., "The Quartiere de'Banchi: Urban Planning in Rome in the First Half of the Cinquecento" (Ph.D. dissertation, University of Pennsylvania, 1977)
CELLINI, BENVENUTO, *The Autobiography of Benvenuto Cellini* (trans. G. Bull; Harmondsworth: Penguin, 1956)
CHASTEL, A., *The Sack of Rome, 1527*, trans. B. Archer, A.W. Mellon Lectures in the Fine Arts, 26; Bollingen Series XXXV, 26 (Princeton: Princeton University Press, 1983)

CIERI VIA, C., "*Characteres et figuras in opere magico.* Pinturicchio et la décoration de la *camera segreta* de l'appartement Borgia," *Revue de l'art* 94 (1991), 11–26

COCHRANE, E., *Italy, 1530–1630* (London and New York: Longman, 1988)

COFFIN, D.R., *The Villa d'Este at Tivoli* (Princeton: Princeton University Press, 1960)

— *The Villa in the Life of Renaissance Rome* (Princeton: Princeton University Press, 1979)

— *Gardens and Gardening in Papal Rome* (Princeton: Princeton University Press, 1991)

COHN, N., *The Pursuit of the Millennium* (New York: Oxford University Press, 1970)

DACOS, N., *La Découverte de la Domus Aurea et la formation des grotesques à la Renaissance*, Studies of the Warburg Institute, 31 (London and Leiden, 1969)

D'AMICO, J.F., *Renaissance Humanism in Papal Rome: Humanists and Churchmen on the Eve of Reformation* (Baltimore and London: Johns Hopkins University Press, 1983)

DAVIDSON, B.F., *Raphael's Bible: A Study of the Vatican Logge,* College Art Association Monographs on the Fine Arts, 39 (University Park: Pennsylvania State University Press, 1985)

DELUMEAU, J., *Vie économique et sociale de Rome dans la seconde moitié du XVIe siècle,* 2 vols (Paris: E. de Boccard, 1957–59)

— "Rome: Political and Administrative Centralization in the Papal State in the Sixteenth Century," *The Late Italian Renaissance, 1525–1630,* ed. E. Cochrane (New York: Harper and Row, 1970), 287–304

DEMPSEY, C., "Mythic Inventions in Counter-Reformation Painting," *Rome in the Renaissance: The City and the Myth,* ed. P.A. Ramsey, Medieval and Renaissance Texts and Studies, 18 (Center for Medieval and Early Renaissance Studies, Binghamton, N. Y., 1982), 55–75

DICKENS, A.G., *The Counter Reformation* (Norwich: Harcourt, Brace & World, 1970)

DUSSLER, L., *Raphael. A Critical Catalogue of his Pictures, Wall-Paintings and Tapestries* (trans. S. Cruft; New York and London: Phaidon, 1971)

EBERT–SCHIFFERER, S., "Ripandas kapitolinescher Freskenzyklus und die Selbstdarstellung der Konservatoren um 1500," *Römisches Jahrbuch für Kunstgeschichte,* 23/24 (1988), 75–218

EINEM, H. VON, *Michelangelo* (London: Methuen, 1973)

ERASMUS, DESIDERIUS, *The 'Julius Exclusus' of Erasmus,* trans. P. Pascal, intro. and critical notes by J.K. Sowards (Bloomington: Indiana University Press, 1968)

ETTLINGER, L. D., *The Sistine Chapel before Michelangelo: Religious Imagery and Papal Primacy* (Oxford: Clarendon Press, 1965)

EVENNETT, H. O., *The Spirit of the Counter-Reformation* (Notre Dame: University of Notre Dame Press, 1970)

FAGIOLO, M. and M.L. MADONNA, "La Roma di Pio IV: la Civitas Pia, la Salus Medica, la Custodia Angelica," *Arte Illustrata* 5 (1972), 383–402

FALDI, I., *Il Palazzo Farnese di Caprarola* (Turin: Edizioni Seat, 1981)

FIRPO, M, "The Cardinal," in *Renaissance Characters,* ed. E. Garin, trans. L.G. Cochrane, (Chicago and London: University of Chicago Press, 1991), 46–97

FREEDBERG, S. J., *Painting of the High Renaissance in Rome and Florence,* 2 vols (Cambridge, Mass.: Harvard University Press, 1961)

FROMMEL, C. L., *Der Römische Palastbau der Hochrenaissance,* 3 vols, Römische Forschungen der Bibliotheca Hertziana, 21 (Tübingen: Wasmuth, 1973)

— "Die Peterskirche unter Papst Julius II. im Licht neuer Dokumente," *Römisches Jahrbuch für Kunstgeschichte* 16 (1976), 57–136

— "Francesco del Borgo: Architekt Pius' II. und Pauls II.," *Römisches Jahrbuch für Kunstgeschichte* 20 (1983), 107–54, and 21 (1984), 71–164

— "Il Palazzo Vaticano sotto Giulio II e Leone X: Strutture e funzione," *Raffaello in Vaticano* (Milan: Electa, 1984), 118–35

— "Papal Policy: The Planning of Rome during the Renaissance," in *Art and History: Images and Their Meaning,* eds. R.I. Rotberg and T.K. Rabb, (Cambridge: Cambridge University Press, 1986), 39–65

— "Il Cardinal Raffaele Riario ed il Palazzo della Cancelleria," in *Sisto IV e Giulio II mecenati e promotori di cultura,* eds S. Bottaro et al, Atti del Convegno Internazionale di Studi, Savona, 1985 (Savona: Coop Tipograf, 1989), 73–85

— "Il Palazzo della Cancelleria," in *Il Palazzo dal Rinascimento a oggi in Italia nel regno di Napoli in Calabria: Storia e attualità,* ed. S. Valtieri, Atti del Convegno Internazionale Reggio Calabria, 20–22 Ottobre 1988; (Rome: Gangemi editore, 1989), 29–54

— "St. Peter's: The Early History," in *The Renaissance from Brunelleschi to Michelangelo,* H.A. Millon et al (Milan, 1994)

FROMMEL, C. L. et al, *Raffaello architetto* (Milan: Electa, 1984)

GAMRATH, H., *Roma Sancta Renovata: Studi sull'urbanistica di Roma nella seconda metà del sec. XVI con particolare referimento al ponificato di Sisto V (1585–1590),* Analecta Romana Instituti Danici, 12 (Rome: L'"Erma" di Bretschneider, 1987)

GEIGER, G.L., *Filippino Lippi's Carafa Chapel: Renaissance Art in Rome,* Sixteenth-Century Essays and Studies, 5 (Ann Arbor: 1986)

GERE, J., *Taddeo Zuccaro: His Development Studied in his Drawings* (Chicago and London: University of Chicago Press, 1969)

GILBERT, F., *The Pope, his Banker, and Venice* (Cambridge, Mass.: Harvard University Press, 1980)

GLEASON, E.G., *Reform Thought in Sixteenth-Century Italy,* American Academy of Religion, Texts and Translations Series, 4 (Chico, Calif.: Scholars Press, 1981)

Gli affreschi di Paolo III a Castel Sant'Angelo: Progetti ed esecuzione 1543–1548 (Rome: de Luca, 1981)

HALLMAN, B. McC., *Italian Cardinals, Reform and the Church as Property, 1492–1563* (Berkeley and Los Angeles: University of California Press, 1985)

HARPRATH, R., *Papst Paul III. al Alexander der Grosse. Das Freskenprogramm der Sala Paolina in der Engelsburg* (Berlin and New York: de Gruyter, 1978)

HAY, D., "The Renaissance Cardinals: Church, State, Culture," *Synthesis* 3 (1976), 35–46

— *The Church in Italy in the Fifteenth Century: The Birkbeck Lectures, 1971* (Cambridge and New York: Cambridge University Press, 1977)

HEYDENREICH, L. and W. LOTZ, *Architecture in Italy, 1400–1600*, trans. M. Hottinger, Pelican History of Art, (Harmondsworth: Penguin, London: 1974)

Hibbard, H., "*Ut picturae sermones*: The First Painted Decorations of the Gesù," in *Baroque Art: The Jesuit Contribution*, eds R. Wittkower and I.B. Jaffe (New York: Fordham University Press, 1972), 29–49

— *Michelangelo* (New York: McGraw-Hill, 1974)

HIRST, M., *Sebastiano del Piombo* (Oxford: Clarendon Press, 1981)

JACKS, P., *The Antiquarian and the Myth of Antiquity. The Origins of Rome in Renaissance Thought* (New York and Cambridge: Cambridge University Press, 1993)

JEDEN, H., *A History of the Council of Trent*, trans. D.E. Graf, 2 vols, (St. Louis: B. Herder, 1957)

JONES, M.D.W., *The Counter Reformation: Religion and Society in Early Modern Europe* (Cambridge: Cambridge University Press, 1995)

JONES, R. and N. PENNY, *Raphael* (New Haven and London: Yale University Press, 1983)

JUNGMANN, J.A., *The Mass of the Roman Rite: Its Origins and Development*, 2 vols (New York: Benziger Brothers, 1951)

KELLER, R.E., *Das Oratorium von San Giovanni Decollato in Rom: Eine Studie seiner Fresken* (Neuchâtel: Institut Suisse de Rome, 1976)

KLIEMANN, J., *Gesta Dipinte: La grande decorazione nelle dimore italiane dal Quattrocento al Seicento* (Milan: Silvana, 1993)

LEE, E., *Sixtus IV and Men of Letters*, Temi e Testi, 26 (Rome: Edizioni di storia e letteratura, 1978)

LEWINE, C. F., *The Sistine Chapel Walls and the Roman Liturgy* (University Park: Pennsylvania State University Press, 1993)

LEWINE, M.J., "The Roman Church Interior, 1527–1580" (Ph.D. dissertation, Columbia University, 1960)

— "Roman Architectural Practice During Michelangelo's Maturity," in *Stil und Überlieferung in der Kunst des Abendlandes*, 2 vols, Akten des 21. Internationalen Kongress. Kunst. Bonn 1964 (1967), II, 20–26

MADONNA, M.L. (ed.), *Roma di Sisto V: Le arti e la cultura* (Rome: de Luca, 1993)

MAGNUSON, T., *Studies in Roman Quattrocento Architecture* (Stockholm: Almquist and Wiksell, 1958)

Michelangelo e la Sistina. La tecnica, il restauro, il mito (Rome: Fratelli Palombi, 1990)

MITCHELL, B., *Rome in the High Renaissance: The Age of Leo X* (Norman: University of Oklahoma Press, 1973)

MORTARI, L., *Francesco Salviati* (Rome: de Luca, 1992)

MURRAY, P., *Bramante's Tempietto*, Charlton Lecture on Art, Univ. of Newcastle upon Tyne (London: McLean, 1972)

O'MALLEY, J., *Giles of Viterbo on Church and Reform: A Study in Renaissance Thought* (Leiden: E.J. Brill, 1968)

— *Praise and Blame in Renaissance Rome: Rhetoric, Doctrine, and Reform in the Sacred Orators of the Papal Court, c. 1450–1521*, Duke Monographs in Medieval and Renaissance Studies, 3 (Durham, N.C.: Duke University Press, 1979)

— *The First Jesuits* (Cambridge, Mass.: Harvard University Press, 1993)

Le Palais Farnèse: École française de Rome, 3 vols (Rome: L'"Erma" di Bretschneider, 1980–81)

PARKS, N.R., "On the Meaning of Pinturicchio's *Sala dei Santi*," *Art History* 2 (1979), 291–317

PARTNER, P., *Renaissance Rome, 1500–1559: A Portrait of a Society* (Berkeley and Los Angeles: University of California Press, 1976)

— *The Pope's Men: The Papal Civil Service in the Renaissance* (Oxford: Clarendon Press, 1990)

PARTRIDGE, L., "Triumphalism and the Sala Regia in the Vatican," *'All the world's a stage...': Art and Pageantry in the Renaissance and Baroque*, eds B. Wisch and S.S. Munshower, 2 vols, Papers in Art History from The Pennsylvania State University, 6 (University Park, Pa., 1990), 22–81

PARTRIDGE, L. and STARN, R., *A Renaissance Likeness. Art and Culture in Raphael's "Julius II"* (Berkeley and Los Angeles: University of California Press, 1980)

PASTOR, L. VON, *The History of the Popes from the Close of the Middle Ages*, eds F.I. Antrobus et al, 40 vols, (St. Louis: Herder, 1912–52)

PIETRANGELI, C., et al, *The Sistine Chapel. The Art, the History, and the Restoration* (New York, 1986)

QUEDNAU, R., *Die Sala di Costantino im Vatikanischen Palast: zur Dekoration der beiden Medici-Päpste Leo X. und Clemens VII.*, Studien zur Kunstgeschichte, 13 (Hildesheim: Georg Olms, 1979)

Raffaello nell'Appartamento di Giulio II e Leone X (Milan: ENEL, Electa, and Edizioni Musei Vaticani, 1993)

REDIG DE CAMPOS, D., *I Palazzi Vaticani*, Roma Cristiana, 18 (Bologna: Cappelli, 1967)

REINHARD, W., "Nepotismus. Der Funktionswandel einer päpstgeschichtlichen Konstanten," *Zeitschrift für Kirchengeschichte* 86 (1975), 145–85

ROBERTS, P.L., *Masolino da Panicale* (Oxford: Oxford University Press, 1993)

ROBERTSON, C., "Il Gran Cardinale": Alessandro Farnese, Patron of the Arts (New Haven and London: Yale University Press, 1992)

ROSENTHAL, E., "The Antecedents of Bramante's Tempietto," Journal of the Society of Architectural Historians 23 (1964), 55–74

SALERNO, L., L. SPEZZAFERRO, AND M. TAFURI, Via Giulia: Una utopia urbanistica del '500 (Rome: Aristide Staderini, 1975)

SANDSTRÖM, SVEN, Levels of Unreality. Studies in Structure and Construction in Italian Mural Painting During the Renaissance, Acta Universitatis Upsaliensis; Figura, N.S.4 (Uppsala: Almquist and Wiksell, 1963)

SCHIFFMANN, R., Roma felix: Aspekte der städtebaulichen Gestaltung Roms unter Papst Sixtus V. (Bern and Frankfurt am Main: Peter Lang, 1985)

SCHROEDER, H.J. (ed.), The Canons and Decrees of the Council of Trent (St. Louis and London: Herder, 1941)

SETTON, K.M., The Papacy and the Levant (1204–1571), 2 vols (Philadelphia: American Philosophical Society, 1976–78)

SHAW, C., Julius II: the Warrior Pope (Oxford: Blackwell, 1988)

SHEARMAN, J., Mannerism (Harmondsworth, 1967)

— "The Vatican Stanze: Functions and Decoration," Proceedings of the British Academy 57 (1971), 369–424

— Raphael's Cartoons in the Collection of Her Majesty the Queen and the Tapestries for the Sistine Chapel (London and New York: Phaidon, 1972)

SMITH, G., The Casino of Pius IV (Princeton: Princeton University Press, 1977)

SPEZZAFERRO, L., and M.E. TITTONI, Il Campidoglio e Sisto V (Rome: Carte Segrete, 1991)

STEINBERG, L., Michelangelo's Last Paintings: The Conversion of St. Paul and the Crucifixion of St. Peter in the Cappella Paolina, Vatican Palace (New York: Oxford University Press, 1975)

STINGER, C.L., The Renaissance in Rome (Bloomington: Indiana University Press, 1985)

THOMSON, J.A.F., Popes and Princes, 1417–1517: Politics and Polity in the Late Medieval Church (London: Allen and Unwin, 1980)

TOMEI, P., L'architettura a Roma nel Quattrocento (Rome: Multigrafica, 1977)

URBAN, G., "Die Kirchenbaukunst des Quattrocento in Rom," Römisches Jahrbuch für Kunstgeschichte 9–10 (1961–62), 75–287

— "Zum Neubau-Projekt von St. Peter unter Nikolaus V.," Festschrift für Harald Keller (Darmstadt: Eduard Roether, 1963), 131–73

WEIL-GARRIS, K., and J.F. D'AMICO, "The Renaissance Cardinal's Ideal Palace: A Chapter from Cortesi's De Cardinalatu," in Studies in Italian Art and Architecture 15th through 18th Centuries, ed. H.A. Millon, Memoirs of the American Academy in Rome, 35 (Rome: Elefante, 1980), 45–123

WEISS, ROBERTO, The Renaissance Discovery of Classical Antiquity (Oxford: Blackwell, 1963)

WEISZ, J.S., Pittura e Misericordia: The Oratory of S. Giovanni Decollato in Rome (Ann Arbor: UMI Research Press, 1984)

WESTFALL, C.W., In this Most Perfect Paradise: Alberti, Nicholas V, and the Invention of Conscious Urban Planning in Rome, 1447–55 (University Park: Pennsylvania State University Press, 1974)

— "Alberti and the Vatican Palace Type," Journal of the Society of Architectural Historians 33 (1974), 101–21

WISCH, B.L., "The Archiconfraternità del Gonfalone and its Oratory in Rome: Art and Counter-Reformation Spiritual Values" (Ph.D. dissertation, University of California at Berkeley, 1985)

WURM, H.W., Der Palazzo Massimo alle Colonne in Rom (Berlin: de Gruyter, 1965)

ZERI, F., Pittura e controriforma: L'arte senza tempo di Scipione da Gaeta (Turin: Einaudi, 1957)

ZUCCARI, A., I Pittori di Sisto V (Rome: Fratelli Palombi, 1992)

Picture Credits

Unless otherwise stated, museums have supplied their own photographic material. Supplementary and copyright information is given below. Numbers to the left refer to figure numbers unless otherwise indicated.

Title pages: see page 34
1 Bayerische Staatsbibliothek Munich
3 Scala, Florence
5 Reproduced by courtesy of the Trustees, The National Gallery, London
6 Araldo De Luca, Rome
7 © James Morris, London
page 19, detail of figure 16
10 The Fotomas Index, Kent
12 © British Museum, London
13 Araldo De Luca, Rome
15 Monumenti Musei e Gallerie Pontificie, Città del Vaticano
16 © James Morris, London
17, 18, 19 Biblioteca Apostolica Vaticana
20, 21 © James Morris, London
page 43, detail of figure 23
23 © James Morris, London
24 Scala, Florence
25 © James Morris, London
27, 28 © James Morris, London
31 The Metropolitan Museum of Art, Harris Brisbane Dick Fund, 1941. [41.72 (3.29)]

32 Alinari, Florence
33 © James Morris, London
34, 35 © British Museum, London
37 Scala, Florence
38 © James Morris, London
page 61, detail of figure 45
42 Scala, Florence
43 © Loren Partridge
45 Scala, Florence
46 © Loren Partridge
48 © British Museum, London
50, 51 James Morris, London
54 Fotografica Foglia, Naples
page 79, detail of figure 65
57, 58 Scala, Florence
59 © James Morris, London
61 Scala, Florence
62, 63 Reproduced by courtesy of the Trustees, The National Gallery, London
64, 65 © James Morris, London
66 The Metropolitan Museum of Art, Purchase, Anonymous Gift, in memory of Terence Cardinal Cooke, 1984 J (1984.74)
67 © James Morris, London
68, 69 Scala, Florence
70 © James Morris, London
page 109, detail of figure 88
72, 73, 74, 75 Scala, Florence
76 Ernst Steinmann, *Die Sixtinische Kapelle*, (Tafeln, Erster Teil, Munich, 1901), folio volume I, pl. VII

77, 78 Scala, Florence
79, 80 James Morris, London
81, 82, 83, 84 Nippon Television Network Corporation Tokyo 1991
85 Scala, Florence
86 © Nippon Television Network Corporation Tokyo 1991
87 Scala, Florence
88 By courtesy of the Board of Trustees of the Victoria & Albert Museum
89 © James Morris, London
90 Original drawing by Peter Schmitt
91 © Nippon Television Network Corporation Tokyo 1991
92, 93 Araldo De Luca, Rome
94, 95, 96, 97 © James Morris, London
page 145, detail of figure 103
98 Monumenti Musei e Gallerie Pontificie, Città del Vaticano
99, 100, 101, 102, 103, 104 Scala, Florence
105 Monumenti Musei e Gallerie Pontificie, Città del Vaticano
106, 107, 108 Scala, Florence
109, 110 © James Morris, London
112, 113, 114 Scala, Florence
115, 116, 117, 118 Araldo De Luca, Rome

Index

blood chemistry, 242

blood pressure, 234–35, 244

C-reactive protein (CRP), 240

frequency of, 245

fructosamine assay, 243–44

for glaucoma, 244

glucose challenge test, 242–43

hemoglobin A1c (HbA1c), 235–37

importance of, 232

lipid profile, 236–40

microalbumin, 241

monofilament test, 244

during pregnancy, 268–69

records of, 233, 246

rights to know results, 232–33

stress test, 173

thyroid panel, 245

urine, 240–42

Therapeutic touch, 80, 81

Thomas, Denise, 122

Thrombosis, 323

Thrush, 261

Thyroid disease, 347–48

Thyroid panel, 245

Toenails, 250–53

Tolazamide (Tolinase), 212

Tolbutamide (Orinase), 211–12

Tolinase (tolazamide), 212

Toohey, Barbara, 142

Transcendental meditation, 75

Transcutaneous electrical nerve stimulation (TENS), 334

Transplantation, 355

Treatment

communication with doctor, 32–33, 41–43

doctor's visits, 33–34, 38–40

health-care team in, 27–31

of low blood sugar, 94–96

multidisciplinary approach to, 27–28, 37–38

Patient's Bill of Rights in, 34–37

plans for, 37–38

selecting a doctor, 29–30

Triglycerides, 239

Troglitazone (Rezulin), 207

Truncal neuropathy, 332

Tumor necrosis factor alpha, 53

Turner, Robert, 20

UKPDS. *See* United Kingdom Prospective Diabetes Study

Ultrasound test, 269

United Kingdom Prospective Diabetes Study, 19, 86, 236

Uremia, 336–37

Urinary tract, 338–40

U.S. Centers for Disease Control and Prevention, 25, 114, 199, 216

Urologists, 337–39, 341–44

USDA Food Guide Pyramid, 130–32

Vacuum cylinder devices, 344

Valentine, Virginia, 142

Vanadium, 154

Vardenafil (Levitra), 343

Vascular complications, 322–25

Vasodilators, external, 344

Vegetarian diets, 144–47

Viagra (sildenafil), 343

Visualization, 77

Vitamins, 149–54

folic acid, 151, 267

in gestational diabetes, 267